# Parables and Presence

## FORMS OF THE
## NEW TESTAMENT TRADITION

*Robert W. Funk*

**FORTRESS PRESS**     **PHILADELPHIA**

**Library of Congress Cataloging in Publication Data**

Funk, Robert Walter, 1926–
    Parables and presence.

    Bibliography: p.
    Includes index.
    1. Bible. N.T.—Criticism, interpretation, etc.—
Addresses, essays, lectures. 2. Jesus Christ—Parables
—Addresses, essays, lectures. 3. Bible. N.T.—
Language, style—Addresses, essays, lectures. I. Title.
BS2361.2.F86    1982    225.6′6    82-71827
ISBN 0-8006-0688-4

*To Ada*

*Parent of the Prodigal
Sire of the Samaritan*

# Contents

Preface     ix
Acknowledgments     xiii

1. Introduction: Language as Perception, Problem, Promise     1

### I. Parables and Presence

2. The Narrative Parables: The Birth of a
   Language Tradition     19

3. The Good Samaritan as Metaphor     29

4. Participant and Plot in the
   Narrative Parables of Jesus     35

5. The Prodigal Samaritan     55

6. The Temporal Horizon of the Kingdom     67

### II. Letters and Presence

7. The Apostolic Presence: Paul     81

8. The Apostolic Presence: John the Elder     103

### III. Language and Tradition

9. Myth and the Literal Non-Literal     111

10. On Dandelions: The Problem of Language     139

11. The New Testament as Tradition and Canon     151

Bibliography     187
Index of Parables     195
Index of Citations     197
Index of Authors     201
Index of Subjects     203

# Preface

*Parables and Presence* explores two forms of the New Testament tradition: the parable and the letter. An investigation of these forms cannot be adequately carried out apart from reflection on language and tradition. Accordingly, this book combines close investigation of particular linguistic forms with the systematic probing of the issues surrounding language and tradition.

The parable and the letter appear at critical points in the development of the language tradition that came to fruition in the New Testament.

The parable stands at the threshold of the tradition, at its inception, and thus can be said to have given fundamental direction, along with the aphorism, to its development as a whole. We do not yet know precisely what that means. However, it is becoming clear that Jesus infringed the symbol system of his religious tradition so that he modified the fundamental structure of the correlative semantic code. The system of oppositions on which every linguistic code depends goes together with the way the world, or reality, is apprehended. In short, the linguistic network is a kind of screen or grid through which one sees the world. As a modification of the semantic code, the parable and the aphorism became an event of language: a new tradition, a new code, with new polarities—and thus a fresh sense of the real, emerged.

The language of the parables almost certainly took shape in Greek: the parables were composed for the ear. It is not impossible that Jesus spoke Greek as well as Aramaic, and that the foundational language of the Christian tradition received its decisive imprint in Greek.

The great narrative parables have a common narrative structure. This structure makes it possible to evaluate the rhetorical strategies of the parables as literary devices; it also reveals the fundamental lines of the message of Jesus.

If the parables are taken as an index to what Jesus said, we are in a position to reevaluate the view, widely held since Albert Schweitzer, that Jesus expected the imminent end of the world. He may indeed have been influenced by common apocalyptic notions, but the temporal horizon of the kingdom seems not to have been borrowed from everyday eschatological hopes. Rather, Jesus' view appears to lie much closer to that mythopoetic mentality in which past and future flow together in a present so intense that the ecstacies of time are indistinguishable.

The parables as an event of language give presence to Jesus; the letters endeavor to give presence to the itinerant apostle whenever he is forced to be away from his congregations.

The letter is a linguistic instrument, an established literary form, utilized and modified by Paul in the management of the congregations he founded. We now know much more about the form and history of letters, both common and literary, in the Hellenistic period than we did two decades ago. This knowledge makes it possible to isolate with considerable confidence features of the letter that are peculiar to Paul. Paul's adaptation of the letter is of special interest because he turns a common linguistic vehicle into a major theological form during the first stage of reflection on the emerging Christian tradition. The Pauline letter thus represents the tradition becoming conscious of itself for the first time.

In his letters Paul speaks regularly of forthcoming visits to his churches, sometimes even threatening unruly members with the power of his presence. These remarks are gathered, as a rule, into a section which may be termed "apostolic *parousia*" (*parousia* may be translated as presence). This section indicates the strong oral orientation of the apostle's ministry, for which he regarded the letter as a weak substitute.

The letters of John the elder echo the Pauline apostolic presence in their form and style, though the characteristic Pauline stamp is lacking.

Underlying these studies of the New Tradition is a view of language as perception, problem, promise. Language as habituated and as containing glimpses of worlds aborning may be discovered in talk of the lowly dandelion populating the spring lawn. To the modern mind, which is given to literal-mindedness, such talk, including mythical and metaphorical parlance, is simply mysterious and mystifying. But myth and metaphor are connected in a fundamental way with the emergence of New Testament language and canon. As such they invite, indeed require, reflection.

The content of these essays is by no means entirely my own. Those from whom I have learned most immediately are indicated in the list of works consulted. But others, students and faculty colleagues alike, have also taught me important lessons, sometimes with no consciousness of having done so. To these, named and unnamed, I am grateful. I am also greatly indebted to Charlene Matejovsky for immaculate typesetting and bibliographic work, and to Meryl Lanning for expert editorial review. Finally, it is to Norman Hjelm and John Hollar of Fortress Press that I am obligated for the encouragement and opportunity to bring this volume to completion.

Robert W. Funk

Riverbend
May Day, 1982

# Acknowledgments

Chapter 2, "The Narrative Parables: The Birth of a Language Tradition," appeared first in *St. Andrew's Review* (Spring–Summer 1974) 299–323. It was included in *God's Christ and His People; Studies in Honour of Nils A. Dahl,* edited by J. Jervell and W. A. Meeks (Oslo: Universitetsforlaget, 1977) 43–58.

Chapter 3, "The Good Samaritan as Metaphor" appeared in *Semeia* 2 (1974) 74–81.

Chapter 4, "Participant and Plot in the Narrative Parables of Jesus," appeared in a different form in *Semeia* 2 (1974) 51–73.

Chapter 5, "The Prodigal Samaritan," is a revision of an essay that appeared in *JAAR Thematic Studies* XLVIII/1 (1981) 83–97.

Chapter 6, "The Temporal Horizon of the Kingdom," appeared in an earlier form in *Journal for Theology and the Church* 6 (1969) 175–191.

Chapter 7, "The Apostolic Presence: Paul," was included in *Christian History and Interpretation: Studies Presented to John Knox,* edited by W. R. Farmer, C. F. D. Moule, R. R. Niebuhr (Cambridge: Cambridge University Press, 1967) 249–268.

Chapter 8, "The Apostolic Presence: John the Elder," was published originally in the *Journal of Biblical Literature* 86 (1967) 424–430.

Chapter 9, "Myth and the Literal Non-Literal," was published in *Parable, Myth, and Language,* edited by Tony Stoneburner (Cambridge, MA: The Church Society for College Work, 1968) 57–65.

Chapter 10, "On Dandelions: The Problem of Language," appeared first in *JAAR Thematic Studies* XLVIII/2 (1981) 79-87.

The author is grateful to these publishers and publications for the right to make further use of these materials.

*Parables and Presence*

# One

# INTRODUCTION: LANGUAGE AS
# PERCEPTION, PROBLEM, PROMISE

*0.* Religious traditions may be said to be linguistic in a broad sense. Linguistic in this context refers to any system of signs or symbols. A religious tradition begins as a special code or new and powerful symbol system. It comes into existence by deforming and reforming the semantic code already present in the tradition that functions as its predecessor. And, so long as that new code gives shape and coherence to the way reality is experienced by believers, the new symbol system remains functional. When, however, a discrepancy opens up between that system and the way in which the everyday world presents itself, that tradition begins to deteriorate and fade. In time, perhaps, a new semantic code or symbol set will arise to take its place. This, in brief, is the cycle of the rise and fall of religious traditions.

The question of the destiny of Christianity and Judaism in the modern West is therefore a linguistic question in some profound sense. As a linguistic question, the study of religious traditions is related to the attention being lavished on the study of languages in allied disciplines: analytic philosophy and phenomenology, linguistics in the narrower sense, anthropology, folklore, literary criticism, and the literary arts. So intense has this preoccupation with language been in the twentieth century that many scholars speak of it as a language crisis (cf. Steiner, 1967).

It is possible, even probable, that the character of man as a speaking animal has fundamental religious dimensions: religion seems a possibility only for the beast that has language. In any case, language and the way in which the world is organized and presents itself to man are somehow bound up together; the question of world is a religious question; religion in most forms is not indifferent to the shape of the cosmos.

If our analytic tools were sufficiently refined, it is possible that we could examine the language of a society and determine its real religious orientation. Certainly the deep structure of a symbol system is an index, perhaps the index, to religion. It is also probable that one is religious to the extent that language permits. We thus need to develop the means of examining religious traditions with sufficient care so that we can discern how they take their rise, how they function as they do, and what happens when they fade and fail. For the study of religion may be organized around language and tradition as the central focus.

*1. Tradition building as layers of talk.* The New Testament is the literary deposit of the early Christian movement. It contains twenty-seven books or writings that were composed over nearly a century beginning about 50 CE and ending about 130 CE. The oldest extant manuscript copies of the New Testament are from III CE, although a few fragments can be dated to II CE. Behind the writings preserved in the New Testament lie months, even years, of oral tradition: from the death of Jesus, about 30 CE, to the composition of Paul's letters in the late forties and early fifties of I CE, the account of what was to be written down about Jesus and his first disciples was taking shape in the mouths of believers. What was eventually written down in the gospels, Acts, and the letters of Paul represents a kind of codification of what was already being said.

In the primitive Christian community, then, there was talk of Jesus, of the adventures of the apostles, of faith, hope, love; but the focal point of this talk was Jesus. The first disciples, too, were preoccupied with talk of Jesus. It should be recalled that Jesus himself was talking about something else: the kingdom of God. So the second generation, or the community, was talking about the disciples talking about Jesus talking about the kingdom of God.

This emerging tradition soon became reflective about itself, as does every tradition. If we add reflective layers to the strata already suggested, it can be said that the first disciples talked about themselves talking about Jesus talking about the kingdom of God. And of course the community sometimes talked about itself talking about the first disciples talking about Jesus talking about the kingdom of God. But Jesus rarely talks about himself talking about the kingdom of God.

A very complex process is being represented schematically here:

Jesus talking about the Kingdom of God
    (e.g., in Parable)
    ⇧

First disciples talking about:
Jesus talking about the kingdom of God
    (e.g., Pronouncement Stories)
    ⇧

First disciples talking about:
Themselves talking about:
Jesus talking about the kingdom of God
    (e.g., Sons of Zebedee, Mark 10:35-45)
    ⇧

Community talking about:
First disciples talking about:
Jesus talking about the kingdom of God
    (e.g., Acts, Gospels)
    ⇧

Community talking about:
Itself talking about:
First disciples talking about:
Jesus talking about the kingdom of God
    (e.g., Galatians 1-2)

In this complex process a religious tradition was taking its rise, and in these layers of talk something considered of great importance was struggling to come to expression.

2. *Accessibility and inaccessibility.* A tradition takes form as something being said about something. There are two "somethings" in this formulation: one is linguistic in character, the other refer-

ential. There is talk or speech or language, and there is the object or referent of that talk or speech or language.

2.1 The referent, about which something was being said before and in the New Testament, was both accessible and inaccessible. It was accessible in that something could be said about it: it was being brought forward, given a presence in speech, made available in talk. But it was also inaccessible—at least in the sense that more remained to be said about it.

2.2 Consider first the matter of accessibility. Events in history are remembered because they are recorded in song, poem, story, and history book. If events do not enter the language tradition in some form, they soon pass from sight and are forgotten. No one knows what Jesus did between his childhood and public ministry because it was not thought worth the telling and repeating. This leads to the startling generalization that without speech man would have no history; memory is dependent upon language.

2.3 Events are inaccessible, on the other hand, when they are lost to memory and history, when they remain untold. But they are also inaccessible in another sense. About everything that happens and is told, something further can always be said. The full concreteness of things and events is never exhausted in words. A description of Mount St. Helens or an account of the Council of Nicea is perpetually incomplete simply because both will always be open to an additional detail, a further nuance, another perspective. Of course, the possibility of that further telling is dependent upon access to the thing or event, either immediately or mediately through a previous telling.

Historic events are also inaccessible in that they can be told with new implications and meanings on future occasions. In this respect, the event, although past in time, is not yet accessible; by being told, a past event continues to be eventful. For example, we cannot say with certainty what the founding of the nation will mean to Americans at its retelling in its tricentennial year, 2076. We cannot even be certain, at least not this close to the telling, what the bicenntenial celebration meant and means.

The commonsensical view, informed as it is by the modern conviction that all true telling is descriptive, is inclined to think that history is reported primarily as it happens: historians tell it like it is. But history also happens as it is reported, and the reporting is never done. What the author of the Fourth Gospel says of Jesus therefore actually applies to every event, no matter how humble: if everything were told, the world could not contain the books. Memory is rescued from this potential profusion, however, because it is selective: it retains the root images and paradigms and feeds on them in its rehearsals and recitals.

2.4 The accessibility and the inaccessibility of the referents—that about which something is being said—are polar tendencies: when the one draws near, the other recedes, like the relation of winter and summer. In dialectical tension they function marvelously in the creation and transmission of traditions, provided one or the other does not get the upper hand permanently. If that occurs, the tradition to which they are related dies.

This way of putting the matter invites further explication.

2.41 When occurrences such as Moses receiving the law on Mt. Sinai or the proclamation of Jesus evoke speech, these events enter memory, or history, and a tradition is born. The linguistic act which launches such a tradition attempts to picture or symbolize the originating events, to fix or anchor them in memory for future reference. Thus those events are viewed in the young tradition from one, or at most several, perspectives; it cannot fasten on many or all perspectives simultaneously, being human and finite. The very act of taking up events into language in order to preserve access to them for posterity crystallizes the initial perspectives from which those events were viewed; the threat posed by this necessity is that memory may be confined to first perspectives.

Picasso, along with many other modern painters, felt the restrictions of the single perspective. In traditional portraiture the face and body are represented from a single perspective. In concert with the revolt against traditional perspectives at the end of XIX CE, Picasso thought that painters should not be confined to the single perspective, and he sought to invent ways of representing more than one viewpoint simultaneously. He sometimes painted noses on faces looking straight on, and then painted them also, in the same picture, from a side view. Similarly, he painted the face viewed from the front, side, and back on the same canvas, juxtaposed. Such pictures look odd to those accustomed to single perspectives. Yet Picasso did not want to sacrifice the truth of multiple perspectives to the single point of view, so he distorted the individual's view of things—renouncing the tyranny of the individual perspective—in order to represent the multidimensional character of reality.

In Picasso multidimensionality is spatial. In the *Alexandrian Quartet*, Lawrence Durell depicts a series of events from multiple perspectives in which both space and time are pluralized. He tells the same story four times in order to place his characters in three-dimensional space to give his story spatial thickness and in order to represent the temporal sequence variously. His aim is to draw fiction closer to the ambiguities of existence and memory.

The tradition which fixes Moses or Jesus in memory from limited perspectives has a similar counterweight: that tradition tends to generate inconsistency and contradiction, to wrap crucial events in an aura of mystery, in short, to obscure. Moses and Jesus are depicted from a variety of seemingly contradictory viewponts. The people could not make up their minds whether God spoke to Moses or whether it had only thundered. The date on which Jesus was born cannot be fixed, his physical appearance is never described, and his first disciples cannot be named with certainty. It is strange that traditions otherwise so strong would have such weak memories for details of this order. The reason, however, is clear: what is made accessible in the tradition must also remain inaccessible for the sake of those who will come after. The potential of primary events is provided for by language that does not close off events, lock them into initial and partial perspectives.

The matter could be put thus: the great events of history precipitate song and poem, drive man to speech, prompt language commensurate with the potential of those events. In other words, the drive to bring forward, to capture in words, to fix in memory is self-defeating, if not counterbalanced by the mystery, by the plenitude of paradigmatic events. If we really *knew* who Abraham and Jesus were, they would not be the father of Israel and the author of the Christian faith. An American Revolution with one set of facts and an American constitution with one catalogue of frozen interpretations would no longer fire the imagination of Americans.

The temple of history is its mystery: what can be seen and told only with the eyes of generations yet unborn. What is told is profaned because it has been cast into the outer court, made public. The vitality of a culture depends upon guarding the secret. Yet without tradition, without the telling, memory would be blank. So man celebrates and recites his past in order to be man, in order to have a future, but the celebration and recitation recall human finitude, remind the celebrant of the fact that the paradigmatic events of the past will require telling all over again in some unspecifiable future.

2.42   The dialect of accessibility and inaccessibility, of the mystery and the profane, has other dimensions worth noting.

Traditions evolve by word of mouth. The first generation of witnesses to epoch-making events is content with oral rehearsal. This contentment is undergirded by the premonition that writing will somehow silence the original voice. Traditions still fresh from their inception take no thought for the morrow; they ask bread only for the day. The link is living.

The second generation is alarmed, and rightly so, by aging and failing memories. The original witnesses begin to pass away—the first disciples and their associates in the case of the Christian tradition—and the living voice is notably weakened; the verbal record becomes increasingly ambiguous without primary interpretation. There is thus a strong impulse to fix in writing what has been said by the first witnesses.

Note the contrary tendencies: on the one hand, the primary voice is still taken to be oral, which means living, developing, open to interpretation, and it is to this voice that the tradition wishes to maintain a reliable link. Yet the tradition can retain that link only at the expense of orality: testimony has to be reduced to writing and thus fixed in order for that witness to abide. Orality among other things means equivocal, for a living voice by definition does not come to rest in a single, univocal assertion. If the living voice is to be preserved, however, it must be fixed in writing, at least in its final form; and, if what it meant at the time of its fixing is to abide, that final form will be accompanied by a body of interpretation. Respect for the tradition prompts its arrest and codification.

How can the unfolding tradition honor its aspiration to fix the testimony of its first witnesses in writing without at the same time entirely sacrificing the oral character of that testimony?

If original testimony is to be fixed in writing it is essential that that testimony be pluralized. The tolerance of the primary witness for ambiguity, contradiction, mystery has already been noted. But there must also be more than a single voice. It was inevitable that there should be four gospels, Irenaeus said in the late second century. He reasoned that this should be so because the earth has four corners and there are four winds and four cardinal directions. But the real, non-figurative reason is that a single voice must not be permitted to tyrannize memory. It is necessary, not that the gospels should agree, but that they should disagree. A strong tradition cannot countenance univocal testimony; it must be supported by at least two diverging witnesses. This permits even written tradition to live and grow.

The early Christian movement took the matter of plurality very seriously, as did its Jewish ancestors. Both movements gave rise to extensive, non-conforming literatures which formed the core of living, vibrant traditions. So lively were these traditions, in fact, that they gave rise to their own excesses.

The creation of still other testimony, in the form of other books, by other witnesses to the same principal events bred a significant apocryphal and pseudepigraphic literature. The apocryphal and pseudepigraphic works accompaning the New Testament, for example, tend to fill in with great detail what is left blank or is only hinted at in the earlier tradition. Thus infancy and resurrection gospels abound, in which Jesus' youth and his post-resurrection talks with his disciples become the focus of attention. And in order to secure recognition for them, these accounts are of course attributed to eye witnesses, although they are mostly written by second- and third-generation (or later) devotees.

The emergence of so large a literature is evidence of the vigor of the tradition. Yet it also poses a threat to that tradition, a threat of the opposite sort. Just as there can be too few voices, there can also be too many: an indefinite number of voices threatens the integrity of the tradition, its link with its originator, its center, its horizon. As a consequence, the plurality of witnesses admitted by the tradition must manifest some integrity in the midst of their diversity.

The tradition can meet this threat by accrediting only those accounts of its origins or formative events which sustain an integral relationship to original witnesses and originator. It does not insist that all accounts be original, only that derivative testimony hold that referent strictly in view. The integrity of the relationship means, among other things, celebrating in the concreteness of speech while maintaining respect for the essential mystery. In other words, the mystery must not be exhaustively profaned. Equivocal does not mean absolutely indeterminate.

These observations raise the question of the New Testament canon. Why are there twenty-seven books rather than one, or sixty-six, or an indefinite number? Put more generally, does the witness to a tradition have any limits?

It has been observed that there is no thing or event about which something further cannot be said. Accordingly, to every event at least two diverging witnesses are required. Two points are necessary to locate a third in space and time, as every surveyor knows. However, only witnesses authentically related to the primary event or the original witnesses can be accredited. This means that the foundation of the tradition cannot be extended indefinitely. It is immaterial, consequently, how many books the New Testament contains, so long as it contains more than one and fewer than infinite number and so long as the witnesses it does contain provide authentic access to the ground of that tradition.

2.5 The New Testament is thus the product of a very complex process by which traditions are created. In and behind the New Testament something is being talked about, brought forward, made available in speech, and that witness reduced to writing. At the same time, what is being talked about remains inaccessible, elusive, ambiguous. Its mystery perseveres and invites subsequent witnesses, if they wish to remain true to the tradition, to bring that thing to speech afresh. This dialectical tension causes the tradition to breathe and grow. Without it, the tradition would atrophy like unused muscules.

These conditions hold, to a greater or lesser extent, for all traditions, religious and secular. It may be that to pose the question of tradition in this fashion is to pose a question that is at bottom religious. However that may be, it is quite possible to explore the function of language in this process.

3. *Language as perception.* In the language tradition of which the New Testament is a depository, something is being brought forward, made available in speech. It is important to inquire what restrictions that language tradition—language as it was received and used in giving expression to the new "something"—imposes upon

the representation of what is being made available. What does the Greek language in late antiquity permit one to see with regard to the foundational events in the formation of the Christian tradition? More specifically, what restrictions did the Jewish tradition impose upon Jesus' ability to speak about the kingdom of God? What limitations did the letter form pose for Paul in communicating with his churches? Neither Jesus nor Paul would have understood these questions, yet they had to give answers in their speech, because they were striving to bring something to speech through and beyond the language of their patrimony.

3.1   We now know that we do not readily see things for which we do not have names. We do not give designations to things once we have recognized them, but rather we recognize things in the act of designation.

In a linguistics seminar, an instructor asked the students to name the color of the shirt one student was wearing. Among the colors named were tan, beige, gold, brown. The first three labels were submitted by the female members of the class; the category, brown, was the choice of every male in the room.

The generalization illustrated here is that females in American society have twice or three times the color discriminations, and hence, the vocabulary, of males. Males know a color, brown, which females divide into two or three other colors. Males may know words like tan or beige, but these are usually employed as non-functional terms unless the male in question is a hairdresser or decorator, both of whom must be able to speak female. Males cannot discriminate as many colors as females; together they cannot discriminate colors for which neither has the vocabulary.

3.2   The anthropologist Edmund Leach postulates "that the physical and social environment of a young child is perceived as a continuum. It does not contain any intrinsically separate 'things.'" (1972: 47) In due course a child is taught to impose a discriminating grid on the surrounding world, and this grid is linguistic in nature. It seems self-evident in English that bushes and trees are different things, but they are not discriminated in all languages. We would not know the distinction had we not been taught it with our language.

Language is thus the means by which we classify things. More important, "it actually molds our environment; it places each individual at the center of a social space which is ordered in a logical and reassuring way." (Leach, 1972: 48) As a warrant for this generalization, Leach advances the verbal categories which distinguish certain types of social space in relation to their distance from the ego-self. There is the set: self / house / farm / field / wilderness, in which each term designates space still more remote from the self. To this set corresponds the classification of animals as pets / livestock / game / wild or zoo animals.

That these are not arbitrary but actually have to do with the way our social space is ordered is proved by an interesting correlative set of taboos.

There is a strong taboo against eating animals in the category of pet in American society. The thought of eating dog, cat, or horse is disgusting to most speakers of English, although dogs are bred for eating in some parts of the world and the French eat horsemeat without qualms. Livestock is edible but only if immature or castrated. Game is edible if hunted in accordance with accepted rituals. Wild animals are not edible. There are thus special restrictions that go with each category and these taboos sustain a close relation to the categories of the language. An African finds monkey meat as pleasurable as Americans find it abhorrent—but then, someone brought up in the heart of the African continent looks at the world through a different set of linguistic binoculars.

The demarcations between and among our categories are made as clean as possible. The child's continuum is broken into things, states, and processes, and the original links between and among them are suppressed. Naturally the world does not fall neatly into discrete bins, so there are ambiguities. And it is those things that fall into categorial interstices—into the cracks—that tend to become taboo laden or have ritual value. One could say that taboos are psychological and social reinforcement for keeping the language clean.

In the set of animal categories, the fox appears to belong to the wild category in certain respects and to the province of game in others. It is hunted under very strict rules, like game, but is considered inedible, like zoo animals. Perhaps this is the reason the fox hunt is so strongly ritualistic and surrounded by such fierce taboos in England.

Speakers of English are aware of the social impropriety of referring to a person as a son-of-a-bitch or a swine. To call the same person a bear or a lion or the son of a giraffe may have figurative overtones but is not obscene. The reason ritual or imprecatory value is attached to dogs and pigs but not to bears, lions, and giraffes is that the former are especially close to man. (In older farm traditions, swine were raised in pens attached to the dwelling and were fed scraps from the table.) Pets may thus be said to be in an ambiguous category, intermediate between man and animal; because they are neither entirely man nor animal, their names may have strong ritual value.

3.3 The effective color spectrum and the organization of man's social space suggest that language is a screen through which the environment is filtered. The eye and ear receive what language has prepared them to receive. The something about which something is to be said is made accessible in the first instance by language as perception. Seeing is linked to saying.

In the gospels Jesus is viewed as an exorcist, a faith healer, and an itinerant prophet, among other things. It should not surprise the modern reader to learn that these are precisely the categories used to describe the so-called divine man or thaumaturge so well known in I CE. Jesus is simply classified in accordance with the terms used to organize social space in his day. He is made to fit a recognizable mold. He may, of course, be made to break the mold, in which case he becomes a new aspect of the grid subsequently used to place other messianic figures.

In the gospels the reader comes across terms like rabbi, prophet, messiah, and kyrios, usually translated "lord." These are ordinary, everyday words belonging to the Jewish tradition. Because the gospels have made them common, they are familiar but alien terms to the modern reader. It is not necessary to use ancient terms to describe the figure of Jesus. It would be possible, for example, to employ designations taken from American speech of the 1970's. He could be depicted as a child prodigy, a juvenile delinquent, a member of the building trades union, as currently on unemployment compensation, without dependents, with no established residence and thus a vagrant, and as clad in tattered levis with long dirty hair: in a word, as a hippie. These characterizations are probably fairly close to the actualities; but contemporary readers have come to accept the linguistic terrain of the New Testament as appropriate to Jesus, whereas the same reader looks at his or her own world through indigenous language. In any case, it is clear that those first given to talk about Jesus took him into linguistic space already established, for the most part, and he became rapidly domesticated there. Biblical literalists are those who insist on the original words but not necessarily the original meaning. Care for the tradition dictates that the reader seek to give the original words their proper space in that tradition. Otherwise, the reader will seek to substitute correlative living speech, in other words, to translate the original set of categories into the corresponding modern set.

4. *Language as problem.* The discussion thus far has concerned language as perception, the established linguistic frame within which things and events are perceived and thus made accessible in the tradition. That same frame, when extended indefinitely, may come to tyrannize sight, permitting only habituated accessibility. In that case, language has become a problem.

Just as a tradition gives access to its referent by making the referent available in talk, so it may also close off or stop down access by trading only in crystallized categories and clusters of one-dimensional terms. The inevitable tendency, prompted precisely by care for the tradition, is to make the language that carries the tradition rigid and flat for fear of loss. This tendency comes to expression as determination to repeat the same terms, the terms in which the tradition first took shape and voice. But to continue to say the same thing, to repeat the same words, is to drift further and further from the original perceptive moorings. That is because both the language and the speaker-perceiver are subject to drift in relation to the object of memory, and the two do not necessarily drift in the same direction. Linguistic drift is a very subtle affair, taking place as it does over a long period of time and at a level that is, at any moment, barely perceptible. We may be well out to sea before we realize the ship of talk has slipped a cable.

Drift is most readily recognized in the lexical stock of a language. Illustrations of this point are difficult without extended explanations and citations, but one or two items from the New Testament lend themselves to a more superficial treatment.

Jesus is a name venerated by the Christian tradition. It is reserved for one person alone, the founder of the faith, in most Western languages employed by Christians (Spanish seems to be an exception).

Jews avoid the name for the opposite reason. The modern student conditioned by one or the other of these attitudes will be startled to run across the name Jesus frequently in Greek papyri and inscriptions of the New Testament period and earlier. Josephus, a historian of I CE, refers to no fewer than twenty persons by the name of Jesus, no one of whom was from Nazareth. If we were to translate the name Jesus into a modern counterpart with a comparable feeling tone, we would have to refer to the speaker of the sermon on the mount as Bill or Dick.

The point seems scarcely worth the making. Yet it is this drift, of both language and user, that alters one's relation to a textual tradition. The name Jesus has acquired a tone in the course of its veneration that it did not originally have, and repetition of that name with its new connotations has subtly altered the relation of every reader, friendly or hostile, to the text of the New Testament. To restore the original tonality, a neutral name is required.

The term kyrios (κύριος) was mentioned earlier. It is usually translated "lord" in modern versions. In our society the range of meanings of this term has been greatly narrowed: it is now used almost exclusively with reference to divinity, owing to its use in the Bible; the Lord is a synonym for God. In the New Testament the term is also used of Jesus, and it is very likely that the modern reader assigns the meaning "divinity" to it whenever it occurs in the text. Nevertheless, the term also means regal person, or person holding a high rank in society; Great Britian still has its lords, and in tales of King Arthur's roundtable we have no difficulty in assigning this meaning to the word. But we have lost the third sense common to the term in the New Testament: in Greek it is often merely an address of respect that is best translated "sir."

Translators of the New Testament endeavor to distinguish overtones of divinity from the term of respect by capitalizing "lord" in the former sense. But most readers undoubtedly ignore the distinction and assign "divinity" to all forms of the word. In other words, the term has atrophied as a term for divinity for readers of the Bible, to the extent that the translator may as well capitalize all occurrences. The apparent solution is to translate as "lord" where divinity is intended and to render "sir" when it functions merely as a term of respect. That practice, however, would force the translator to decide the issue in every instance, and that is not always possible.

In Mark 10:51, blind Bartinaeus says to Jesus, "Master, let me receive my sight." In the parallel passages in Matthew and Luke (Matt 20:33, Luke 18:41), the blind man (or men: Matthew) says: "Lord, let me receive my sight." The translators dutifully render with "Lord" and capitalize it. The justification they would give is that Matthew and Luke probably so understood the term: Bartimaeus is made to address Jesus as Son of God. However, that may not have been the intention of Bartimaeus on the original occasion.

The language cannot be made to stand still. By continuing to utilize the terms "Jesus" and "lord," we are in fact saying something different from the meanings carried by those terms at the time the New Testament language tradition was formed. Were we to restore to the language of the New Testament, in English translation, something like its original semantic range and flavor, the notes and explanations, together with alternative translations and paraphrases, would run to several volumes for each book. Indeed, commentaries have come to run to hundreds of tedious pages. It somehow spoils the effect of a succinct parable like that of the Good Samaritan to have to stop at the outset and give a thirty-minute sketch of the history of the Samaritans in order for the reader or listener to appreciate what that story is about. And yet the auditor who does not know who the Samaritans were and has no feeling for their relationship to the Jews will scarcely be able to appreciate that parable. For those who aspire to better understanding, it is almost easier to learn Greek and immerse oneself in Hellenistic history than it is to grapple in frustration with words and phrases whose meaning was arrested eighteen centuries ago.

Language that conceals rather than reveals, that obstructs rather than constructs, is a problem. It is out of time, out of place, out of rhythm. Much of the language of the New Testament has become problematic in this sense.

5. *Language as promise.* In language usage and development, particularly in its higher levels, abstraction is inevitable and also desirable. Abstraction is the process of ignoring certain qualities of an object in order to attend to others. For example, one may ignore the shape and color of the leaves on a tree, perhaps even the leaves themselves, in order to attend to the structure of the trunk and branches. The result is an abstraction. Or, the process of abstraction

may entail isolating in the imagination the common properties of all known trees—ignoring the features which distinguish particular trees from one another—in order to arrive at a definition of tree as such. This, too, is an abstraction.

By grouping similar but distinguishable things or processes, man gains knowledge of and control over the environment. Abstraction is thus a highly beneficial activity which is characterisitc of all advanced societies.

It is easy to see that abstractions help us see what is around us in relation to established scientific categories. Abstract language is thus related to perception. But abstract language, too, may become ossified, in which case it may also tyrannize sight, and then it becomes a problem. In either case, abstracting from concrete particulars is a blinking of the amazing richness of the panorama that surrounds us. We could say: abstraction is a denial of reality.

It is not our purpose here to pursue the question of the value and limitations of abstract thinking and the language that is correlative with that thinking. It is our purpose, rather, to note that abstract language may lose its worldly bearings. By that is meant that a particular language may be become so abstract that it loses all reference to particulars: it no longer refers to anything. Logic is such a language, but as a language it is designed for a specific purpose: to manipulate a set of arbitrary signs or counters. Abstract language of a less specialized sort may and often does become a threat to perception: our categorical affirmations become too powerful to permit us to see the richness, the variety, the metamorphoses before our eyes.

This way of stating the problem permits us to come to language as promise: language that is full of promise is language that has been reassembled around concrete things; it is words that have been brought around to full senuous contact with the real world; it is words plucked, as Thoreau puts it, from the earth with dirt still clinging to their roots. This language is promise-laden because language traditions are born and renewed by virtue of their contact with the real world.

To the magician of words we sometimes give the name poet. The poet is the one who rediscovers language. He or she takes words from the tradition and defamiliarizes them by bringing them into contact with referents and qualities and glimpses of lost worlds. Words pour from the pen of the poet full of fresh energy, charged with the power to provoke new sight, freed from the weight of habituated usage. The term poet is of course used here in a root sense: not just as the creator of verse, but as creator of threshold language opening onto vistas forgotten or worlds aborning. Poet thus refers to all who stand at the foundation of language traditions. In this sense, Moses was a poet, Socrates was a poet, Jesus was a poet. It would then not be incorrect to say that Jesus, as a maker of parables, invites his hearers, by means of his tales or riddles, to pass over from the attenuated world of jaded senses to some fabulous yonder he sees before him. He calls this fabulous yonder the Kingdom of God, and he wonders why others about him cannot see what is so evident to him. He admonishes them: you cannot point to the Kingdom there or here, as though it were an object among other objects; rather, the Kingdom is in your midst, if you would but look. The poet and the parabler produce language of promise.

Language that is sparkling with promise comes in surprising forms. Jacques Lacan, a Parisian French psychoanalyst, holds that psychoanalysis is nothing other than an exchange of words. Freud worked, of course, primarily with dream material and free association, including puns and slips of the tongue. Lacan becomes fully explicit at one point: what is analyzed is reports of dreams and other linguistic material. Analyzing a patient's language is a fruitful enterprise, Lacan says, because the structure of language corresponds to the structure of the unconscious.

Lacan believes that each person is essentially a story, a narrative: persons are constituted by the memory of the tales they have lived. Psychological trauma erupts when pieces or segments of the story or narrative are lost or suppressed. The analyst is most successful, consequently, when he or she helps the patient to recover his or her story. In this transaction the analyst listens and prompts, and the patient is passive or nearly so; the story of the patient must tell itself, must be renewed of its own accord.

A parable is also a story, at the hands of Jesus, that invites the reader or hearer to join the narrative and live it out. It is not, perhaps, an old story of our own to be recovered, but a new story, one that opens onto a new world, where things run the other way around: the poor and the destitute are surprised by their good fortune, while the established and comfortable are shaken from their lethargy. If the parable is a threat to the habituated, crystallized world, it is full of promise for those who are ready to quit that world. One could even say: the kingdom for Jesus is the invitation to quit the received world.

George Steiner, the literary critic, has written: "language is . . . an intensely energized beam of light, shaping, placing, and organizing human experience." (1971: 133) In the mouth of the poet, the teller of parables, the singer of songs, language releases dormant powers of perception and brings us before vistas previously unsuspected.

Religious tradition, then, consists of language which presides over perception, which precipitates problems when habituated, and which, when renewed and fresh, may produce promise.

# Two

# THE NARRATIVE PARABLES:
# THE BIRTH OF A LANGUAGE TRADITION

*1.1*   The Christian movement embodied its extant traditions in the common tongue of the Hellenistic world, Koine Greek. Yet the language of this incipient movement was not simply congruent with the Greek vernacular as attested elsewhere, however difficult it is to define the difference. The emerging tradition adapted Greek to its ends, and Greek, for its part, took the tradition to its bosom. The union gave birth to a language tradition.

In pursuing the question of the specific vernacular in which the Christian tradition took shape—and to which it, in turn, gave shape—it is necessary to move as close as possible to the fountainhead of that language tradition. Chronologically speaking, it is probably in portions of the synoptic tradition attributed to Jesus that we stand closest to tradition and language aborning in the new idiom. Within the Jesus tradition the major narrative parables will be subjected to analysis for the purpose of ascertaining whether the language of these parables bears the stamp of a linguistic tradition in process of formation.

*1.2*   The analysis will focus on one group of major narrative parables consisting of the Laborers in the Vineyard, the Talents, the Ten Maidens, the Great Supper, the Good Samaritan, and the Prodigal Son. These parables each have three principal characters and comparable plot structures.

The analysis will move from the more general to the more detailed. The point will be scored wherever possible in English. In some instances it will be necessary to resort to Greek.

*2.0* The major narrative parables give evidence of having been carefully composed and constructed.

*2.1* There is first of all the matter of vocabulary. Words and expressions are used parsimoniously, as though drawn from a stock dangerously low. Vocabulary is the simplest: there are no freighted terms, only everyday words like *laborer, field, go, rejoice, five.* Abstract nouns are lacking. Some very common terms appear to be especially suited to the concrete realism of the parable: *vineyard, go away, servant* (Gaston: 43). These few words come preciously to the tongue of the narrator, like water to parched lips in a city under siege. Or, to change the figure, words are polished like mirrors: an image is reflected in them unblurred.

*2.2* Descriptors and adjectives are kept to a minimum; characters are defined by what they do. Feelings and emotions are mentioned only where essential. The background of persons and events is not made explicit but is left to the imagination. There is a penurious economy of words in depicting actions. Where details are given, however, they are concrete in the extreme. Such details often afford clues to the direction of the narrative. Direct speech is preferred to third-person narration.

*2.3* The parsimony of words is joined by an economy of characters and conciseness of plot. Only the necessary persons appear. The plot is simple. Only two sets of relationships are developed, even in the full narrative, for example, younger son/father, older son/ father. Little appears in the narrative that is non-functional.

*2.4* There is repetition by two's and three's, and occasionally more, with variation. Together with other forms of rhythm and assonance, this endows the prose of the parables with certain poetic qualities.

*2.5* Some of these characteristics are common to folk literature of other types, but many appear to be specific features of the synoptic parables. It is of course difficult to attain certainty in every detail because of the editing to which the earliest traditions were subject.

*3.0* The narrative or story line of the six parables is divided into three parts: opening, development, and crisis-denouement. The parts are signaled by certain surface markers hitherto unnoted by biblical critics.

*3.1* The development and crisis-denouement are initiated, as a rule, by temporal sequence phrases. In the Talents, the principle characters are introduced in two sentences (=opening), then the text reads:

Matt 25:15 *Immediately* the five talent man . . .

The crisis-denouement begins with:

Matt 25:19 *After a good while,* the master . . .

In other words, temporal sequence phrases indicate where the two principal subdivisions of the parable begin.

The first temporal marker in the Ten Maidens comes after an elaborate opening:

Matt 25:6 *In the middle of the night* came a cry . . .

And the brief denouement begins with the notice:

Matt 25:11 *Later* came the rest of the maidens . . .

In the Laborers in the Vineyard the opening appears to be conflated with the development. The first temporal phrase appears in the first sentence.

Matt 20:1 [a householder] . . . went out *early in the morning* . . .

The reason for this move is the long, repetitive development, in which the householder ventures forth to hire laborers five times. The opening is therefore incorporated into the development, which serves also to introduce the principals. The Laborers in the Vineyard is an exception in this respect, although openings elsewhere are sometimes minimal, as in the Prodigal Son.

The development in the Laborers in the Vineyard ends with verse 7. The crisis-denouement opens with these words:

Matt 20:8: *When evening came* the master . . .

There can be no doubt about the division of this and other parables on the basis of temporal sequence markers alone.

*3.2* The principal character, functioning as the axis of the story, so to speak, is introduced in the opening by a common noun:

*householder, a man, a certain man.* As a rule, reference in the development is by pronoun or by zero anaphora. At the opening of the crisis-denouement, however, this same figure is reintroduced by a new common noun, that is, the participant is identified by nominal substitution. The *householder* of the Laborers in the Vineyard becomes *the master of the vineyard* at the opening of the crisis-denouement. *A man going on a journey* of the first sentence of the Talents becomes *the master of those servants* at the beginning of the third division. In the Great Supper, *a certain man* becomes *a householder* at the commencement of scene three. There are some exceptions to the rule, but in general a shift in identification indicates the beginning of a new division.

3.3  There is another type of marker that indicates, as a general rule, that the crisis or denouement has arrived. As the Samaritan comes down the road and sees the victim in the ditch, he has "compassion" on him (ἐσπλαγχνίσθη, Luke 10:33). When the host in the Great Supper learns that the invited have rejected his summons, the closing scene opens: "Then the householder became angry..." (ὀργισθείς, Luke 14:21). Affective terms expressing compassion or wrath thus appear to mark the crisis or denouement.

The parable of the Unmerciful Servant belongs to another group of parables with a slightly different dramatic structure. There are actually two crises in the parable, one when the servant first encounters his master and the master has "compassion" on him (σπλαγχνισθείς, Matt 18:27), the second when the master calls the servant to account for failing to have "compassion" on a fellow servant. On the second occasion, the master becomes "angry" (ὀργισθείς, Matt 18:34) and calls him a "worthless servant" (δοῦλε πονηρέ, Matt 18:32). In the Talents, the master also calls the one talent servant a "worthless servant" (πονηρὲ δοῦλε, Matt 25:26) and deals with him angrily, although the term ὀργισθείς does not appear.

The Prodigal Son can be read in two ways. The first episode can be taken as a parable in its own right. In that episode the father has "compassion" (ἐσπλαγχνίσθη, Luke 15:28) on his younger son when he returns home. The second episode can be read as the crisis-denouement going with the first episode as the development (the opening is very brief). In episode two, the older son becomes "angry" (ὠργίσθη, Luke 15:28) and will not join in the celebration underway.

The terms σπλαγχνίζω and ὀργίζω thus appear to be linked to the parable in a special way and are associated with the crisis or denouement. The terms are preserved in single tradition parables appearing in both Matthew and Luke.

*4.1*   According to Charles Taber, a carefully planned and executed narrative in Sango, an African language, involves precise doses of repetition mixed with novelty (I, 87). Repetition and novelty in exact measure appear to be characteristic of the narrative parables also.

In the Laborers in the Vineyard, Act I (the first division), scene i, consists of three sense lines or themes:

(a)   who went out early in the morning to hire laborers for his vineyard
(b)   Upon agreeing with the laborers for a denarius a day
(c)   he sent them into his vineyard

These three lines are repeated in scene ii with significant variation and in different order:

(a)   Going out at the third hour he saw others squatting idle in the marketplace
(c)   He said to them, You also go into the vineyard
(b)   and whatever is right I will give you.

Scenes iii and iv are carried by a repetition of a fragment of the opening clause and what amounts to ditto marks:

(a)   Again going out at the sixth and ninth hours he did likewise.

In the final scene, (b) is omitted, (c) is repeated from scene ii, and (a) is considerably expanded:

(a)   And going out at the eleventh hour he found others squatting (abbreviated from scene ii)
And he says to them, "Why have you stood here idle all day?"
They reply, "Because no one hired us."

Note that the same thematic words and phrases appear: going out at *x* hour, squatting idle, hire, go, vineyard. Act I is then rounded off by (c).

(c)   You also go into the vineyard.

It is difficult to get a clear impression of the repetition and variation in Act I without reading the lines aloud or setting them down on paper in a schematic arrangement and then examining closely. There is, first of all, the broad a/b/c pattern with the variations indicated above. Further, some phrases run like a thread through the entire act: εἰς τὸν ἀμπελῶνα (αὐτοῦ) ("into the [his] vineyard"): twice repeated in scene i, once in scenes ii and v, always at the end of clauses. In scene i the householder ἐξῆλθεν ἅμα πρωΐ ("goes out early in the morning"); this phrase is repeated in scenes ii, iii–iv (καὶ ἐξελθὼν περὶ τρίτην ὥραν; πάλιν ἐξελθὼν περὶ ἕκτην καὶ ἐνάτην ὥραν), with the elements in the same order. In the final scene, the order of the two principal phrases is reversed: "At about the eleventh hour he went out" (περὶ δὲ τὴν ἐνδεκάτην ἐξελθών). The variation in phrase order after so much repetition invites renewed attention. And the expanded form of (a) with the omission of (b) in the final scene of Act I confirms that a significant development in the story is taking place.

4.2   Repetition and variation can be pursued, on a slightly smaller scale, through the parable as a whole.

In Act II, at the close of the parable, the master of the vineyard singles out one of the grumblers and directs several remarks to him. In the first, "Friend, I do you no injustice," the verb ἀδικῶ picks up a note struck in Act I, scene ii: "Whatever is right (δίκαιον) I will give you." There is thus a play on δίκαιον/ἀδικῶ across a considerable expanse of narrative. The master's second remark, "Did you not agree with me for a denarius?" renews a theme expressed in Act I, scene i: "Upon agreeing with the laborers for a denarius a day . . ." And these two initial closing remarks of the master,

Friend, I do you no injustice.
Did you not agree with me for a denarius?

are also related to each other in that they both renew what was identified as theme (b) in Act I.

The Master next tells the protester to take his denarius and be gone (ὕπαγε). Ὕπαγε recalls item (c) of Act I, which was twice repeated: ὑπάγετε καὶ ὑμεῖς εἰς τὸν ἀμπελῶνα. The householder told them to go into the vineyard; now tells them to get out. This represents still another verbal link between Acts II and I.

In what is probably the final remark of the householder, he says, "I choose to give to this last fellow exactly what I gave to you." The verb δοῦναι picks up δώσω of (b) in Act I, scene ii: "Whatever is right I will *give* you." Meanwhile, the master has instructed his steward to "pay" (ἀποδίδωμι) the wages at the beginning of Act II. The verb δίδωμι represents a theme running through the entire parable. Moreover, the designation "last" for one of the workers hired at the eleventh hour goes back to the dichotomy also introduced at the outset of Act II: ". . . pay the wages, beginning with the *last*, up to the first." Subsequently, those hired at the first hour are referred to as "the first" (οἱ πρῶτοι), and they, in turn, call their lazy colleagues "the last" (οἱ ἔσχατοι). Again, there is wordplay on first/last in the second half of the parable.

The play upon or renewal of δίκαιον/ἀδικέω, συμφωνέω δηναρίου, ὑπάγω, δίδωμι, πρῶτοι/ἔσχατοι across a large expanse of the narrative gives the story a textual unity and subtlety that would not have been missed by the ear, difficult as it may be to catch by the untrained eye.

4.3   Some of the forms of repetition and variation indicated above are explored by J. D. Denniston in his work *Greek Prose Style*. In the final chapter, Denniston takes up various forms of assonance, which he defines as "the recurrence of a sound in such a manner as to catch the ear" (124). According to W. B. Stanford, the primacy of the spoken word in ancient Greek, and in other languages, before the age of printing had a significant effect on composition. Prose as well as poetry was composed by the ear rather than by the eye. Euphony therefore played a large rôle in Greek rhetoric and composition.

Matthew Black has endeavored to make a similar case for Aramaic (160–185). He finds many examples of alliteration, assonance, and paronomasia (wordplay, pun) by translating portions of the New Testament back into Aramaic. His work confirms the importance of the ear for the common languages of Hellenistic-Roman Palestine.

4.31   The relation of sound to content need not be argued here. At the threshold of language—in poiesis in the root sense: the naming of the gods and in creation—it is taken for granted. It is no less obvious in the lullaby and the jingle, ancient and modern. In an age dominated by the eye, the precincts of the ear are mostly void.

Yet for those laboring to say something unheard of in the common tongue, the ear must have been crucial. And one expects rhythm and assonance in folk literature, to which the parables are closely related.

4.32 Repetition and variation in themselves contain forms of rhythm and assonance: the parallelism of clauses with variation; the repetition of thematic phrases; the play upon theme words; and the like. It is not surprising to find such cadences and euphony in prose that borders on poetry. It is perhaps somewhat surprising that the parables exhibit other interesting forms of assonance involving the sounds of Greek.

Act I of the Laborers in the Vineyard concerns a householder who goes out to hire ἐργάτας "laborers," some of whom stand ἀργούς "idle" in the ἀγορᾷ "marketplace." The use of these three terms exemplifies anagrammatic assonance (sound play on the same consonants in varying order). The juxtaposition of ἐργάτας/ ἀργούς/ ἀγορᾷ calls attention to Act I, scene ii: εἶδεν ἄλλους ἑστῶτας ἐν τῇ ἀγορᾷ ἀργούς. In this line, in addition to ἀγορᾷ ἀργούς, there is alternating alliteration with iota and alpha sounds (ε, α, ε, ε, α, α). This alliteration is continued in the first part of the next line: καὶ ἐκείνοις εἶπεν, ὑπάγετε καὶ ὑμεῖς εἰς τὸν ἀμπελῶνα, this time with ε and υ; the last phrase in the line of course renews a phrase already twice used. These two lines from scene ii thus exhibit at least three forms of assonance: anagrammatic assonance, alliteration of initial vowel sounds, and repetition of theme phrase.

The next line of scene ii runs: καὶ ὃ ἐὰν ᾖ δίκαιον δώσω ὑμῖν. The alliteration in δίκαιον δώσω is striking in this context, especially when one recalls that δίκαιον and δίδωμι are both theme words, alluded to in the final line of the parable.

In Act II of the same parable, the protest of those hired first is introduced with the verb ἐγόγγυζον, itself an onomatopoeic word. And this is what they murmur: οὗτοι οἱ ἔσχατοι/μία ὥραν ἐποίησαν/καὶ ἴσους αὐτοὺς/ἡμῖν ἐποίησας τοῖς βαστάσασι τὸ βάρος τῆς ἡμέρης καὶ τὸν καύσωνα. The repetition of -οι -οι -οι/-αν -αν -αν/-ους -ους, called homoeoteleuta (Denniston: 135; Bl-D §488[3]), appears to reinforce the sound effect succession of the verb. In the latter part of the line there is a succession of sounds with terminal σ· -ας, -οις, -ος, -ης (nine times), with a similar effect. And there is alliteration with β in βαστάσασι, βάρος.

4.4 The kinds of assonance noted in §4.3 undoubtedly occur, to a certain degree, in all levels of language—not just in poetry—when spoken by competent native speakers. The texture of the narrative parables is such that one has the impression they were "heard" originally in Greek by a competent native speaker.

5.1 The structural and surface evidence adduced from the parables is of more than one type. Some features may belong to deep structures which are translatable without essential loss into any language, for example, the law of the parsimony of characters in folk tales. Whether all deep structures are universally translatable is a question which cannot be broached here. Some surface features may be suited to either Aramaic (Hebrew) or Greek and readily translatable into the other language. Temporal sequence markers would presumably belong to this category. Many so-called Semitisms can also be explained either as translation Semitisms or as spoken Semitic-Greek (Bl-D §4). Other features are difficult to account for on the basis of a Semitic (Aramaic or Hebrew) original, of which the Greek text preserved for us is a reasonably close translation. On balance, it seems to me that the major narrative parables provide ample evidence of having been composed in Greek.

5.2 J. Barre Toelken has suggested that the more significant aspects of Navaho coyote tales lies in their texture—in any *coloration* given a traditional narrative as it is unfolded (222f.). He then cites Alan Dundes with approval: "the more important the textural features are in a given genre of folklore, the more difficult it is to translate an example of that genre into another language" (Dundes: 254; Toelken: 223). The texture of the narrative parables would make it difficult to achieve the same effect in another language.

5.21 The Greek of the parables strikes one not so much as translation Greek as Greek which has been thoroughly vacuumed for the occasion. The greek of the parables is as clean of resonances as the German of Franz Kafka or the French of Samuel Beckett— both of whom were writing in a second language. Aramaic may well have been the first language of the narrator of the parables. However that may be, the composer employs Greek as though it were derived from a beginner's manual with only the immediate ordinary sense attached, just as Ionesco used beginner's English as the basis for his first play, *The Bald Soprano*. The Greek of the parables has been shorn of its rich history. Nevertheless, the unadorned and unnuanced simplicity of the style and diction marks an uncommon solemnity. The bare, uninterpreted act, such as a man going down from Jerusalem to Jericho, bristles with anticipation. The way the narrator manipulates this language is therefore not unlike the way Kafka polishes German or Beckett washes French.

5.22 These less tangible features are joined by more obvious traits, such as repetition with variation, and assonance in various forms. Taken together, they indicate that creativity has been inscribed into the parables both on the surface and at the depths. As Leo Spitzer claims, poetic genius touches the linguistic act at all levels (18).

5.3 The conclusion to which these features point, then, is that the narrative parables were composed in Greek. This claim has long been thwarted by the assumption that a Palestinian tradition could not have taken shape in Greek. Now we have reason to believe differently. Further, from the distance of greater options, it becomes incredible that the original language of the tradition should have disappeared with only odd traces. Given the tenacity with which cultures and institutions cling to originating languages—the Latin church and French Canada, to cite only two examples—it is almost implausible that the Christian tradition took shape in Aramaic and then disappeared in that form in a few years or decades. Freedom from the earlier assumption and conclusion may permit us to examine the synoptic tradition with an eye to the ear.

5.4 There has been a steady refusal in this analysis to attribute the narrative parables in their Greek form to Jesus. Such an attribution is by no means ruled out. But the present argument extends just this far: the narrative parable tradition took shape in Greek, whether at the hands of Jesus or someone else, at some point proximate to the threshold of the Christian tradition.

# Three

# THE GOOD SAMARITAN AS METAPHOR

*0.* Literary and biblical critics have always deemed it important to determine the kind of language being used in any text to be interpreted. In some cases this is crucial. For example, the argument over whether the tale of the Good Samaritan (Luke 10:30–35) is a parable or an example story can be settled only in conjunction with determining the nature of the language. The view advocated here is that the Good Samaritan is metaphorical and therefore not an example story (cf. Funk, 1964; 1965; 1966: 199–22). This understanding runs counter to both ancient and modern traditions of interpretation. John Dominic Crossan has joined the battle on the side of metaphor, while Dan Via has supported the older view with structuralist arguments (*Semeia* 1, 1974).

The Good Samaritan is a particularly interesting case because the story is felt to be a powerful symbol in the Jesus tradition, yet it is taken literally by most interpreters. Linked to this is the timely question whether metaphor is native to the modern positivistic mentality, or whether it constitutes an endangered species among classic modes of speech. In any case, the determination of the language of the Good Samaritan would be an important contribution to biblical criticism.

*1.1* Traditionally, the parables in the Jesus tradition were taken either as example stories (models of right behavior) or as allegories (coded theologies). Even after the revolutionary work of Adolf Jülicher and his successors, the most influential of whom were C. H. Dodd and Joachim Jeremias, the parables were understood as example stories or as illustrations of a point that could have been made, without essential loss, in discursive, non-figurative language. In all these cases, the parables were understood literally: as example stories, they were taken as literally literal and, as allegories and illustrations, they were understood to be literally figurative.

The literal understanding of figurative language implies that something conceptually known and statable is to be communicated by means of non-literal language: the figure is a vehicle for a univocal tenor. The metaphor, by contrast, is the means by which equivocal because pre-conceptual knowledge is discovered to both speaker (writer) and hearer.

The parable as metaphor thus has an altogether different locus in language, and it was as metaphor that the parables originally functioned, in my judgment. It is not possible to discuss here why, in the transmission of the tradition, the metaphorical horizon of the parables of Jesus—of all parables, not just the Good Samaritan—was lost. That is a very interesting question, however, and its answer might throw light on our own interpretive dilemma.

1.2   The parable communicates in a non-ordinary sense because the knowledge involved in the parable is pre-conceptual: it is knowledge of unsegmented reality, of an undifferentiated nexus, of a seamless world. Conceptual knowledge is knowledge of reality segmented, differentiated, classified. Knowledge communicated by the parable lies at the threshold of knowledge as commonly understood.

The parable does not, therefore, involve a transfer from one head to another of information or ideas about an established world. In the parable reality is aborning; the parable opens onto an unfinished world because that world is in course of conception. This means that both narrator and auditor *risk* the parable; they both participate the narrative and venture its outcome. He or they do not tell the story; *it* tells *them*.

These generalizations, and others that could be made, are derivative; their source is a concrete example

2.   The parable of the Good Samaritan is commonly understood as an example story. Everyone knows its "meaning," including the

synoptic writer, Luke, who included it in his Gospel. Jesus is asked: who is my neighbor? He answers: a neighbor is someone who helps another in need. The parable therefore makes the Good Samaritan an example of what it means to be a neighbor. There is no figurative element in the parable, and the parable is taken as commending this kind of behavior.

It is quite possible that the parable can legitimately be read in this way. But I believe it can also be read as a parable, and specifically as a parable of grace. The primary reason for my conviction, in addition to structural considerations (see Chapters 4 and 5 below), is this: *the parable does not invite the hearer to view it as an example of what it means to be a good neighbor.*

Every narrative is constructed so that the reader views events from a certain perspective. Put differently, a narrative is a device to make the audience observers (Gleason: 41). The key question in determining whether the Samaritan is literal or metaphorical is how the parable places the auditors in relation to the events of the narrative.

A glimpse of the original register of the parable can perhaps be evoked by a fresh "reading" of the parable. By "reading" is meant "placing the auditor," by means of "criticism," so that he/she is enabled to attend the parable in the appropriate key. A "critical reading" of the parable is thus an effort to allow the narrative itself to "place" the hearer.

The parable runs as follows:

A man was going down from Jerusalem to Jericho, and he fell among robbers, who stripped him and beat him, and departed, leaving him half-dead. Now by chance a priest was going down that road; and when he saw him he passed by on the other side. So likewise a Levite, when he came to the place and saw him, passed by on the other side. But a Samaritan, as he journeyed, came to where he was; and when he saw him, he had compassion, and went to him and bound up his wounds, pouring on oil and wine; and then he set him on his own beast and brought him to an inn, and took care of him. And the next day he took out two denarii and gave them to the innkeeper, saying, "Take care of him; and whatever more you spend, I will repay you when I come back."

The lead clauses in each section will indicate how the narrative places the auditor.

*3.1    A man going down from Jerusalem to Jericho . . .*

The first question is: who is this anonymous man going down the road? The question arises because the narrative is a piece of everydayness which commands the immediate recognition and assent of the auditors. Naturally, this man is any Jew, like those in the audience, who has traveled that dangerous, precipitous road many times, or at least has heard stories of the robbers who lurk there. The listeners are anxious for him; they are not surprised when he is waylaid by robbers. The scene is well known and the listeners are able to respond with a certain recognition: "Yes, that's the way it is on the Jericho road."

The initial perspective therefore draws the listener into the narrative on the side of the victim in the ditch: they sympathize with him, shuddering at the danger because they know the story is true to life and, as a consequence, they take up a vantage point in the ditch to await developments.

*3.2*    From the ditch the victim observes

*by chance a priest passing by on the other side . . .*

As the man lying in the ditch, the auditors are nevertheless alert to what transpires next.

The listeners who are clerical or have clerical sympathies hesitate: they ask for a delay in the proceedings to consider whether they like the turn of events. They want to protest, not because the behavior depicted is not natural, but because callous indifference is being attributed to those who might have legitimate reason to act differently (ritual defilement, for example—let's disarm the point). But the story does not pause. It moves immediately to a new figure coming down the road.

The anti-clerical interests in the audience applaud. Exactly what one would expect, they say to themselves, of the clergy.

It is to be noted that those belonging to the religious establishment identify with the priest and thus resent being so (rightly) represented. Those excluded from the religious establishment have their opinions of priests and so watch the priest pass by with glee—from the ditch. The auditors have now been divided into two groups: one retains the perspective of the victim, the other moves away—down the road.

*3.3*    Then

*a Levite also passes by on the other side . . .*

This sub-scene reinforces the previous scene with its attendant reactions. The righteous have become angry; the religious outcasts begin to snicker. The first group is being herded down the road, reluctantly, on the other side; the second is lolling mirthfully in the ditch, having forgotten the beating and the robbery.

3.4 Neither group is prepared for
*a Samaritan who has compassion* . . .

The account of the Samaritan is relatively the longest part of the narrative and deliberately so. The Samaritan was the mortal enemy of the Jew because he was a half-brother. His appearance as friend sows confusion everywhere: all auditors are Jews. Particularly dismayed are those in the ditch, the religiously outcast, because they have been snickering and because they are now being lavishly befriended. A smile comes momentarily to the faces of the clerics as the spotlight shifts from them. But only momentarily. The narrator looks around to see whether a smile lingers on any face for more than a moment.

A Jew who was excessively proud of his blood line and a chauvinist about his tradition would not permit a Samaritan to touch him, much less minister to him. In going from Galilee to Judea, he would cross and recross the Jordan to avoid going through Samaria. The parable therefore forces upon its hearers the question: who among you will permit himself or herself to be served by a Samaritan? In a general way it can be replied that only those who have nothing to lose by so doing can afford to do so. But note that the victim in the ditch is given only a passive rôle in the story. Permission to be served by the Samaritan is thus inability to resist. Put differently, all who are truly victims, truly disinherited, have no choice but to give themselves up to mercy. The despised halfbreed has become the instrument of grace: as listeners, the Jews choke on the irony.

In the traditional reading of the parable the significance of the Samaritan has been completely effaced: the Samaritan is not a mortal enemy, but a good fellow, the model of virtuous deportment. Further, the auditors were no longer Jews but goyim. These are just two reasons the parable soon lost its original resonances.

4.1 To summarize: if the auditor, as Jew, understands what it means to be the victim in the ditch in this story, he/she also understands what the kingdom is all about.

*Understand* in the context of parable means to be drawn into the narrative as the narrative prompts, to take up the rôle assigned by the narrative. The parable is therefore also an invitation to comport oneself as the story indicates: it does not suggest that one behave as a good neighbor like the Samaritan, but that one become the victim in the ditch who is helped by an enemy. Indeed, the parable as metaphor was meant to be permission to so understand oneself. The metaphor is permission because it gives reality that shape.

4.2    The meaning of the parable cannot be made more explicit because it is non-literal: it lacks specific application.

The parable does not dictate the outcome: although auditors are prompted, they may be drawn into the story as they will. That applies both to those privileged religiously and to the religiously disinherited. The terms of the story, in other words, are not literal. Everyone is invited to smile. Anyone may move over into the ditch.

The "meaning" of the parable is the way auditors take up rôles in the story and play out the drama. Response will vary from person to person and from time to time. The parable is perpetually unfinished. The story continues to tell itself, to "tell" its hearers.

5.    It is possible, to be sure, to reflect on the parable as metaphor and endeavor to raise its meaning into discursive language. To do so on the basis of the reading just given, however, results in an abstract interpretation quite unlike the traditional meaning assigned to the parable. For one thing, the abstract language should retain some of the metaphorical quality of the parable itself. With these precautions in mind, the parable of the Good Samaritan may be reduced to two propositions:

(1) In the Kingdom of God mercy comes only to those who have no right to expect it and who cannot resist it when it comes.

(2) Mercy always comes from the quarter from which one does not and cannot expect it.

An enterprising theologian might attempt to reduce these two sentences to one:

(1) In the kingdom mercy is always a surprise.

# Four

## PARTICIPANT AND PLOT IN
## THE NARRATIVE PARABLES OF JESUS

*1.* We can speak much more confidently now than C. H. Dodd could four decades ago about the definition of a narrative parable. Dodd had to rely on imprecise criteria for his definition: a narrative parable has a series of verbs in a historical tense (18). With the assistance of discourse structure, a new form of linguistic analysis, we are able to plot new and precise grids for the definitions of parables and other types of narrative.

A narrative parable may be defined initially as a parable with at least three major participants. Some parables have only two participants (for example, Unjust Judge, Servant's Wages, Pharisee and Publican) and some only one (for example, Lost Coin, Lost Sheep, Sower). The parables with three principals include:

| | | | |
|---|---|---|---|
| (1) | Laborers in the Vineyard | Matt 20:1–15 | Huck §190 |
| (2) | Talents | Matt 25:14–30// Luke 19:12–27 | §228 |
| (3) | Ten Maidens | Matt 25:1–13 | §227 |
| (4) | Great Supper | Luke 14:16–24// Matt 22:1–10 | §170 |
| (5) | Good Samaritan | Luke 10:30–35 | §144 |
| (6) | Prodigal | Luke 15:11–32 | §173 |
| (7) | Unjust Steward | Luke 16:1-9 | §174 |
| (8) | Unmerciful Servant | Matt 18:23–34 | §136 |

| (9) Wicked Tenants | Mark 12:1–9// | §204 |
| | Matt 21:33–41// | |
| | Luke 20:9–16 | |
| (10) Rich Man and Lazarus | Luke 16:19–31 | §177 |

To this list could be added the Two Sons (Matt 21:28–31a, §203), which, if a narrative at all, is a narrative only in the most skeletal form.

A second criterion is this: a narrative parable must have at least two scenes. This feature eliminates the Two Sons, as well as items (9) and (10) in the list above, about which further idiosyncrasies will be noted.

*1.1* In counting principal participants, groups are treated as one if members of the group act in concert, for example, the five talent and two talent servants in the parable of the Talents, the priest and Levite in the Good Samaritan. The foolish and wise maidens in the Ten Maidens of course represent two principals (cf. Bultmann, 1968: 188).

*1.2* Subordinate characters are not counted. They are used sparingly and in no case play more than ancillary roles. Subordinate figures may be stage pawns representing the buffer between social superiors and inferiors or between social groups of equivalent status. Examples are the steward in the Laborers in the Vineyard (Matt 20:8) and the servant in the Great Supper (Luke 14:17, 21ff.) and in the Prodigal (Luke 15:26). They may also supply missing links in the narrative which are necessary but cannot be supplied by one of the principals. Examples are the servants who inform on the servant in the Unmerciful Servant (Matt 18:31) and the robbers in the Good Samaritan (Luke 10:30). Subordinate figures may fill out the body of the narrative by repetition without adding to the content—for example, the laborers hired at the third, sixth, and ninth hours in the Laborers in the Vineyard (Matt 20:3–5).

*1.3* The scale on which participants are viewed may change during the course of a narrative. The scale may contract from a large group to a few members or to one member of the group, or it may expand in the opposite direction. In the Laborers in the Vineyard, for example, those hired first are represented by a single person in Matt 20:13. Changes in scale do not increase the number of participants.

*1.4* The ten parables with three principals will not be given equal attention in the analysis which follows. The Rich Man and Lazarus will receive comment only in passing, and others, notably the Wicked Tenants, will also be slighted for reasons that will eventually become apparent.

*2.* The major parables with three principals fall into two distinct groups.

*2.1* In Group I, consisting of parables (1)–(6), one of the principals functions as what may be called the *determiner* (similar to but not identical with the ordainer: Via, 1974: §2.122); the other two represent contrasting *responses* to the *focal actuality* of the parable. The focal actuality of the parable is the situation or action represented in or created by the determiner: money given in trust, banquet hall standing ready for guests.

In the Ten Maidens, the maidens take their lamps and go out to meet the bridegroom in order to conduct him, in festal procession, to the bride. His delay has been occasioned according to custom by bargaining over the gifts to be made to relatives of the bride: the longer the delay, the greater the compliment to the bride because extended bargaining indicates reluctance on the part of kinfolk to relinquish her.

Some of the maidens go prepared to light the way for the bridegroom, others do not. As the night wears on, lamps grow dim and all fall asleep. Suddenly, a cry announces the imminent arrival of the bridegroom. The five imprudent maidens try to borrow oil for their lamps, are rebuffed, and then go off to buy for themselves. Meanwhile the five wise maidens trim their lamps and enter the banquet hall with the bridegroom. In the final scene judgment is pronounced on the foolish girls by the bridegroom through the closed door.

In this parable, the bridegroom is the figure on which the story turns, the participant who determines the situation in relation to which the action takes place. He may therefore be called the determiner, or D. In addition to D, there are two other sets of participants, the wise and the foolish maidens. Their responses to the situation set by D are in some sense contrasting or opposed. For the sake of convenience, these participant sets may be labeled R1 and R2 (R for respondent). The three participants may thus be termed D, R1, R2.

The parable of the Talents is similarly constructed. The master entrusts money to two sets of servants. One set trades with the money and increases it, the other buries or hides it out of fear. Upon his return, the master rewards the first group and punishes the second.

In parables (1)–(6), D thus sets the terms or situation to which responses are made. In this sense, D determines the course of the narrative. One could therefore say that D provides the axis on which the parable turns, either as something D is or as something D does. Sometimes D is highly visible in the narrative, as the householder in the Laborers in the Vineyard, for example, but D may also play a subdued role, such as the bridegroom in the Ten Maidens. In the Good Samaritan, D is silent and passive throughout but nevertheless functions as the focal actuality of the parable.

Because D creates the focal actuality, directly or indirectly, to which R1 and R2 respond, D may be said to be the middle term between the two other participants.

R1 and R2 represent contrasting (or opposite) responses to the terms of the situation established by D.

This description is derived from the first six parables in the list:

(1) Laborers in the Vineyard
    D = householder
    R1 = hired first
    R2 = hired last
(2) Talents
    D = master
    R1 = 5 + 2 talent servants
    R2 = 1 talent servant
(3) Ten Maidens
    D = bridegroom
    R1 = foolish maidens
    R2 = wise maidens
(4) Great Supper
    D = host
    R1 = invited
    R2 = uninvited
(5) Good Samaritan
    D = robbed
    R1 = priest, Levite
    R2 = Samaritan

(6) Prodigal
   D = father
   R1 = younger son
   R2 = older son

*2.2* In the second group of parables having three principal characters, there is also what might be called a determiner (D), to whom there is *one* principal respondent (R), who sustains narrative contact with D on the one hand and with a second, subordinate character (r) on the other. In this case, R is the mediating term between D and r.

In the parables of Group II, R and r do not represent contrasting responses. Rather, r provides the occasion for development in the relation of R to D. Thus R more nearly approximates the unifying subject of the narrative in Via's sense (1971: 180; 1974: §3.23), whereas r serves as a foil for R.

In this group, too, D initiates or evokes the action (Via, 1967: 164), to which a response is made. Participant D is visible only in that portion of the narrative involving contact between D and R: D sets the terms for R, disappears from the narrative during the contact between R and r, and then returns at the end of the narrative for the denouement. The determiner is also absent from the narrative line part of the time in some of the parables of Group I (Talents, Ten Maidens, Prodigal).

The chief difference observed thus far between the two groups of parables is that R1 and R2 represent contrasting responses to D in Group I, whereas the narrative in Group II permits response only on the part of R. In the latter, the response of R looks two ways, in one direction toward D, in the other toward r.

This decription is derived from:

(7) Unjust Steward
   D = master
   R = steward
   r = debtors
(8) Unmerciful Servant
   D = king
   R = first servant
   r = second servant

It is possible that

(9) Wicked Tenants
    D = owner
    R = tenants
    r = servants, son

also belongs to Group II, but I am not confident of this judgment.
It is also probable that

(10) Rich Man and Lazarus

belongs to Group I.

2.3   It was noted that D is the middle term between R1 and R2
in the parables of Group I: R1–D–R2. In the second group, R is the
middle term: D–R–r. The lines connecting symbols stand for both
deep (fundamental relationships) and surface (narrative contact)
stucture.

These relationships could also be expressed in the form of a
triangle:

| Figure 1 | Figure 2 |

In all ten of the narrative parables only two of the three possible
sets of relationships are expressed in any given parable.
In figure 1 there is D–R1 and D–R2, but not R1–R2. In figure 2
there is R–D and R–r, but not D–r.

Bultmann (1968: 188; cf. Olrik: 134f.) has observed that the law
of *stage duality* is operative in the parables: only two persons
(groups) may speak or act at one time. To this can now be added the
further observation: in the narrative parables with three principals,
only two of three possible sets of relationships may be developed.
This could be called the law of relationship duality, or the law of the
open triangle.

2.31   If R1 and R2 represent contrasting responses to D in
parables of Group I (if figure 1 represents the deep structure of the
parables of Group I), are the relationships R1–D and R2–D always

expressed and the relationship R1–R2 always left open in the surface structure of the parable? In other words, does the surface structure always coincide with the deep structure?

The six parables listed in §2.1 are relatively monotonous in this regard. In all except the Ten Maidens, the deep and surface structures match. In the Ten Maidens, however, the foolish maidens (R1) and the wise maidens (R2) sustain significant narrative contact among themselves (Matt 25:8-9). Only the foolish maidens (R1) have any real narrative contact with D (we are told only that the wise maidens entered the hall when D arrived, Matt 25:10). The triangle representing the two sets of surface relationships in the narrative would thus be:

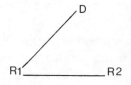

Figure 3

Nevertheless, the deep structure of the Ten Maidens is clearly identical with other parables in the group.

The surface structure of the Rich Man and Lazarus is similar to figure 3, but the deep structure appears to be accurately represented by figure 1.

*2.4*  To summarize: the major narrative parables with three principals may be divided into two subgroups. In the first, the determiner (D) sets the stage for contrasting responses on the part of R1 and R2. In the second, D sets the stage for the response of R, which is worked out in narrative contact with r, a third principal.

In Group I, D is the middle term between R1 and R2; in Group II, R is the middle term between D and r. In both groups only two sets of narrative relationships are developed.

In both groups D functions as the axis on which the story turns.

*3.*  We may now investigate the relation of the principal participants, identified in §2, to the narrative line of the parable.

*3.1*  The relation of the participants to the narrative line in the parable of the Laborers in the Vineyard may be charted as follows:

the householder (D) hires laborers early in the morning: $D > R1$. After repeating this action at the third, sixth, and ninth hours (repetition to heighten the tension), the householder returns to the marketplace and engages eleventh hour idlers: $D > R2$.

When evening comes, the householder orders that R2 be paid their unearned wages first: $D > R2$. When they are paid the same amount, R1 protests: $D < R1$. The determiner responds with a final pronouncement (= denouement): $D > R1$.

Although not the subject of the narrative in the customary sense (Via, 1967: 149f.), D nevertheless serves as the axis of the story. Because D sets the terms of the narrative, the D line may be permitted to coincide with the narrative line:

D ————————————————————————→

The two respondents represent contrasting responses to the situation created by D, and in this parable they are made to witness each other's fate. Moreover, R1 and R2 appear in the second scene in reverse order in relation to their initial appearances (noted by Crossan, 1974c: §3.55). The fate of R1 turns downward (tragic), whereas the fate of R2 turns upward (comic). The two may therefore be represented on the narrative line as follows:

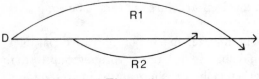

Figure 4

The Talents and the Ten Maidens may be diagramed in a comparable way but with significant differences, to be noted subsequently.

Parables diagramed (figure 4) may be designated Group Ia.

*3.2* The determiner is also the thread on which the parable of the great Supper is strung. However, the exchange between D and R1 (those invited) takes place and is concluded before the uninvited (R2) appear on the scene; the two respondents confront their fates in isolation. Once again, the fate of R1 turns downward and the fate of R2 is comic. The Great Supper may be represented diagrammatically as:

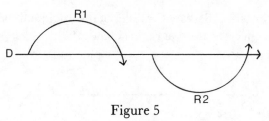

Figure 5

The diagram for the Good Samaritan would be identical: R1 = priest, Levite; R2 = Samaritan.

The diagram of the Prodigal would also be identical, except that the order of the tragic and comic curves is reversed:

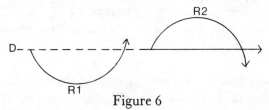

Figure 6

Parables with the diagram (figure 5) or (figure 6) may be designated Group Ib.

The difference between Groups Ia and Ib may be stated this way: in Ia the sets of relationships between D and R1/R2 are intertwined on the narrative line; in Ib the two sets of relationships are discrete.

3.3 In the parables of Group II, the determiner appears at the beginning of the narrative, sets the stage by encountering R, then drops out of the narrative during R's encounter with r, until the denouement. Nevertheless, D remains the axis on which the story turns. The presence and absence of D from the narrative may be represented as solid and broken lines, respectively (cf. figure 6).

In these parables R is subject to a double reversal: once in connection with D, a second time as a result of contact with r. In the Unjust Steward, R is threatened with ruin by D, but R then treats D's debtors in such a way that his fate is reversed. The parable could therefore be diagramed as:

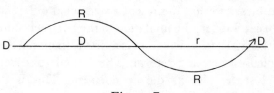

Figure 7

In the Unmerciful Servant the order of the tragic and comic curves is reversed; otherwise the diagram is identical:

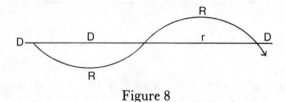

Figure 8

*3.31* The parable of the Wicked Tenants may be diagramed as (figure 8), except that the fate of R1 (the tenants) does not appear to turn down initially. The fact that r (servants, son) are sent by D (cf. §1.2) also raises a question about the fundamental structure of the parable.

*4.* Via observes two episode patterns in the narrative parables (1971: 174ff.; 1974: §4.2 and fig. 2), one consisting of action / crisis / denouement, the other of crisis / response/ denouement. The relation of these formal categories to surface markers in the narrative requires investigation. The Laborers in the Vineyard, for example, is clearly divided into two (not three) scenes by correlative temporal markers (Matt 20:1, 8). Nevertheless, it may be asked how the clusters of participants (§2) and their relation to the narrative line (§3) are correlated with the sequence of episodes as proposed by Via.

The parables of Group Ia follow the pattern action / crisis / denouement, in agreement with Via's analysis.

The Unjust Steward and the Unmerciful Servant in Group II follow the pattern crisis / response / denouement, also in agreement with Via.

The Wicked Tenants follows the pattern action / crisis / denouement, according to Via (1974: fig. 2), yet it belongs for other reasons to Group II. This discrepancy raises further questions about the parable (cf. §3.31).

The parables of Group Ib present a somewhat different pattern.

In the Great Supper, the invitation to the banquet could be taken as a disguised crisis, to which there is a first response in the form of a series of excuses denoting refusal. The second (passive) response follows and serves also as the denouement. This is the precise pattern of the Good Samaritan, except that it is the first response, rather than the second, that is passive in that parable.

|  | "crisis" | response 1 | response 2 (denouement) |
|---|---|---|---|
| Great Supper | invitation | R1: invited excuses | R2: uninvited: swept in |
| Good Samaritan | victim in ditch | R1: priest, Levite passby | R2: Samaritan first aid |

This pattern may be designated: crisis / response 1/ response 2 (denouement).

The Prodigal Son presents a rather more complicated picture.

Via charts only the first part of the parable (the story of the younger son), which manifests the pattern: action / crisis / response (1974: fig. 2; 1971: 175). Via regards part 2 (the story of the older son) as authentic, so he is not justified in ignoring it in his analysis (1967: 163, 167). It is also necessary for him to blink the law of end stress, which he otherwise frequently invokes.

Unlike any of the other narrative parables, the Prodigal is clearly episodic (episode is used here in a different sense than in the phrase "sequence of episodes"): part 1 could stand by itself as a parable with two principals, just as Via takes it, and part 2 can be understood as a response to the conclusion of part 1, to which the father's pronouncement at the end provides the denouement. It is this episodic arrangement that gives the Prodigal its peculiar structure.

The two parts of the Prodigal overlap, so to speak, to the extent of the father's reception of the younger son upon his return: the father's reception is the denouement of the episode of the younger, yet it serves as the focal actuality to which the older son responds. D (= father) is thus quite literally the middle term between R1 and R2. However, just as the father provides two types of denouement (receives the younger son, reprimands the older son), he also sets the situation twice, once in receiving the younger son back. Nevertheless, R1 and R2 represent contrasting responses to a reasonably consistent D.

Part I, as Via has rightly pointed out, follows the pattern action / crisis / denouement. Part 2 follows this pattern: crisis (father's reception of the younger son) / response (older son's protest) / denouement (father's final word). Two patterns thus appear in a single parable, depending on whether one is looking primarily at the first or the second part. The Prodigal therefore belongs to both Groups Ia and II, so far as sequence of episodes is concerned; but it belongs to Group Ib so far as the diagram of the relation of its participants to the narrative line is concerned.

Assigning the Prodigal to Group Ib depends on reading the parable as a whole (§3.2). This fact and the sequence of episodes observed in the Great Supper and the Good Samaritan (§4) suggest still another way of viewing the parable. The Prodigal could be read, as a whole, on the pattern: "crisis" / response 1 / response 2, when we note that the younger son actually evokes the action (Via, 1967: 164) and sets the terms to which the father and the older son respond.

|  | *"crisis"* | *response 1* | *response 2* |
|---|---|---|---|
| Prodigal | fall, return of younger son | father's reception | older son's reception |

In this case, the younger son is D, R1 is the father, and R2 is the older son. The reception of the younger son is taken to be the issue on which the parable turns: the father accepts, the older son rejects. And the younger son certifies that grace is actual, as in the case of the victim in the Good Samaritan (note §6.2).

There are, of course, features of the Prodigal which work against this third sequence of episodes, but that would be true of any multi-layered narrative. Bold as it may be, it is still possible.

So far as I can see, the Prodigal is the only parable which offers the prospect of three different readings, owing to its episodic nature. Perhaps this is another reason for the admiration of this parable in the tradition.

5.    The principals D, R1, R2, R, and r have been treated thus far in a purely formal way. It is now necessary to speak of their *functions* in the several narratives. In so doing we shall be speaking of them as *actants* (= function, role, or status, Via, 1974: §2.122). Observations will be confined initially to the actants in parables of Group I.

5.1    It is appropriate to begin with R1 and R2 in the parables with the formal structure R1–D–R2.

In the Laborers in the Vineyard, those hired first agree with the householder for wages of a denarius a day. When wages are dispersed at the end of the day, they observe that those hired at the eleventh hour receive a denarius for their inconsequential labor. They are therefore led to expect more, the narrative instructs us, but they, too, receive the agreed wage. The rising expectations and then the dashed hope is created by the realism which permeates the parable. That is, the logic of everydayness, which infuses the narrative up to the point of reckoning, except for one or two glimmers of an impending "turn," requires that those hired first respond as they do. Those hired first are thus those who give the appropriate response in accordance with the realism of everyday, and the protest they mount against the householder can be said to be "justified" in accordance with this same logic. This type of response might be labeled RJ for "response of the just," or "justified response." In the Laborers in the Vineyard, those hired first are R1 (they appear first), yielding the equation $R1 = RJ$.

In the Prodigal Son, the behavior of the older son is exemplary, in accordance with contemporary standards. His protest against the exaggerated reception of the younger son is therefore justified: $R2 = RJ$.

One way of describing the behavior of RJ is to say that it is expected. This characterizes the non-involvement policy of the priest and the Levite in the Good Samaritan, which may reflect an everyday anticlericalism of the period. The priest and Levite also have what might be called establishment status, which may be compared with the status of the older son and of the Pharisee in the Pharisee and Publican. All these responses are, of course, also expected.

The same may be said of the invited in the parable of the Great Supper in its Lukan form. I have argued that the invited are so depicted as to suggest social status; in the narrative, however, their status is unmarked, except by contrast with the street people. In any case, they are marked as invited guests, and that specifies status of some order in relation to the uninvited from the street. The response of the invited is also expected, that is, realistic.

These observations lead to the definition of RJ as the one or ones in the narrative who give the expected response in accordance with the canons of everydayness; who are justified in protesting, if they do; who are on the right side of the fence religiously or socially, or whose status is otherwise marked as superior to the other R in the narrative. In spite of these "positive" qualifications, RJ never gets what he thinks he is entitled to, what he in fact may be entitled to, or what he aspires to. Put more broadly, RJ gets a poor shake as the narrative comes to denouement. For RJ the story invariably turns downward (tragic).

5.2 The characterization of RJ in §5.1 makes it possible to abbreviate the description of the other respondent in parables with the structure R1–D–R2.

By contrast with RJ, the other respondent customarily does not expect anything, and has no "right" to expect anything, is not especially justified in his position, but in the end he is pleasantly surprised by the way things turn out. In general, he is passive in relation to events unfolding in the narrative. Because this respondent gets what he does not deserve, he may be designated RG (= recipient of grace). For RG the story regularly turns in a comic direction.

There is no difficulty in recognizing RG as those hired at the eleventh hour in the Laborers in the Vineyard, as the uninvited street people in the Great Supper, and as the younger son in the Prodigal. It is surprising, though no less evident, that the victim in the ditch is the recipient of grace in the Good Samaritan. This fact suggests that the functions RJ and RG may be mapped onto D, R1, R2 in more than one way, since the victim in the Good Samaritan is D in the formal structure of the parable.

Before pursuing this point, a third function in the narrative parables with three principals should be noted.

5.3 RJ and RG represent the contrasting responses referred to in §2.1. In the earlier discussion it was assumed that these responses were always represented in the narrative by R1 and R2; that is not, in fact, always the case, though it is predominantly so. A third function in the narrative parables is represented by the figure that dispenses grace or justice (IG/J = instrument of grace or justice). This function is usually but not always embodied in D, who customarily is an authority figure. The instrument of grace is he who receives, admits, rewards, helps; as instrument of justice he excludes, pays what is due, rebukes, refuses aid.

5.4 It should be observed that RJ and RG are juxtaposed in the respondent (R) in the parables of the Unjust Steward and the

Unmerciful Servant. The steward faces impending ruin (= justice) before he acts to gain reprieve; the master's approval is unexpected. The unmerciful servant, on the other hand, is the recipient of surprising grace before he foolishly cashes it in for justice of his own, which trails disaster in its wake.

In these parables, the master and the king are instruments of justice and grace (Unjust Steward: IJ/G; Unmerciful Servant: IG/J).

The actants IJ/G, RJ, and RG are thus mapped onto the formal structure of the parables of Group II in a way which differs from any of the options finding expression in Group I.

6.1    The fortunes of RJ and RG in the parables discussed in §5 are always reversed in relation to expectations. Those hired at the beginning of the day expect to be paid more but are not; those who worked only an hour do not expect a full day's wage but receive it. The younger son does not expect to be taken back as a son, but he is; the older son does not anticipate the reception his brother is given, but he has to swallow it nevertheless. The reversal in the Unjust Steward and the Unmerciful Servant was noted in §5.4.

In the case of the Great Supper, it is no less evident that those invited to the banquet do not expect to be deliberately excluded, although there is no recognition scene or surrogate; the people in the street do not anticipate an invitation, but they get it. Similarly, in the Good Samaritan, the priest and Levite are handled brusquely in the narrative; they are not allowed to protest visibly, as there is nothing resembling a recognition scene. The Samaritan, on the other hand, is a surprise to everybody, especially to the man in the ditch, whose fortunes are suddenly reversed.

The reversal of the fortunes of RJ and RG carries with it a more profound reversal. Put succinctly, the fortunes of all those who are justified or require justice suffer tragedy; the fates of those who expect or require nothing, to the contrary, swing upward in comic relief.

6.2    The determiner was defined in §2.1 as the figure which sets the terms of the narrative. In relation to the reversals discussed in §6.1, the preeminent function of D appears to be to *certify those reversals.* Just as the old order of reality is certified by authorities represented in the narrative by RJ, the new reality also has its sanctions, and the sanction in each case is D.

The determiner is most frequently an authority figure (owner of vineyard, rich man, bridegroom, host, father, king) and in those parables in which this is so, D dominates the denouement, which may consist simply of a pronouncement. In the same parables, D is not always highly visible and is "not drawn into the vicissitudes of the plot" (suggested by Via, 1967: 160). It is the supreme temptation of parable interpretation to assume that D, as the one who certifies the reversal, is represented in the narrative by an authority figure because such a figure is an appropriate model for God. The fact that D is not drawn into the vicissitudes of the story reinforces this proclivity.

It is possible that this factor is a fundamental weakness in the parables of Jesus. I say weakness for aesthetic reasons: if Jesus chooses an authority figure each time to model God, we are driven in spite of ourselves back in the direction of allegory.

There are at least two good reasons for resisting the supreme temptation. The first is that the authority figure does not always provide a suitable analogue for God (for example, the doting father in the Prodigal, the master in the Unjust Steward; for other examples, see Jeremias: 179).

A second and more impressive reason is that in the Good Samaritan D is not an authority figure but the victim in the ditch. The parable calls on the man in the ditch to certify the new reality, and that means, to Jesus' hearers, that he who is a recipient of grace can certify that grace has come, even at the hands of a Samaritan. In the Samaritan, therefore, we have an interesting correlation of formal and functional aspects: $D = RG/R1 = RJ/R2 = IG$. As a consequence of this parable it is necessary to distinguish certification from IG; in other words, D and the certifier of the new reality (now designated C) are always the same, but D or C do not always coincide with IJ/G.

If the Prodigal is given the third reading sketched in §4, it, too, requires that D and C be distinguished from IJ/G. In that reading, the younger son $= D$; at the same time, he is the recipient of grace (RG) and therefore certifies the reversal. The father is R1 and also IG/J, and the older son is $R2 = RJ$.

6.3  The elements D, C, IJ/G, R1, R2, RJ, and RG, analyzed in §6.1–2, may be summarized in tabular form:

| GROUP I | D(C) | | R1 | | R2 | |
|---|---|---|---|---|---|---|
| (1) Laborers | IG/J | Owner | RJ | Hired First | RG | Hired Last |
| (2) Talents | IG/J | Master | | 5+2 Talent | 1 | Talent |
| (3) Ten Maidens | IG/J | Bridegroom | | Foolish | | Wise |
| (4) Great Supper | IG/J | Host | RJ | Invited | RG | Uninvited |
| (5) Samaritan | RG | Robbed | RJ | Priest, Levite | IG | Samaritan |
| (6) Prodigal | IG/J | Father | RG | Younger Son | RJ | Older Son |

| GROUP II | D(C) | | R | | r |
|---|---|---|---|---|---|
| (7) Unjust Steward | IJ/G | Master | RJ/RG | Steward | Debtors |
| (8) Unmerciful Servant | IG/J | King | RG/RJ | First Servant | Second Servant |
| (9) Wicked Tenants | IJ | Owner | | Tenants | Servants, Son |

Notations for the parables of the Talents, Ten Maidens, and Wicked Tenants are not complete. There are no notations, of course, for the r column in parables of Group II.

7.  If Parables (1), (4)–(8) are taken as indicative of the "message" of Jesus, it may be said that Jesus announces a fundamental reversal of the destinies of men. This reversal is related to expectations as informed by the received or everyday world. Further, this reversal is a perpetual state of affairs in the kingdom: whatever man comes to expect as owed to him is perpetually refused, but to him who expects nothing, the kingdom arrives as a gift.

Those who hear the parables are at liberty to take up positions vis-à-vis the parable as they will. They may elect to insist on justice or they may settle for grace. How one chooses depends not a little on where one comes from and where one is going. RG is forever leaving home in order to return; he is always crossing over to that fabulous yonder of Kafka. RJ cannot come home because he never leaves; he clings to the certainties of the everyday.

The "message" cannot be specified further: the hearers cannot be identified in advance of the telling, and the reversal is a perpetual state of affairs.

The received world is always the world RJ comes to trust, on which he depends for the right of it; it is always in the process of crystallization and can never be specified with exactness. The new reality, on the other hand, is only on its way; were it to arrive, it would forthwith become the old reality, the received world.

Who will be the invited and the uninvited, those hired first and those hired last, depends on how the hearer comports himself in relation to the movement of the narrative: is he unwilling to quit the solid comfort of the expected, or is he ready to venture forth?

Similarly, the determiner and the certifier remain a cipher because God does not "appear." That means only that Jesus is not heavy handed: he offers the new reality on the authority of the parable, as a comic inversion of received certainties, that the hearer is free to cross over or not, as he chooses. There is no coercion; God does not "appear" to force the issue. The issue is joined only by the metaphor.

It is of course clear that Jesus sides with RG in the parables. All the parables are fundamentally comic, on Via's terms, because they are all parables of grace, even when the narrative formally turns down. This is proved by the fact that RG always wins; RJ never does. So the teller pronounces the parable as an incantation for those who are willing to accept the certification of a new reality.

For the reason articulated in §§6, 7, I dimly perceived the major parables as double paradigms or declensions of reality (1966: 193f.). The first paradigm brings the logic of everydayness to the surface and confirms that logic as self-evident or self-validating. The first paradigm is shattered on the second, which disrupts the order of everydayness by reversing certainties or turning things upside down. This analysis is confirmed by the structure of the narrative parables as sketched in §§1-7.

8.7   It became necessary to allow for exceptions in the analyis of the Talents and the Ten Maidens already in §3.11 and especially in §§5ff. Why is this the case?

The diagram (figure 4, §3.1) does not satisfactorily express the relation of the participants to the narrative line in these two parables because the destinies of R1 and R2 do not follow an ascending and then descending, or descending and then ascending, movement, as in the parable of the Laborers. Rather, the destinies of the two principals rise steadily or fall steadily.

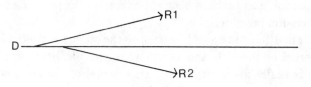

Figure 9

The master distributes the money according to ability (Matt 25:15), and the participants act accordingly; the wise and foolish maidens are wise and foolish to the end. There is thus no reversal in these two parables (§6.1; cf. Crossan, 1974c: note 41). As a consequence, R1 and R2 cannot be designated R J or RG. In other respects, however, the two parables are structurally like the Laborers in the Vineyard.

8.2  In the Wicked Tenants, the destiny of R does not suffer a double reversal as suggested by diagrams (F7) and (F8). Letting out the vineyard may be understood as an act of grace, of course, but that act does not reverse a previously grim situation, as the initial act of grace does in the Unmerciful Servant. From the vantage point of tenancy the narrative does turn downward at the close, or so the tradition implies.

It is possible that the Wicked Tenants is to be understood as a narrative parable with two principals only. The servants and son would then be subordinate figures who play no essential role (cf. §3.31). The observation that servants serve as a narrative buffer between different social strata supports this view. Aquisition of tenancy would represent the upward movement, and the ouster of the tenants would then be comparable to a diagram of the second episode of the Prodigal:

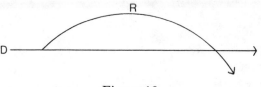

Figure 10

Viewed in this fashion, the Wicked Tenants would not be a parable with three principals and thus should be eliminated from the list in §1.

The parable has perhaps been too effaced in the tradition to make a firm decision possible.

*8.3* The Rich Man and Lazarus, on the other hand, does involve the reversal of the rich and the poor in the life beyond. But the parable is really about an attempted reversal of the reversal. And there are other peculiarities which make this parable difficult to classify.

*8.4* At least six of the narrative parables have a common deep structure, as indicated above. Of the four that diverge from that common structure, it is against three (Ten Maidens, Wicked Tenants, Rich Man and Lazarus) that a question of authenticity is most often set.

# Five

# PARABLE, PARADOX, AND POWER:
# THE PRODIGAL SAMARITAN

*1.* As a consequence of the pioneering work done by Vladimir Propp on the Russian folktale, and the development of that work principally by the French structuralists, we can now say that there appear to be at least two basic plot structures possible in narrative literature. The narrative parables of Jesus seem to conform to one of them.

Propp defined the Russian folktale as any development proceeding from an act of villainy or a lack or misfortune, through intermediary functions, to marriage, reward, or the liquidation of the lack or misfortune. Such a three-phase development Propp terms a *move*.

In the Gospels, the healing miracle story appears to follow this general pattern. The healing miracle is developed out of a lack or misfortune: a sufferer is introduced, usually with some indication of the gravity of the malady (for example, a woman who had been infirm for eighteen years). This misfortune is overcome in the act of healing. The testimony of bystanders often serves as the conclusion, and this type of conclusion connects the narrative to its larger context in the Gospels: the witness to Jesus of Nazareth as a wonder worker.

The French structuralist A. J. Greimas has developed an analysis of what he terms the *contractual syntagm* (see Patte, 1974). In order to keep our terminology uniform, this type of plot will be called a *contractual move*.

The contractual move consists of three basic functions: contract, test, judgment. The contract is normally made between the hero and a superior power who has the authority to set the terms and to reward success or punish failure. The contract always comes at the beginning, the reward or punishment at the end. The test, obviously, must come between. No other order is possible.

The actors in this scheme are contractor / contractee, tester / tested, judge / judged. The six possible participants may in fact be represented by only two characters, the hero and the superior power. It is also possible, of course, to have two "heroes," one who fulfills the contract and is rewarded, the other who does not fulfill the contract and is punished. It is also necessary to have the same superior power running through the story, or implied in it, in order to have a narrative at all.

The contractual move as developed by Greimas appears to fit well the plot structure of most parables in the Jesus tradition.

The contract in the Ten Maidens is formed when the Ten Maidens take their lamps and go out to meet the bridegroom. Some go prepared and some do not. The test takes place when it is announced that the bridegroom is arriving. The imprudent maidens fail the test, the wise maidens are prepared and pass it. In the final scene, judgment is pronounced on the foolish girls through the closed door. The move—contract, test, judgment—thus serves as the plot structure of this parable and of the other narrative parables as well.

2. In identifying sets of participants and their interrelationships, and in identifying the basic plot structure of the parables, we have been trading in items too general to be discriminating. The analysis must be sharpened so as to be able to distinguish among specific parables—narrative parables only, it should be noted—and perhaps even grade them in relation to their literary quality, their power to draw listeners into their orbit, and the profundity of the message they bear.

The remarks that follow will be more readily appropriated if the results are presented in advance. I propose to demonstrate that the Great Supper and the Laborers in the Vineyard are rather more sophisticated and compelling metaphoric instruments than the parables of the Talents and the Ten Maidens. Further, the Prodigal Son and the Good Samaritan are even more subtle and complex in spite of their evident simplicity: listeners are drawn into and captivated by them whether they will or not. In my view, the Prodigal Son and the Good Samaritan stand at the apex of Jesus' parabolic creativity; the Laborers in the Vineyard and the Great Supper follow closely; the Talents and the Ten Maidens are only fair representatives of the genre by comparison.

3. In the parables of the Talents and Ten Maidens, the determiner (D) is an authority figure. In the one case he is a landed master, in the other a bridegroom. It is this figure that sets the situation to which R1 and R2 respond. D also serves as the thread on which the story is strung.

The two respondents in the Ten Maidens are identified from the outset as wise and foolish. We do not have to wait to see how the story turns out; we know in advance that the foolish will do something unwise and be punished. There are no surprises. Furthermore, the wise maidens achieve something positive, something quite in accordance with normal expectations, to merit their designation and reward: they take extra oil along with their lamps for the vigil. The Ten Maidens is therefore heavy-handed: its message is hammered home unsubtly, like a commercial.

Similarly, the Talents introduces the listener to two groups of servants, one receiving plural talents, the other a single talent. Though they are not specifically identified in all versions at the outset as good and bad, the reader is reasonably certain that the number of talents given in trust corresponds to the level of the servants' competence. We are therefore not surprised that the story turns out as it does. It meets common expectations. The trusted servants, moreover, do as we anticipate: they trade with the master's money and earn him interest. For this positive achievement they are rewarded.

These observations on the Ten Maidens and the Talents may be summarized in four points, to which a fifth and concluding point may then be added.

(1) The determiner, or D, is an authority figure who rewards and punishes two sets of respondents in accordance with their behavior. D: it is this way because I say it is.

(2) The two sets of respondents are identified as good and bad, wise and foolish, from the outset of the narrative.

(3) Those who are rewarded merit their reward by achieving something positive.

(4) The narrative affirms the hearer's everyday expectations: the story turns out as anticipated.

(5) The last three features just enumerated make it possible for the hearer to hold the story at arm's length, to relate to it as a bystander rather than as a participant: (1) the hearer does not have to decide for him/herself who the good characters are; (2) the good characters achieve something the hearer is expected to value (preparedness, thrift); (3) the story turns out as the hearer expects. This means that the Ten Maidens and the Talents are robbed of their provocative power: the hearer is not caught in a parabolic snare because there is no snare.

The narrative structure of these two parables is represented in figure 9, Chapter 4, §8.1.

*4.* The Laborers in the Vineyard and the Great Supper, together with the Prodigal Son and the Good Samaritan, constitute a group which may be termed *parables of grace.* In examining these parables, we must now distinguish functions from participants, as we did in the participant analysis in Chapter 4, and thus develop a second grid.

The Laborers in the Vineyard and the Great Supper also present us with determiners who are authority figures. The owner of the vineyard and the host of the feast reward and include, rebuke and exclude, as does D in the Talents and Ten Maidens. In respect of D, the second pair of parables is comparable to the first.

Those hired first in the Laborers in the Vineyard are prompted, by virtue of the full day's wage paid those hired last, to protest their treatment. This protest is lodged in accordance with the canons of everydayness, as observed earlier. Participant is not distinguishable from function: those hired first give a justified response, which has been labeled R J, for the sake of convenience (in this case, R1 = RJ).

In the Prodigal Son, the response of the older son is justified, expected, in accordance with contemporary standards (R2 = RJ). The noninvolvement policy of the priest and Levite in the Good Samaritan is prudent, safe, commonplace (R1 = RJ). Those invited to the banquest in the Great Supper are expected to decline, given the responsibilities they shoulder (R1 = RJ); the hearer would be surprised if they didn't. In all these cases, one respondent in the story is marked as RJ: the one who is justified in protesting. Yet RJ is never treated in the story as he thinks he ought to be; his expectations, and the expectations of all those dominated by everydayness, are frustrated. For RJ the story regularly turns in a tragic direction.

By contrast with RJ, the other respondent in these parables usually does not expect anything but is pleasantly surprised by the way things turn out. Because this respondent gets what he does not deserve, he has been given the designation RG (recipient of grace). For RG the story regularly turns in a comic direction.

Those hired at the eleventh hour in the Laborers in the Vineyard, the uninvited street people in the Great Supper, and the younger son in the Prodigal are RG. It is no less evident that the victim in the ditch is the recipient of grace in the Good Samaritan.

(1) As in the Talents and Ten Maidens, D is an authority figure who rewards or punishes two sets of respondents in accordance with their behavior.

(2) Unlike R1 and R2 in the Talents and Ten Maidens, the two respondents in the parables of grace are *not identified in advance.* However, native responses prompt the hearer to identify RJ as the good and RG as the bad participants.

(3) In the Talents and Ten Maidens, the good characters are rewarded for positive achievements. In the parables of grace, the recipients of grace are either passive (street people in the Great Supper, victim in the Samaritan), indolent (those hired at the eleventh hour), or wasteful (prodigal son). They appear to be rewarded in spite of non-achievement.

(4) As a consequence of the two preceding points, it has to be said that the four parables of grace *do not confirm everyday* expectations. Indeed, those expectations are regularly frustrated. Grace, in fact, comes as a surprise.

(5) Because these parables are realistic, the hearer is drawn into them by way of unstudied affirmation: the initial situation prompts the listener to affirm, "Yes, that's the way it is!" However, the parables take a turn in which that lazy affirmation is jarred and then upset. This turn intensifies the relation of the listener to the story: the hearer must now pay attention to see how the narrative turns out. Furthermore, the listeners will be disposed to join those who protest equal payment, if they consider themselves industrious and

just, or they will smile if they have been sitting on their haunches in the marketplace all day. In sum, in these parables *listeners are provoked to choose up sides.*

It is for these reasons that the parables of grace may be taken to be more compelling, more provocative, more carefully constructed, and closer to the heart of the message of Jesus.

The narrative structure of the parables of grace was diagramed as figure 4 in Chapter 4.

It should be noted that the respondents are now labelled RJ and RG, rather than R1 and R2. Because the diagram indicates how the story turns out (it turns downward for RJ and upward for RG), function labels are required; however, the neutral labels R1 and R2 would remind us that the participants are not identified at the outset.

5.   Two of the functions in the parables of grace have been identified as RJ and RG: the justified response and the recipient of grace. A third function in the parables of grace is the dispensation of grace or justice (IG/J = instrument of grace or justice) to common expectations. The preeminent function of the determiner in these parables appears to be to dispense grace and justice, and that involves a fundamental reversal in relation to habituated expectations. Just as the everyday or received order of things is undergirded by the initial realism of the parable and the hearer's unstudied response, so the new reality announced by the parable is sanctioned by D, the determiner around whom the whole story revolves.

Earlier, we were led to the question: is D always the instrument of grace and justice, as he is in the Laborers in the Vineyard and the Great Supper? Or is this function, IG/J—and consequently also the functions RJ and RG—mapped onto the narrative in different ways? A preliminary answer was provided earlier; we may renew it now with respect to the parables of the Prodigal Son and the Good Samaritan.

6.   The parable of the Prodigal Son can be read in at least three different ways (see Chapter 4, §4), which will be sketched here in relation to both the participants and the plot structure.

In the predominant understanding of the parable, which may be designated Prodigal 1 for convenience, the father is understood as the determiner and the two sons as contrasting respondents. In this reading, the division of the father's estate between the sons functions as the contract. The test consists of the way each son handles his inheritance, and the judgment consists of the response of the father. These relationships are represented by figure 11.

*Prodigal 1*

D = Father = IG/J

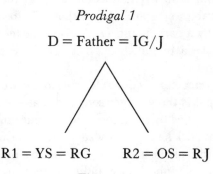

R1 = YS = RG    R2 = OS = RJ

Figure 11

Although this view of the Prodigal appears to have predominated in both ancient and modern times, two things may be said against it.

In the first place, the test or response of the older son is not related directly to his share of the inheritance, but to the reception of the young prodigal on the part of the father. Second, the father is not quite the thread on which the story is strung; the younger son appears to play this rôle.

Further, if we take the Prodigal as a parallel to the Lost Sheep and the Lost Coin, with which it is grouped in Luke, the first episode may be construed independently: the contract consists of the father giving the younger son his inheritance; the test is his performance in a foreign land; and the judgment is his repentance and reception by his father.

If the second episode is authentic—and some scholars hold that it is not—it is then necessary to understand the first episode as a whole as the contract, in relation to which the test of the older son is how he relates to his father's acceptance of the young prodigal's prodigality. And the judgment is the rebuke spoken by the father to the older son.

Read in this way, Prodigal 2 (to use a brief designation) is a complex parable, in the sense that one parable of the Lost Sheep type serves as the contract for another simple parable. The first simple parable as a whole serves as a constituent element in the second.

If this reading is correct, the structure of Prodigal 2 is unique among the parables of Jesus, so far as I can see.

In spite of its possible formal uniqueness, it is just possible that Prodigal 2 is, in fact, the more traditional reading.

A third reading of the Prodigal is suggested by the structure of the other three parables of grace. Recall that this formal structure is given its shape by a participant, D, who sets the terms of the narrative and runs like a thread through it. To D there are two contrasting responses.

If this formal structure is our sole criterion, it would appear that D in the Prodigal is the younger son, and that the two contrasting responses are supplied by the father and the older son, as our observations on Prodigal 1 have already suggested. In this case, the contract, or the terms of the narrative, are set by the account of the prodigal wasting his inheritance and then returning home to seek mercy. The test consists of how the father and the older son receive him. The judgment is not given as a separate item but is implied in the contrasting responses. This reading is represented by figure 12.

*Prodigal 3*

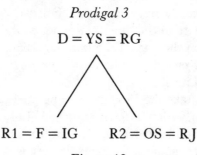

$$D = YS = RG$$

$$R1 = F = IG \qquad R2 = OS = RJ$$

Figure 12

One difficulty with Prodigal 3 as a reading is that D in the parables is customarily an authority figure. There is thus a strong proclivity to interpret the father as D simply because the father is an authority figure. As an authority D means: it is this way because I say it is.

There are three good reasons for resisting this supreme temptation. The first is that the authority figure is not always a suitable model for God: for example, the doting father in the Prodigal and the master in the Unjust Steward. To these could be added the Great

Supper: would God invite the socially respectable first and only then turn to the outcasts, as is suggested by the narrative sequence? In the Laborers, would God pay a subsistence wage and insist on its justice?

The second reason has to do with interpretive consistency. If we read the father as a figure or model for God, should we not also read the other two participants as models? The older son is often taken, to be sure, as representing the Pharisees, so we have the equations: father = God; older son = Pharisees. In that case, what about the younger son? Should he not also be taken as the literal model of the sinner? In sum, those who take the father (and the older son) literally or figuratively are bound to take the younger son on the same terms.

The third reason is that there is one parable in which D is clearly not an authority figure: the Good Samaritan. In the Samaritan, D is the victim in the ditch. The parable calls on the Jewish man in the ditch to certify, even in his inertness, that grace has come, $D = RG$: it is this way because I have experienced it so. It follows, too, that D is not always the instrument of grace or justice. In others words, the Prodigal and the Good Samaritan open up new ways of understanding sets of participants and sets of functions. On the basis of the first four parables examined, it could have been concluded that the relationships between participants and functions are constant; the Prodigal and the Samaritan point to other and richer possibilities.

The reading of the Prodigal as Prodigal 3, which has not been proposed in the scholarly literature so far as I know, is suggested by the structure of the Good Samaritan. In both parables, D is a figure who has suffered misfortune. In both cases, D is the recipient of grace. The father and the priest and Levite are authority figures, but they are respondents. In one case, the father as R1 functions as the instrument of grace; in the other, the priest and Levite function as RJ, the justified response. And in neither case is judgment a discrete narrative item—by contrast with the Ten Maidens, Talents, Great Supper, and Laborers.

That the Prodigal is carefully constructed is proved by the fact that it can be read in several ways. It is a narrative of no little subtlety. We are probably attracted to it by virtue of its structural ambiguities, even though we may tend to read it predominantly in one way. And finally, since there seems to be no way to arbitrate among the structural claims on this parable, the three ways of reading it would appear to contribute to its plurisignificative character as parable and metaphor.

7. The discussion of the Prodigal anticipates the analysis of the Good Samaritan in large measure.

On the formal side, D in the Samaritan is the fellow in the ditch: it is he upon whom the story turns. There are two contrasting responses, one by the priest and the the Levite, the other by the Samaritan. The priest and the Levite are therefore R1, the Samaritan R2. With regard to parabolic functions, D is the recipient of grace and thus RG; R1 (priest and Levite) functions as RJ, the response to be expected; R2 (the Samaritan) is the instrument of grace, or IG. There is no explicit judgment, although IJ may be said to be implied. the Samaritan is therefore not heavy-handed, in contrast to the other narrative parables, including, perhaps, even the Prodigal (does the father function as IJ in relation to the older son?).

The Samaritan is diagramed in figure 13.

*Samaritan*

D = Victim = RG

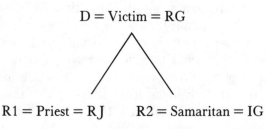

R1 = Priest = RJ      R2 = Samaritan = IG

Figure 13

I must confess that reading the Good Samaritan in this way, indeed, reading it as a parable at all, runs contrary to the history of interpretation.[1]

---

[1] I first advanced the reading of the Samaritan as metaphor in 1964, developed the reading in 1965 and 1966 (199–22), then consummated it in *Semeia* (1974b; Chapter 2 above). The case was taken up by J. Dominic Crossan (1973:57–66 and 1974a) and approved by Norman Perrin (1971 and 1976:138–41). It goes without saying that this reading has not been universally accepted.

The Good Samaritan as parable forces on its hearers the question: who among you will permit himself or herself to be served by a Samaritan? In a general way it can be replied: only those who are unable to refuse. Permission to be served by the Samaritan is thus inability to resist. Put another way, all who are truly victims, truly disinherited, truly helpless, have no choice but to give themseves up to mercy. And mercy comes from the quarter from which it is least expected. Grace is always a surprise.

As a parable the Samaritan is a very powerful instrument. It sets the message of Jesus in unequivocal terms for its audience. No one could mistake. It explains why IRS officials and prostitutes understand the kingdom, whereas theologians, Bible scholars, and professional pietists do not. It explains why a hated alien must be the instrument of grace. It makes pretense on the part of the listener impossible. There is no other parable in the Jesus tradition which carries a comparable punch. The Christian community moralizes it in order to be able to live with it, and that is inverted testimony to its power.

# Six

# THE TEMPORAL HORIZON
# OF THE KINGDOM

*0.* There is perhaps no more difficult problem in current New Testament scholarship than to determine the temporal horizon of the kingdom of God. The problem is difficult because historical and theological questions are intimately and subtly interlaced. It is thus necessary to ask, as independent but correlative questions, what firm historical bases have been established from which to face the theological issue squarely, and what conceptual hostages are likely to be given, on the part of particular interpreters, to any examination of the historical problem. Only by addressing these questions simultaneously can we hope to reach some fundamental clarity regarding the problem.

*1.* The historical and theological questions appear to be intertwined to this extent: there are those who assume some form of material continuity between Jesus and the primitive church, and who are therefore inclined to credit that body of synoptic material which confirms such continuity. On the other hand, there are those who assume a real and radical break at Easter, and who are therefore disposed to discredit the synoptic material that attributes an Easter faith to Jesus. The differences between these two groups impinge directly upon the question of Jesus' self-consciousness, which goes together but is not identical with the question of Jesus' view of the future.

The historical and theological questions are correlative in another, though less obvious, respect. The universally acknowledged principle that Jesus' proclamation of the kingdom is to be explicated with reference to its Jewish milieu may be taken to mean either that Jesus' eschatology is more or less identical with one or the other of the eschatologies prevalent in his day, or that his message is to be identified by those points at which it allegedly differs from Jewish antecedents. Once again, the problem of continuity / discontinuity may take on theological overtones, especially for scholars who have a stake in the uniqueness of the Christian faith and who seek to link the rise of that faith to Jesus.

As a clean means of avoiding theological bias, one might, of course, become a consistent advocate of continuity and draw a straight line from Judaism through Jesus to the primitive church. But if one posits a unilinear development in order to avoid the theological pitfall, has one not then fallen into the historiographical ditch? Aside from the resistance the data offer, the price paid for the proximate continuity of history in terms of causal antecedents is the particularity of persons and events. If history is to be done justice, it is the interplay between continuity and discontinuity, as Ernst Käsemann puts it, that is the key to sound historical analysis. Those who posit a break at Easter, and those who distinguish Jesus from antecedent Judaism are right, not for theological but for historical reasons. Who Jesus was and what he taught is to be established, in the first instance, out of those points at which he differed from both his predecessors and his successors. Any other procedure is to reduce him—and any other historic figure—to an undifferentiated cog in a universal historical gear box.

For this reason, Norman Perrin's work *Rediscovering the Teaching of Jesus* is built on a firm methodological foundation. Perrin employs dissimilarity as his fundamental criterion in establishing the authentic voice of Jesus; that is, he is willing, initially, to regard as authentic only those traditions which can be shown to be dissimilar in characteristic emphasis to both Judaism and the early church on the grounds that the early church, oriented as it was to Judaism, would have been inclined to interpret Jesus in accordance with its own everyday understanding of the religious subject matter. The significance of this point is obvious: the church's memory that it was the genius of Jesus which gave rise to the Christian way over against common Judaism is invoked as the basis of the criterion that his most characteristic emphases must have been, in some respects at least, dissimilar. The church is made to witness against itself, that is, against its own leveling memory, in the interests of witnessing for itself, that is, in support of its consciousness that it was not simply a carbon copy of current Judaism.

Although there are other good reasons for regarding Perrin's work highly, I have chosen to single out the criterion of dissimilarity for special notice, because this criterion touches most directly on the problem of Jesus' understanding of the temporal horizons of the kingdom, and thus on his relation to apocalyptic. With this criterion as vantage point, it is possible to see how Jesus' peculiar understanding of temporality got leveled in the subsequent history of the tradition, that is, how the process of handing the Jesus tradition around and on made inevitable the assimilation of his understanding to the everyday, and presumably apocalyptic, notion of time. With this last remark, however, we anticipate. We must first ask what firm historical bases have been established from which to face the theological issue realistically. Perrin's works on Jesus (1963, 1967, 1976), especially the later volumes, can provide us with reliable historical leverage—about as reliable as we could hope to have—on the conceptual and theological problems involved in tracking the rôle of apocalyptic in early Christian thought. His analysis is supported in outline and most particulars by Günther Bornkamm in his *Jesus of Nazareth* (64–95).

2.  It is universally agreed that Jesus proclaimed the eschatological kingdom of God (Perrin, 1967: 56). According to Perrin, certain events in the ministry of Jesus are understood and interpreted by Jesus as "nothing less than *an experience* of the Kingdom of God" (67). Everything else in his teaching turns on this central conviction (77f.). At the same time, the present experience of the kingdom of God, "although it is truly fulfillment, still only anticipates the consummation in the future" (164). If Jesus proclaimed in word and deed that the kingdom had come, he nevertheless looked forward to its coming: there is thus a fundamental and pervasive tension between present and future in Jesus' understanding of the kingdom (Bornkamm: 92f.).

Of the present experience of the kingdom, that is, of its arrival in the word and deed of Jesus, a great deal can be said. Among the items gleaned from the more or less undisputed Jesus tradition are the following: (1) God's intervention in history takes place in a situation of conflict in which penultimate defeat is a real possibility (Perrin, 1967: 67, 77); (2) the coming of the kingdom is not marked by visible signs which can be read objectively (72ff.); (3)the kingdom is aimed not at the community (Israel) as a whole, but at the individual (67); (4) the kingdom offers a new point of departure in that it breaks through the traditional categories and expectations of Judaism (81); (5) the discovery of the kingdom is accompanied by surprise and joy to such an extent that the newly found treasure completely dominates the present and future of the discoverer (89); (6) the kingdom as God's redeeming activity is experienced primarily as the radical or eschatological forgiveness of sins in that those who had no reason to anticipate forgiveness—the mortal sinners—are unexpectedly favored by grace (90–108).

These remarks on the nature of the inbreaking of the kingdom in Jesus' activity could be considerably expanded on the basis of other fairly reliable traditions. Even without such elaboration it is striking, by contrast, how little can be specified regarding Jesus' anticipation of the future consummation of the kingdom. Perrin, in effect, allows only two basic points: (1)Jesus did anticipate a future consummation (1967: 161, 163f.), and (2) he conveyed the utmost confidence that the God who is acting in the present is also the God to whom the future is to be entrusted (159). In sum, Jesus affirmed that the present activity of God harbingers a future fulfillment that will do nothing other than put a period to the present experience of the inbreaking of the kingdom.

In view of the sharp discrepancy between the specifiable content of the present experience of the kingdom and the vacuity of future expectation beyond its "that," Perrin summarizes: "Almost all the elements in the tradition which give a definite *form* to the future expectation in the teaching of Jesus fail the test of authenticity" (203). The apocalyptic expectation of Mark 13 (pars.), the "parousia," and the apocalyptic Son of man belong to early Christian apocalyptic and interpretations of the resurrection. The difference in expectation between Jesus and the early church, on the one hand, and contemporary Judaism, on the other, is spectacular (203).

3. It is probably accurate to claim that the views of Perrin and Bornkamm represent an emerging consensus: Jesus thought of the kingdom as in some sense present, in some sense future. Those views which see the kingdom as wholly realized or entirely futuristic may therefore be set aside; "realized" and "consistent" eschatology alike appear to be one-sided distortions of the data. But beyond the acknowledgment of an elusive tension between the two tenses, the scholarly consensus rapidly dissolves. The dissolution is especially apparent when the question of imminence is introduced.

Rudolf Bultmann holds, for example, that Jesus shared the imminent and futuristic hope of late Judaism, although with a sharp reduction in apocalyptic detail (1951: 4ff.). W. G. Kümmel, among others, shares this historical judgment (1957: 88, 104, 141). But when Bultmann and Kümmel come to assess the significance of Jesus' hope, they part company. Bultmann insists that hope must be reinterpreted, precisely as regards its cosmological eschatology, because every informed person knows that history will continue to run its course (1957: 5). However, Bultmann appears to retain the note of the imminent future because he understands eschatological existence in faith as "interim," as "a *brief* transitional span" between the old and new aeons (1960: 251, italics mine). Kümmel regards the imminent expectation as mistaken and hence dispensable, but insists that a real chronological future must be regarded as essential because the kingdom still must be realized (1957: 152f.).

The *imminent* expectation is both a historical and a theological problem. It is a historical problem in the sense that the primitive church was evidently exercised about the contradiction between *its* imminent hope—whether derived from Jesus or not—and *its* experience of history as ongoing. This problem is known as the "delay of the *parousia*." The question is whether the problem of the delay arises out of a proper understanding of the tension between present and future in Jesus' message or out of a misunderstanding of that tension, and particularly out of the imminence which seems to be ingredient to his message. It is by no means certain that Jesus experienced anything like a delay (83–7). It is quite possible, and it would have been expected, that an acute juxtaposition of present and future in Jesus would be assimilated to popular apocalyptic expectations as his message was handed around and on. The prospect of assimilation is enhanced by the fact that eschatology cannot be transmitted in the same way as, for example, christology (Conzelmann: 27). At all events, the modern theological problem of the delay stems from imminence as understood in the primitive church, and its experience of a delay. All of this says nothing about how matters stood with Jesus. Perrin has concluded that those sayings which express an imminent expectation fail to pass the test for authenticity; he holds, specifically, that Jesus never expressed his expectation in terms of a time element (1967: 203f.; Kümmel, 1957: 149ff.). Yet he unequivocally allows that Jesus held the critical hour for decision to be *now*, as exemplified in the parables of the Great Supper and the Unjust Steward (Perrin, 1967: 110–5). If the critical hour is now, if now is the time of ultimate decision, how can Jesus' expectation be understood as anything other than imminent?

Joachim Jeremias is undoubtedly correct in asserting that the twin parables of the Treasure in the Field and the Pearl of Great Price (Matt 13:44–46) do not call for complete surrender, but rather express the surprise and then the joy at happening upon the treasure (200f.).[1] Surprise there is, and in a double sense: the two men are pleasantly surprised at their good fortune and the hearers of the parable are surprised at the modest character of the treasure (299, 32). Nevertheless, a point cannot be singled out for exclusive attention if the parable is coherent metaphor and not reduced allegory. The narratives as wholes depict two men who, having chanced upon a modest treasure, resolutely abandon what they have in order to claim it: "No man who puts his hand to the plough and looks back is fit for the kingdom of God" (Luke 9:62) (Perrin, 1967: 142).

The two parables reflect what might be called the naïve fusion of temporal aspects: the new reality of the kingdom is surprisingly present, and yet it belongs to the future as something to be resolutely entered into. The future impinges upon the present as what is "really real" in the present and consequently determines the future trajectory of the present. The kingdom arrives as both the "out of which" and the "into which" of existence that is caught up in the transition from man's present to God's future. Just as concrete

---

[1] Jeremias notes that joy is not specifically mentioned in the parable of the pearl, but he states that the words of the first parable apply to the second as well.

spatiality means co-presence in the world, authentic temporality means the coincidence of the horizons of time.

The element of surprise in the first sense indicated above—surprise at happening on the treasure—occurs repeatedly in various though related contexts in the parables. In the parable of the Great Supper (Luke 14:15-24 // Matt 22:1-10), surprise is written all over the faces of idlers in the street who were startled at the course of events that brought them into the banquet hall. And the hearer, too, is caught napping by the unexpected turn of events. What does this element of surprise signify in a temporal horizon? The kingdom comes shrouded as a commonplace, veiled as the obvious, which means that it arrives when it is least expected. In temporal terms, the kingdom's coming is characterized by the indefiniteness of its *when*.

The indefiniteness of the when and the coincidence of present and future of course go together. The metaphorical bridge linking present and future is the imminence of the kingdom, which is expressed both positively and negatively: the kingdom is near; the time of its arrival is indefinite.

The tension between present and future in the proclamation of Jesus is not adequately understood if it is expressed as the highest possible degree of imminence. It is not a matter of an interim between sign and reality, however brief that interim is, but a matter of the coincidence of the two modes of temporality. On the one hand, the kingdom is present in Jesus' own appearance: "If it is by the finger of God that I cast out demons, then the kingdom of God has come upon you" (Luke 11:20//Matt 18:28). On the other hand, although no apocalyptic signs will be given (Mark 8:12//Luke 11:29, Matt 12:39), the signs of the time are already present and are being acted out in the person of Jesus (Perrin, 1967: 191-5), if they could but read them (Luke 11:29, 32). The kingdom is so near that it completely overwhelms and dominates the present; it can no longer be looked for, awaited. So long as the kingdom is anticipated in a chronological sense, it is still possible to view its coming from a distance. But for Jesus this is impossible. He therefore transcends the question of the time as such. If one still asks about the date, it is only because the signs are misunderstood. Whether one fixes the date near or far, the question has been converted into an apocalyptic one (Conzelmann: 10f.).

There is a second sense in which the kingdom comes as a surprise. The treasure in the field is not sufficient to erect a palace and purchase a train of slaves, as a rabbinic parallel has it (Jeremias: 32, cf. 200), nor is the pearl as magnificent as represented in parallels (Jeremias: 200, citing Strack-Billerbeck, I: 674ff). The original invitees to the supper were not able to grasp the significance of the banquet because the invitation came to them shrouded as a commonplace. And the parable of the Mustard Seed is certainly to be read against the background of Ezek 17:34 and Dan 4, as most exegetes agree. Yet it is rarely noticed that the ephemeral mustard plant is but a burlesque of, and serious satire on, the mighty cedar as a symbol of the kingdom. The kingdom arrives with comic relief: it is the manifestation of divine power, all appearances to the contrary notwithstanding.

The indefinite date and the ambiguous signs of the kingdom's arrival do not make its coming less but more certain. It is as certain as the seed growing of itself, the leaven leavening the loaf, the harvest from seed scattered upon the ground. This overwhelming certainty does not arise from an announcement tenaciously believed, but out of the fact that men already participate in the kingdom's coming. This is made most evident by the so-called parables of grace, for example, the Two Debtors, the Prodigal Son, the Lost Sheep and Coin, the Laborers in the Vineyard. The mercy of God does not wait upon some future—near or remote—but is already "there" for those who care to quit the immense solidity of the mundane world and step through the looking glass of the parable. The kingdom is "there" as certainly as Jesus goes in to eat with sinners.

The matter might be summed up thus: the imminence of the kingdom is the metaphorical bridge linking present and future—a bridge made necessary by the pervasiveness of the everyday understanding of time, which tends to fragment temporality into discrete moments, which, in turn, are divided up into three tenses. The isolation of the present moment is the means by which past and future are held at arm's length and time is "objectified" as chronological time. In Jesus' naïve understanding of time, as opposed to an everyday perspective, the present moment is nothing other than the coincidence of past and future in the horizon of the reality of the kingdom. But the reality of the kingdom does not universally and hence objectively cancel out the evil powers of this age: the wheat and the weeds grow up together (Matt 13:24–30). The kingdom comes in and through the ambiguities of the present age as something out of which and into which existence is to be lived.

*4.* Given the necessity of handling the Jesus tradition around and on, it was inevitable that the temporal horizon of the kingdom as Jesus understood it should have been assimilated to the mundane notion of time. What evidence is there that such assimilation took place, and how did it transpire? In developing this aspect of the problem, I am particularly indebted to Hans Conzelmann's significant essay "Present and Future in the Synoptic Tradition" (26–44).

We may take for granted that the earliest church shared the imminent apocalyptic expectations of contemporary sectarian Judaism for which Paul is a later and secondary witness. (See Bultmann, 1951, I: 37ff., for the eschatological consciousness of the early church; cf. Conzelmann: 37f.). Yet it is a curious fact that the earliest forms of the kerygma (for example, 1 Cor 15:3ff.), do not employ the Son of man title or mention the *parousia* (Conzelmann: 31). The kerygma focuses on the lordship of Jesus and the redemptive significance of his death-resurrection, or on his humiliation and exaltation. No connection has yet been made between his resurrection and his return. Thus there is, on the one hand, the kerygma as the church's response to Jesus' "history," particularly his death and resurrection, and, on the other, the expectation of the *parousia,* which is now the apocalyptic hope linked specifically to Jesus. But the community has not yet thought through the connection between resurrection and return; it has not yet worked out the sense in which the redeemer has already come, and the sense in which he is still to come.

It has now to be asked: what time consciousness serves as the frame of reference for working out the connection between Jesus' death-resurrection and his return in triumph? We must content ourselves with illustrative data from the synoptic tradition and Acts that can be attributed with a degree of certainty to the primitive community.

There is, first of all, rudimentary reflection on the difference between the time of Jesus and the time of the post-Easter church. In Mark 2:18ff., of which verses 19b–20 are almost certainly community formulations (Conzelmann: 40; Bultmann, 1951: 18ff.;

Perrin, 1967: 77-80), the present is viewed as a time of mourning and fasting, in contrast to the time of Jesus, which was a time of feasting. The present is therefore understood as a time between the bridegroom's departure and his return.

The rise of the consciousness of a "time between" brought with it a looking back to the past and, at the same time, a different mode of anticipating the future. On the one hand, the church now looks back to Jesus as the one who came but was denied his claim. This point of view is represented by the parable of the Wicked Tenants (Mark 12:1–12), which, in its present form at least, is evidently the product of the church (Jeremias: 70ff.). The true heir is killed and cast out of the vineyard (Mark 12:8). On the other hand, the church, which regards itself as living in the ambiguous time between, anticipates that the Messiah will not leave his servants long to wait. The brevity of the wait is most clearly expressed in Mark 13:30 ("Truly, I say to you, this generation will not pass away before all these things take place"), which Perrin attributes to the community (1967: 200). The summary of the eschatological preaching of John (Matt 3:7–10, par.), which the early community placed at the head of Q, and Matt 10:23b ("Truly, I say to you, you will not have gone through all the towns of Israel, before the Son of man comes")—which Bultmann (1968: 122), Grässer (138), and Perrin (1967: 202) attribute to an early Christian prophet—both express the lively expectation of the post-Easter church.

The difference in the times, coupled with looking back and looking forward from the "time between," means that the redemptive events must now be divided into two groups: those which belong to the time of Jesus and those which have yet to take place (Conzelmann: 38). The earliest church had not yet reflected on the eschatological significance of Jesus' first appearance, but its own consciousness that it is "between the times" indicates that the history of Jesus has fundamentally altered man's situation in the world (Bultmann, 1951, I: 37ff.). The church is caught, so to speak, in the contradiction between its purely apocalyptic hope and consciousness that it owed its existence as the eschatological congregation to Jesus. The church must therefore look to the eschatological significance of Jesus' first coming, which it already does in the first forms of the kerygma.

The line of development beyond the first community is reasonably clear. Mark has not yet historically distinguished the time of Jesus from the now of his church, he has not drawn a line from Jesus to the past, that is, to the history of Israel, and he has not worked out the connection of Jesus' first coming with his second coming across the interim period of the church (Conzelmann: 38f.). Luke, on the other hand, has separated apocalyptic from history and divided history into periods: the time of Israel, the time of Jesus and the apostles, and the time of the church. He can actually permit a reintensification of apocalyptic because of the firm distinction between the times. Such apocalyptic reintensifications as occur sporadically in the ancient church do not necessarily recover the temporality of Jesus, but arise out of the memory of Jesus' juxtaposition of present and future, on the one hand, and the impacted situation of the church in the world, on the other.

One final point requires notice. As the history of salvation schema was worked out, it was also necessary to work out the difference between the two groups of eschatological events. Those connected with the time of Jesus have the character of hidden revelations; at the consummation, what was hidden will become openly manifest. Hiddenness and openness are correlative with humiliation and exaltation. With the breakup of the coinherence of the modes of time, it became necessary to dissolve also the inner connection between humiliation and exaltation as posited by the primitive kerygma. As Jeremias has it, at the end time the Christian community will lose its servants' form and take on its true character (226). There will thus be a reinversion of the inversion: he who is first will really be first, and he who is last really last. With this development, the inner unity of Jesus' ethical message and his eschatological proclamation is also broken.

It is understandable that when the church endeavored to imagine the future from the vantage point of its time between, it did so in apocalyptic terms. Apocalyptic lay ready to hand as the means of embodying eschatological futurity. Consequently, Jesus' restraint in this connection is the more remarkable and significant. The intensity with which present and future were fused for him undoubtedly stimulated apocalyptic speculation in the early community, yet his restraint also served as an inhibiting factor. It would not be accurate to say that apocalyptic reemerged after Easter, but rather that Jesus bracketed apocalyptic out in order to let his own time consciousness emerge (Conzelmann: 38). The future impinged on his present to such a degree that he could no longer contemplate it from a distance, however brief.

5. The foregoing sketch has endeavored to show that New Testament scholars have been driven, almost in spite of themselves, onto an elusive conceptual problem touching temporality. Assuming that Jesus proclaimed both the imminent coming and the present efficacy of the kingdom, W. G. Kümmel has formulated the problem concisely: "We must ask whether this juxtaposition is due to historical accident or whether it expresses precisely the particular quality of Jesus' eschatology" (1957: 141). It would be agreed, presumably, that the juxtaposition was not merely accidental. In that case, can it be accommodated conceptually, or must the New Testament scholar "adjust" Jesus' time consciousness to his own notion of time, whether for historical or theological reasons, or both?

Setting aside "realized" and "consistent" eschatology as "adjustments" of one kind or another, there is the further option, Kümmel suggests, of eliminating time altogether (1957: 143ff.). By this he means the elimination of a real future consummation of the kingdom. Kümmel's willingness to detach imminence from the message of Jesus and retain a purely chronological future may be the result of his conviction, however, that no other conception of futurity is legitimate, indeed possible (1957: 148f., and n. 16). Oscar Cullmann is certainly of this opinion (1950: 28ff., 48f., 53 and n. 4 and *passim*), and a distinguished American scholar affirmed, not so many years ago, that he did not want his "eschatology de-eschatologized" (Burrows: 8). His appeal, to be sure, was to what *everybody* takes futurity to mean. On these views, it seems, we are faced with the choice of assimilating Jesus' temporal horizon to that of the primitive church, and thus to that of common apocalyptic, or of eliminating altogether so-called "real" time.

I for one do not like the choice. Amos Wilder and others have been trying to persuade us for years that we need to come to some appreciation of the mythopoeic mentality, and thus of an "ecstatic mythical intensity" that dissolves and transcends the common temporal categories (1959; especially 236ff.). Such an ecstatic fusion of temporal aspects is not uncommon among the poets, and even philosophers and theologians have been known to offer conceptual accounts of it (Fackenheim: 34–40; Cassirer: 162–90; Heiddeger:

Division Two). We are not, then, faced with the choice set by Kümmel and others, but we may infer from the data that Jesus was governed by a different mode of temporality than that current in the marketplace. In so doing, we are not necessarily detemporalizing Jesus' message. We may, in fact, be faced with what Ernst Cassirer calls the "pure intuition of time" (n. 55, pp. 169f.; cf. 167, 189f.).

A resolute passion for hard historical data, for *wie es eigentlich gewesen ist,* has its special merit which no serious scholar would care to contest. Let it be granted that this merit often appears where the collector and interpreter has no special case to plead, no hobbyhorse to ride. Nevertheless, the historian who mounts the evidence for a particular slice of historical reality functions ever and again as the great disillusioner by bringing to nought those interpretations built on fragmentary evidence and limited perspectives. He does so by enlarging and/or constricting the data and/or the perspectives in relation to which or from which a particular phenomenon or constellation of phenomena is seized.

There is a tendency in some quarters to think that the historian functions best as disillusioner when he knows least about the speculative aspects of the problem he is addressing qua historian. In no other sphere is this tendency so blatant in modern New Testament scholarship than in the sphere of apocalyptic, together with its attendant catchwords: eschatology, end of the age, futurity, time, history, and so forth. I should like to enter a caveat against this tendency and the correlative confusion of objectivity and lack of conceptual sophistication. I propose that conceptual sophistication is precisely what is needed if we are to attend to the data relative to the question of apocalyptic. This caveat is not to be understood as a plea for more philosophy and less history, but precisely as a plea for more history and less everyday, drawing-room philosophy. For the historian is free to disillusion only when he himself is free from the tyranny of what everybody takes as self-evident.

# Seven

# THE APOSTOLIC PRESENCE:
# PAUL

*0.* In his letters, Paul often indicates his reason for or his disposition in writing, his intention or hope to dispatch an emissary, and his intention or hope to pay the congregation a personal visit. These items tend to converge in one more or less discrete section of the letter. In an earlier study, this section was identified as the "travelogue," and an attempt was made to isolate and establish it as a structural element in the Pauline letter (1966: 264–274). The designation "travelogue" suggested itself because the passages in question appear to be concerned primarily with Paul's movements, as indeed, in a sense, they are.

Upon further reflection, however, it has become clear that Paul regarded his apostolic presence (in Greek: *parousia*) to his congregations under three different but related aspects at once: that of the letter, that of the apostolic emissary, and that of his own personal presence. All three are media through which Paul made his apostolic authority effective in the churches. The underlying theme is therefore the apostolic *parousia*—the presence of apostolic authority and power—of which the travelogue in the narrow sense is only one element.

The apostolic *parousia* may be analyzed, first, by setting out its formal structure, and, second, by considering its significance in relation to Paul's understanding of his own apostolic authority. The appropriateness of the designation will emerge in connection with the latter. The analysis yields two specific consequences that touch two of the many provocative suggestions and proposals put forward by John Knox.

*1.* The following passages may be identified, on the basis of both form and content, as specifically concerned with the apostolic presence: Rom 15:14–33 with its parallel in 1:8ff.; Phlm 21f.; 1 Cor 4:14–21; 1 Thess 2:17–3:13; Phil 2:19–24. Although 1 Cor 16:1–11 comes under the heading of "concerning the collection" (16:1; cf. 16:12), it treats the movements of Paul and Timothy, thus manifesting some of the same characteristics as those passages which refer to entire letters. Both 2 Cor 8:16–23 and 9:1–5, which again occur in passages (or letters?) that concern the collection that Paul was taking up for the poor saints in Jerusalem, may be included for the same reason.

Phil 2:25–30 (Epaphroditus) and 1 Cor 16:12 (Apollos) treat the movements or sending of associates, and are attached in each case to sections having to do with Paul's apostolic presence. They are thus secondary but related passages.

In 2 Cor 12:14, Paul introduces the subject of his third visit to Corinth, which leads him to remark again on the economics of his previous visits (cf. 11:7ff.; 12:13); this in turn prompts him to refer to previous visits by his emissaries (12:17f.). In 12:19 he reviews his reason for writing, which is directly coupled with the character of his impending visit: "I write this in order to spare the sharp exercise of authority when I come" (13:10). He refers to his forthcoming visit again in 13:1 and is occupied through 13:10 with that visit and the preparations the Corinthians should make for it. 2 Cor 12:14–13:10 could thus be termed the section on apostolic *parousia.* It is, however, woven into the warp and woof of the letter, undoubtedly because 2 Cor 10–13 as a whole is a defense of Paul's apostleship and hence of the apostolic presence (cf. 10:1ff., 8ff.), but it is no less discernible as a structural element for that.

In the letter to the Galatians, towards the close of his principle arguments and before beginning the *paraenesis,* Paul again turns to the subject of his presence in Galatia (cf. 1:6–12, with reference to his preaching in Galatia). He reviews his first welcome there and ends with the wish that he might be with them just now (4:12–20).

Although this passage skimps on formal elements, as the letter does elsewhere (for example, thanksgiving, closing), it nevertheless functions structurally in a way comparable to the apostolic *parousia* in the other letters.[1]

2. The most elaborate and formally structured of these passages having to do with the apostolic presence is Rom 15:14–33. It therefore serves as a provisional model for both individual items and order.

Paul begins (1) by stating his disposition in writing (15:14–15a), to which he adds (2) an elaboration of the basis of his apostolic relation to the recipients, in this case the Gentiles generally (15:15b–21). The implementation of the apostolic presence forms the major theme of the passage (3): Paul indicates that he has been hindered from coming (15:22), that he has longed to come (15:23), and that he now hopes to see them (15:24b). The same three items appear also in Rom 1:11ff. and 1 Thess 2:17ff., but the first item is last. The order may be arbitrarily resolved in favor of the majority: (3a) an expression of the desire or eagerness to come; (3b) an expression of the hope, intention or wish to come; (3c) the statement that he has so far been hindered or prevented from coming. He occasionally adds (3d) the wish to be sent on by them to wherever he is going next (15:24b). There follows in Rom 15 the statement that when he has completed his mission to Jerusalem he will come to them on his way to Spain (15:25–29); this item announces the definite prospect of a visit.

In parallel passages elsewhere, for example, 1 Cor 4:17, 1 Thess 3:2ff., before announcing a prospective visit of his own, Paul first indicates that he is dispatching an apostolic emissary. Because this item was not relevant in Romans, it may be assumed that 1 Corin-

---

[1] I omit consideration of 2 Cor 1:1–2:13, 7:5–16, the so-called "letter of reconciliation," which is concerned as a whole with Paul's proposed and previous visits and letters, and thus with the apostolic presence in retrospect. It may therefore be described as a letter in which the apostolic *parousia* forms the body. Inclusion here would entail developing the Pauline notion of the reciprocal presence of apostle and congregation to each other—also encountered, for example, in Philippians and 1 Thessalonians—and treating the thorny question of the integrity of 2 Corinthians. In any case, the "letter of reconciliation" does not offer a discrete section which can be labeled apostolic *parousia,* and it is with such segments that we are concerned here.

thians and 1 Thessalonians represent the fuller form at this juncture. The items and order would therefore be: (3e) the dispatch of an apostolic emissary; (3f) the announcement of an apostolic visit.

Having announced his future arrival, Paul then appeals to the recipients to join him in the prayer that he may be delivered from peril and that he may finally come to them (15:30–32). In so doing, he suggests that his coming is dependent upon "God's will" (15:32). The first of these motifs may be designated (4a), the second, more conventional qualification (4b).

Paul anticipates, finally, that his presence among them will bring some benefit to him (15:32b). In Rom 1:11, 13, he suggests that some benefit will accrue to the recipients by virtue of his presence, and in 1:12 he modifies this note to the extent that his presence will be mutually beneficial. This theme in its various nuances may thus be designated 5a, 5b, and 5a–b.

After making allowance for some minor modifications of the rubrics on the basis of parallel passages—and following the order proposed above—the item analysis can be summarized in tabular form:

(1) γράφω (ἔγραψα) ὑμῖν, . . . stating Paul's (1a) disposition (participle) or (1b) purpose (ἵνα-clause) in writing.
(2) The basis of Paul's apostolic relation to the recipients.[2]
(3) Implementation of the apostolic presence.
    (3a) Desire, eagerness to see (come to) them (ἐπιποθέω, σπουδάζω and cognates).
    (3b) Hope (ἐλπίζω), wish (θέλω), intention (προτίθεμαι) to see (come to) them.[3]
    (3c) Hindrance to his coming (ἐνκόπτω, κωλύω), or delay.
    (3d) "To be sent on by you" (προπέμπω).
    (3e) Dispatch of an emissary, which takes the form: (a) "I sent to you . . ." ἔπεμψα ὑμῖν (name); (b) "who . . ." ὃς (credentials); (c) "in order to . . ." ἵνα (or infinitive: purpose).

---

[2] This item does not appear to be consistently accommodated in the apostolic *parousia*, being peculiar to Rom 15 (15b–21) and 1 Cor 4 (15–16).
[3] The justification for dividing into (3a) and (3b) is that both motifs appear in Rom 15, Rom 1, 1 Thess.

(3f) Apostolic presence, which takes the form of an announcement or promise of a visit, or expresses that a
visit is expected, hoped or prayed for (cf. 3b, 4a).

(4) Invocation of divine approval and support for the apostolic
presence.

(4a) The prayer for his presence may be a request for
prayer, their prayer, his own prayer.[4]

(4b) The convention "if God wills."

(5) Benefit from the apostolic presence accruing
(5a) to Paul
(5b) to the recipients
(5a–b) to the two mutually.

The benefit in (5) may be derived from Paul's presence to them by
letter, by emissary, or by his appearance in person. The internal
relationship, but not identity, of these media is thereby confirmed.

To a certain extent this scheme is a theoretical construct, based as
it is primarily on Rom 15:14–33. In order to indicate the range and
persistence of items, together with the variety in order, it is necessary
to tabulate them for each passage in the order in which they occur. It
should be observed that items are sometimes worked up together,
and that one occasionally finds doublets. The numerical shorthand
proposed above will serve for this purpose: an item number in
parentheses indicates phraseology thematically comparable—or,
where two notations are given, that the first includes the function
given in parentheses; brackets indicate that the theme in question
does not occur in the apostolic *parousia*, but in proximity to it. The
reference in each case is to Paul unless otherwise indicated.

*Apostolic "Parousia": Items and Order*

| (1) | | (2) | | (3) | |
|---|---|---|---|---|---|
| Rom 15:14–33 | | Rom 1:8ff. | | Phlm 21f. | |
| 1a | 14–15a | 4a | 10b | [5a | 20b] |
| 2 | 15b–21 | 4b | 10b | 1a | 21 |
| 3c | 22 | 3a | 11a;cf.15 | 3f | 22a |

---

[4] The prayer to be delivered from some peril (Rom 15:31) occurs also in 2
Cor 1:10, 2 Thess 3:2 (there also in requests for prayer). Cf. 2 Tim 3:11, 4:17f.
But it does not appear to be a constitutive element in the apostolic *parousia*.

| 3a | 23b | 5a–b | 11b–12 | 3b | 22b |
|----|-----|------|--------|----|-----|
| 3b | 24b | 3b | 13a | 4a | 22b |
| 3d | 24c | 3c | 13b | | |
| 3f | 28b | 5b | 13c | | |
| 4a | 30ff. | | | | |
| 4b | 32 | | | | |
| 5a | 32b; cf.24d | | | | |

---

| (4) | | (5) | | (6) | |
|-----|---|-----|---|-----|---|
| 1 Cor 4:14–21 | | 1 Cor 16:1–11 | | 1 Thess 2:17–3:13 | |
| 1a | 14 | (1) | 1* | 3a | 17b;cf.3:6b |
| 2 | 15–16 | 3f | 2b* | 3b | 18a |
| 3e | 17 | 3e | 3b† | 3c | 18b;cf.2:16 |
| 3f | 19a | 3f | 4† | 3e | 3:2–5 |
| 4b | 19a | 3f | 5f. | 5a | 3:6–9‡ |
| 5b | 18,19b–21 | 3d | 6b | 4a(3f) | 3:10a |
| | | 3b+3b | 7 | 5b | 3:10b |
| | | 4b | 7b | 4a | 3:11 |
| | | (3c) | 8–9 | | |
| | | (3e) | 10–11 | | |

*Ref.: collection.     † Ref.: delivery of collection.
‡ Ref.: from Timothy's return to Paul.

---

| (7) | | (8) | | (9) | |
|-----|---|-----|---|-----|---|
| 2 Cor 12:14–13:13 | | Phil 2:19–24 | | Gal 4:12–20 | |
| 3f | 14a | 3e | 19–23 | 3b | 20a |
| 3e | 17–18* | 5a | 19b† | 5b(?) | 20b |
| (1) | 19 | 3f | 24 | | |
| 5b | 19b | In 1:1–2:18, note: | | | |
| 3f | 13:1a | 3a | 1:8 | | |
| (1) | 13:2 | 4a(?) | 1:19 | | |
| 1b | 13:10 | 3f | 1:25f. | | |
| 5b | 13:10b | 5a–b | 1:25b–26; cf.2:16b–18 | | |

*Ref.: former sending     † Ref.: Timothy's coming.

| (10)      |       | (11)       |         | (12)       |        |
|-----------|-------|------------|---------|------------|--------|
| 2 Cor 9:1–5 |     | 2 Cor 8:16–23 |      | Phil 2:25–30 |      |
| 1         | 1     | 3a         | 16–17*  | 3e         | 25–28  |
| 3e        | 3–5   | 3e         | 18ff.   | 3a         | 26a†   |
| 3f        | 4     | 3e         | 22ff.   | 5a–b       | 28b‡   |
|           |       |            |         | 5a         | 30b§   |

| (13)      |       |
|-----------|-------|
| 1 Cor 16:12 |     |
| 3e        | 12a   |
| 4b        | 12b—  |
| 3f        | 12c—  |

*Ref.: Titus    †Ref.: Epaphroditus.
‡ Ref.: Epaphroditus' coming. § Ref.: retrospective
of Epaphroditus' service.    — Ref.: Apollos.

---

Before attempting to interpret the preceding data with respect to
the shape of the whole, the internal structure of one item within this
complex may be considered.

3.   The basic formula for (3d), the sending of an apostolic emissary, is similar to the formula used to express the purpose in writing
(1b).[5] When employed in connection with (3e), however, it is
expanded in such a way as to give (3e) a characteristic structure of its
own.

The simple form occurs at 1 Cor 4:17:

---

[5] It is not possible in this context to analyze the two formulae which appear
as items (1a) and (1b). Suffice it to say that Paul developed his own characteristic way of expressing this theme in dependence upon the common Graeco-
Roman epistolary tradition. The same could be said of items (3a), (3b) and (4b),
to cite further examples. The present analysis is thus to be understood as a
preliminary step in the direction of a full comparative study. In anticipation of
that study, it may be said that Paul reflects the common epistolary tradition to an
extent unsuspected even by the readers of Deissmann and Moulton-Milligan, but
that he deforms that tradition in characteristic ways.

a Therefore I sent to you Timothy,
b who is my beloved and faithful child in the Lord,
c who will remind you of my ways in Christ Jesus, . . .

a διὰ τοῦτο αὐτὸ ἔπεμψα ὑμῖν Τιμόθεον,
b ὅς ἐστίν μου τέκνον ἀγαπητὸν καὶ πιστὸν ἐν κυρίῳ,
c ὃς ὑμᾶς ἀναμνήσει τὰς ὁδούς μου τὰς ἐν Χριστῷ ᾿Ιησοῦ, . . .

In this construction, a stands for the introductory formula, b for the credentials clause, and c for the purpose clause.
The same structure occurs at 1 Thess 3:2–3a:

(Therefore when we could bear it no longer . . .)
a and we sent Timothy,
b our brother and God's servant in the gospel of Christ,
c to establish you in your faith and to exhort you,
that no one be moved by these afflictions.

(διὸ μηκέτι στέγοντες . . .)
a καὶ ἐπέμψαμεν Τιμόθεον,
b τὸν ἀδελφὸν ἡμῶν καὶ συνεργὸν τοῦ θεοῦ ἐν τῷ εὐαγγελίῳ τοῦ Χριστοῦ,
c εἰς τὸ στηρίξαι ὑμᾶς καὶ παρακαλέσαι ὑπὲρ τῆς πίστεως ὑμῶν τὸ μηδένα σαίνεσθαι ἐν θλίψεσιν ταύταις.

But Paul then expands on the theme of tribulation (vv. 3b–4), and returns with 3:5 to items a and c:

a For this reason, when I could bear it no longer (renewing 3:1) I sent
c that I might know your faith,
for fear that somehow the tempter had tempted you and that our labor would be in vain.

a διὰ τοῦτο κἀγὼ μηκέτι στέγων (renewing 3:1) ἔπεμψα
c εἰς τὸ γνῶναι τὴν πίστιν ὑμῶν,
μή πως ἐπείρασεν ὑμᾶς ὁ πειράζων καὶ εἰς κενὸν γένηται ὁ κόπος ἡμῶν.

The expansion in 3:3b–4 may be regarded as an expansion of c. Moreover, the first formulation of c, which expresses the immediate purpose for which Timothy is sent, is altered in the second to reflect the apostle's own perspective: it should therefore be called *c'*; *b* is omitted in the repetition.

The identical structure is found at Phil 2:25–30, which has to do with the dispatch of Epaphroditus:

*a* I thought it necessary to send Epaphroditus to you,
*b* my brother and fellow worker and fellow soldier,
and your messenger and minister to my need,
*c* since he has been longing for you all,
and has been distressed because you heard that he was ill.

. . .

*a* I am the more eager to send him, therefore,
*c'* that you may rejoice at seeing him again, and that I may be less anxious.

*a* ἀναγκαῖον δὲ ἡγησάμην ᾿Επαφρόδιτον
*b* τὸν ἀδελφὸν καὶ συνεργὸν καὶ συστρατιώτην μου,
ὑμῶν δὲ ἀπόστολον καὶ λειτουργὸν τῆς χρείας μου,
*a* πέμψαι πρὸς ὑμᾶς,
*c* ἐπειδὴ ἐπιποθῶν ἦν πάντας ὑμᾶς, καὶ ἀδημονῶν,
διότι ἠκούσατε ὅτι ἠσθένησεν.

. . .

*a* σπουδαιοτέρως οὖν ἔπεμψα αὐτόν,
*c'* ἵνα ἰδόντες αὐτὸν πάλιν χαρῆτε κἀγὼ ἀλυπότερος ὦ

In this case, *c* states the reason Paul is sending Epaphroditus back, and that reason is expanded in verse 27. In *c'* Paul states the reason for sending him back from the point of view of the Philippians and himself. The only variation is that *b* breaks into *a*.

With this structure may be compared Phil 2:19–23:

*a* I hope in the Lord Jesus to send Timothy to you soon,
*c* so that I may be cheered by news of you.
*b* for I have no one like him,
who will be genuinely anxious for your welfare.
They all look after their own interests, not those of Christ Jesus.
But Timothy's worth you know,
how as a son with a father he has served with me in the gospel.

*a*  I hope therefore to send him
    just as soon as I see how it will go with me.

*a*  ἐλπίζω δὲ ἐν κυρίῳ 'Ιησοῦ Τιμόθεον ταχέως πέμψαι ὑμῖν,
*c*  ἵνα κἀγὼ εὐψυχῶ γνοὺς τὰ περὶ ὑμῶν.
*b*  οὐδένα γὰρ ἔχω ἰσόψυχον,
    ὅστις γνησίως τὰ περὶ ὑμῶν μεριμνήσει·
    οἱ πάντες γὰρ τὰ ἑαυτῶν ζητοῦσιν, οὐ τὰ Χριστοῦ 'Ιησοῦ.
    τὴν δὲ δοκιμὴν αὐτοῦ γινώσκετε,
    ὅτι ὡς πατρὶ τέκνον σὺν ἐμοὶ ἐδούλευσεν εἰς τὸ εὐαγγέλιον.
*a*  τοῦτον μὲν οὖν ἐλπίζω πέμψαι
*c'* ὡς ἂν ἀφίδω τὰ περὶ ἐμὲ ἐξαυτῆς.

In this form, *b* is omitted from the initial formulation, only to be given expanded treatment in middle position. It would appear that expansion is permissible only in middle position and only in relation to the immediately preceding item. Here *c'* reverses, so to speak, the perspective of *c*: just as Paul is anxious to learn about the Philippians, they are anxious to learn about him (cf. 2:17f.). He will send Timothy as quickly as the issue of his present crisis can be reported (cf. 1:12–26).

The form in 2 Cor 9:3–5 omits *b* altogether but is nevertheless a double form (like 1 Thess 3:2–5; Phil 2:19–24, 25–30), with an extended *c* in middle position:

*a*  But I am sending the Brethren
*c*  so that our boasting about you may not prove vain in this case,
    so that, . . . lest . . . (through verse 4)
*a*  So I thought it necessary to urge the brethren
*c'* to go on to you before me and arrange . . .

*a*  ἔπεμψα δὲ τοὺς ἀδελφούς,
*c*  ἵνα μὴ καύχημα ἡμῶν τὸ ὑπὲρ ὑμῶν κενωθῇ ἐν τῷ μέρει
    τούτῳ, ἵνα, . . . μή πως . . . (through verse 4)
*a*  ἀναγκαῖον οὖν ἡγησάμην παρακαλέσαι τοὺς ἀδελφοὺς
*c'* ἵνα προέλθωσιν εἰς ὑμᾶς καὶ προκαταρτίσωσιν . . .

Once again, *c'* alters the perspective of *c*. In this instance, the immediate purpose is expressed by *c'*, whereas *c* views the matter from Paul's own perspective.

The forms in 2 Cor 8:18ff., 22f., on the other hand, omit c in the interests of the delicate situation in Corinth but strongly emphasize b, which is repeated in end position:

    a  But I am sending the brethren
8:18 a  With him we are sending the brother
    b  who is famous
8:22 a  And with them we are sending our brother
    b  whom we have tested
8:23 b  As for Titus,
        he is my partner and fellow worker in your service;
        and as for our brethren,
        they are messengers of the churches, the glory of Christ.

8:18 a  συνεπέμψαμεν δὲ μετ᾽ αὐτοῦ τὸν ἀδελφὸν
    b  οὗ ὁ ἔπαινος . . .
8:22 a  συνεπέμψαμεν δὲ αὐτοῖς τὸν ἀδελφὸν ἡμῶν,
    b  ὃν ἐδοκιμάσαμεν . . .
8:23 b  εἴτε ὑπὲρ Τίτου,
        κοινωνὸς ἐμὸς καὶ εἰς ὑμᾶς συνεργός·
        εἴτε ἀδελφοὶ ἡμῶν,
        ἀπόστολοι ἐκκλησιῶν, δόξα Χριστοῦ.

In 2 Cor 12:17–18, there is an allusion to a previous dispatch of emissaries; 1 Cor 16:10–11, 16:12 refer to the coming of associates rather than to their dispatch, with the consequence that these passages do not manifest the characteristic structure.[6] Into his dis-

---

[6] It may be that 1 Cor 16:10f. is not an isolated note on Timothy, with reference, perhaps, to 4:17, but that it also comes under the rubric "concerning the collection." Paul's discussion of his prospective sojourn in Corinth (16:5–9) bears at least oblique reference to his instructions concerning the collection (cf. 16:2). It is just possible that Timothy was to assist in the preparation of the collection, though this is not explicitly said. Though 16:10f. lacks the characteristic language of (3e), its structure is nevertheless suggestive:

  *(a)*  When Timothy comes
  *(c)*  see that you put him at ease among you,
  *(b)*  for he is doing the work of the Lord, as I am.
       So let no one despise him.
  *(a')*  Speed him on his way in peace,
  *(c')*  that he may return to me.

cussion of the collection in 1 Cor 16:1ff., however, Paul inserts the prospective sending of approved messengers to carry the offering to Jerusalem (1 Cor 16:3), with this result:

And when I arrive,
b whomever you accredit
a by letter I will send
c to carry your gift to Jerusalem.

ὅταν δὲ παραγένωμαι
b οὓς ἐὰν δοκιμάσητε,
a δι' ἐπιστολῶν τούτους πέμψω
c ἀπενεγκεῖν τὴν χάριν ὑμῶν εἰς Ἱερουσαλήμ.

That Paul arrived at a consistent pattern of articulating these sections, while exercising the liberty to modify that pattern in accordance with the situation, is fairly evident. His skill in this regard goes together with the care he lavishes on the apostolic *parousia* as a whole.[7]

4.0 In considering the apostolic *parousia* as a whole, it should be recalled that Rom 1:8ff., which anticipates 15:14–33,[8] does not constitute an independent example of the apostolic *parousia*. As noted, 1 Cor 16:1–9 (10–11); 2 Cor 8:16–23, 9:1–5 come under the heading of the collection. The sections Phil 2:25–30 and 1 Cor 16:12 are notices concerning associates. Although closely related to the apostolic *parousia*, these passages cannot be pressed to the same degree for structure as can the passages which represent the apostolic *parousia* proper: Rom 15:14–33; Phlm 21f.; 1 Cor 4:14–21; 1 Thess 2:17–3:13; 2 Cor 12:14–13:13; Gal 4:12–20; Phil 2:19–24.

4.1 Items (1) (letter), (3e) (dispatch of emissary), and (3f)

---

(a) ἐὰν δὲ ἔλθῃ Τιμόθεος,
(c) βλέπετε ἵνα ἀφόβως γένηται πρὸς ὑμᾶς·
(d) τὸ γὰρ ἔργον κυρίου ἐργάζεται ὡς κἀγώ· μή τις οὖν αὐτὸν ἐξουθενήσῃ.
(a') προπέμψατε δὲ αὐτὸν ἐν εἰρήνῃ,
(c') ἵνα ἔλθῃ πρός με.

The terms, of course, are not those noted above, with the exception of a and b.

[7] The language of (3e), particularly b, borders on the language of the letter of recommendation, for example, Rom 16:1ff.; 1 Cor 16:15ff. The latter requires investigation before the relationship between the two can be determined.

[8] The significance of this point will be considered subsequently.

(Paul's presence) represent the implementation of the apostolic *parousia* in ascending order of significance. The presence of Paul will therefore be the primary medium by which he makes his apostolic authority effective, whether for negative (1 Cor 4:19) or positive (Phil 1:24ff.) reasons. Letter and envoy will be substitutes, less effective perhaps, but sometimes necessary. The shape of the apostolic *parousia* as a whole could be considered from this perspective.

The significance that Paul attached to his personal presence relative to letter and emissary could have been deduced from the structure of the apostolic *parousia,* had Paul not made the point explicit.[9] The characteristic trajectory is from (1) through (3e) to (3f), from the weaker to the stronger medium. As a rule, (3f) can be followed only by items (4) and (5) (Rom 15; 1 Cor 4; 1 Thessalonians; Phil 2:19–24), that is, only by the invocation of divine approval and the reference to the benefits of his presence. Where this is not the case, Paul wishes to soften the coercion implied by his presence (Phlm 22—a very subtle formulation!); or, his coming is advanced as an open threat and the letter conceived as a means of softening the blow (2 Cor 12:14ff.).

If Paul aspired for compelling reasons to pursue his apostolic oversight of the congregations through the medium of his own personal presence, the absence of (3f) as a particular case would at least require explanation. The absence of (3e), on the other hand, might be occasioned by circumstances, and the explicit mention of his purpose in writing (1) might depend on emphasis. Among the major passages, the constellation (1) + (3e) + (3f) is found in 1 Cor 4; (1) + (3f) occurs in Rom 15; Philemon; 2 Cor 12:14ff; (3e) + (3f) in 1 Thessalonians and Phil 2:19–24. It is only in Galatians that not one of these items is to be found. Among the secondary passages, 2 Cor 9 and possibly 1 Cor 16:1–11 (see above, n. 6) exhibit all three elements, whereas 2

---

[9] For example, in 2 Cor 2:3f., 9, he makes it clear that he chose to write instead of visiting on this particular occasion in order to prepare them for his coming, or rather, to spare them the pain of his coming (1:23; if he had come under the circumstances, he would be seeking to control their faith: 1:24a). The same thought exactly is expressed in 13:10. The letter does not therefore bear the apostolic power to the same degree as would Paul's personal presence. The subordinate rôle of the emissary is obliquely expressed in 1 Cor 4:17ff.: Timothy will remind them, but Paul will put their power to the test.

Cor 8 manifests only (3e): in view of the history of his relations with the congregation at Corinth, Paul may have deliberately suppressed mention of his direct rôle in the gathering of the collection in order to avoid the suggestion that his coming might again be a threat (cf. 2 Cor 1:23ff., 12:20ff., 13:2ff, 10). Since Phil 2:25–30 occurs in conjunction with 2:19–24, the absence of (3f) there occasions no surprise.[10] The remaining passage, Rom 1:8ff., contains only (3a) and (3b)—the desire and intention to come, which is striking in view of Rom 15:14ff. In this case, moreover, (4a) and (4b) precede even the expression of his desire and intention, occasioned formally no doubt by the fact that Paul works the apostolic *parousia* into the thanksgiving. But there may be another reason for this arrangement.

A number of apparently heterogeneous elements are grouped together under (3). The logic of this grouping is not obvious in Rom 14 because (3d) is missing. When (3e) is inserted, the logic becomes evident: Paul is eager to come (3a), hopes to come (3b), but he has suffered delay, encountered some obstacle (3c), which forces him to send an envoy in his place in the meantime (3e). However, his hopes will eventually be realized, God willing, so that he can announce his coming in advance (3f). The movement from (3a) to (3f) thus constitutes one integral unit. This structure reveals the rank of the apostolic emissary: he substitutes for the apostle himself, whereas the letter is at best written authority for what the emissary has to say. Because Paul gives precedence to the oral word, the written word will not function as a primary medium of his apostleship.[11] It is for this reason that item (1) does not loom so large in the Pauline letters as it does in the non-literary papyri.[12]

---

[10] 1 Cor 16:12 occurs in conjunction with (3f), but this point may not be relevant: is Apollos being urged to come as an envoy?

[11] Such a statement as 1 Cor 14:37f. must be viewed as a counterweight to the enthusiasts who placed exaggerated emphasis on the free, spirit-inspired word.

[12] Heikki Koskenniemi (77ff.) has identified the formula γέγραφα οὖν σοι ὅπως ἂν (ἵνα) εἰδῇς ("I have written to you so that you may know . . .") as a common formula in the papyri, both in private and official letters, which extends from Ptolemaic times down into IV CE. It occurs in the Ptolemaic period characteristically as the final item before the ἔρρωσο or other closing formula, but later it also occurs elsewhere in the letter. This convention has obvious affinities with item (1b) in the Pauline letters, as well as with the formula employed in (3e).

The complete movement (3a)–(3f) is present only in 1 Thessalonians.[13] An abbreviated example, lacking (3a)–(3c), is 1 Cor 4, evidently because Paul wants his coming to be regarded as an imminent threat and because an expression of eagerness is not appropriate under the circumstances. It is perhaps not by accident that where (3a)–(3f) is curtailed, for whatever reasons, (1) tends to come to expression (Rom 15; Philemon; 1 Cor 4; 2 Cor 12:14ff.; cf. 2 Cor 9). Philippians is only an apparent exception. In this regard Galatians again constitutes the real exception, though attention should perhaps be directed to 6:11; having failed to call attention to the letter itself at the customary place, is he led to underscore it at the end?[14]

In sum, where the letter comes to the fore—where (3e) is lacking—the movement tends to be more directly from (1) to (3f) (Philemon; 2 Cor 12:14ff.; Rom 15 nevertheless gives expression to (3a)–(3c)). Where emphasis is placed on the apostolic emissary, (1) tends to be suppressed (1 Thessalonians; Phil 2:19–24; cf. 2 Cor 9:1!). The formula in 1 Cor 4 is blunt: (1)–(2)–(3e)–(3f).

4.2 Items (4a), (4b) and (5) in its various nuances are dependent, as it were, upon (3f); (4a) is a convention (well represented also in the papyri), and for that reason less subject to nuance. The authentic prayer (4b), on the other hand, tends to be suppressed where Paul's coming constitutes a threat (1 Cor 4; 2 Cor 12:14ff.); it is therefore the friendlier invocation (Rom 15; 1:8ff.; Phlm 22; 1 Thessalonians). Item (4) is regularly omitted in passages having to do with the collection and in Phil 2:25–30 (Epaphroditus); (4b) is found, however, in 1 Cor 16:12 (Apollos).

Of course, benefits from the apostolic presence accruing either to the apostle (5a) or to apostle and congregation mutually (5a–b) indicates a friendlier letter than emphasis on benefits accruing to the recipients (5b): 1 Cor 4; 2 Cor 12:14ff.; Gal 4.

It remains to consider the apparently chaotic order of 2 Cor

---

[13] Less (3d), which is not constitutive.

[14] This can hardly be regarded as more than a suggestion, though the fact that the assertion of his apostolic authority in Galatia depends solely on the letter perhaps supports it. It is also worth noting that in 1 Thessalonians, where item (1) is also missing, Paul calls attention to the letter among closing matters (5:27). The signature in his own hand at 1 Cor 16:21 (cf. 2 Thess 3:17) is another matter. Yet Philippians constitutes an important exception: Paul nowhere calls attention to the letter itself.

12:14ff. and the apparent incompleteness of Phil 2:19–24 (in addition to the problem of Rom 1:8ff. and Galatians). The reason for the former has already been suggested: The passage 2 Cor 12:14–13:10, though discernible as the apostolic *parousia,* is woven into Paul's defense of his apostleship as the final element. Because it constitutes a phase of the major argument, it is less formally structured.

On the other hand, Phil 1:1–2:18 is a seamless robe with two parallel letters of recommendation joined on. The substance of the letter is anticipated already in the thanksgiving (1:3–11; cf. Philemon); the *paraenesis* is begun in characteristic Pauline fashion in 1:27, then reintroduced in 2:1, after a brief return to the subject of the body (1:28ff.); and the apostolic *parousia* is anticipated by the thanksgiving (1:8), worked into the theme of the body (the issue of Paul's current crisis: 1:19–26),[15] alluded to twice more (1:27, 2:12), and expressed finally in the section having to do with the sending of Timothy (2:19–24; note v. 24). That the apostolic *parousia* is woven into the body of the letter is indicated by the presence of language characteristic of the apostolic *parousia* in 1:25ff. and 1:27 ("Whether I come and see you or am absent, I may hear of you"; εἴτε ἐλθὼν καὶ ἰδὼν ὑμᾶς εἴτε ἀκούω τὰ περὶ ὑμῶν). The tightly conceived unity of theological body and *paraenesis,* not altogether characteristic of the Pauline letter, and the integral significance of the apostolic *parousia* to the theme of the body, explain why Paul distributes the elements of the apostolic *parousia* over the whole letter (cf. 2 Cor 10–13) and subjoins the two recommendations, which he could not easily have worked into the body so conceived. In this case, therefore, it seems legitimate to fill out the apostolic *parousia* from elsewhere in the letter (see the tabular summary above). The character of Phil 1–2

---

[15] It is very likely that εἰς σωτηρίαν (1:19) does not refer to the immediate outcome of Paul's present crisis, but to his ultimate destiny. The prayers of the Philippians and the support of the spirit of Christ will thus also have that reference. But, as vv. 20b and 24ff. make clear, Paul's ultimate destiny is intimately connected with his present dilemma: since he is confident (πεποιθώς, 1:25) that it is necessary for him to remain in the flesh (1:24), he knows (οἶδα, 1:25, of his certainty in faith; cf. 1:19) that he will remain (1:25) in order to continue his fruitful labor (1:22), which, through his presence again to them, will benefit their progress and joy in faith (1:25b–26). The prayers of the Philippians (1:19) thus eventually come to bear upon Paul's presence again to them.

illustrates all the more forcefully that Paul incorporates the same structural items of the apostolic *parousia,* even where he does not group them in the customary fashion.

The initial model for the apostolic *parousia* was Rom 15:14–33, supplemented at one point (3e). This has proved to be a reliable index to Paul's pattern in the other letters. Yet it would have been possible to reconstruct the substance of it out of 1 Cor 4, 1 Thessalonians and Philemon, in content if not in order.[16]

*5.1* It may legitimately be asked whether any significance is to be attached to the apostolic *parousia* as a structural element in the Pauline letter other than as a natural inclination to issue news regarding renewed contact between apostle and/or emissary and congregation—especially, one would suppose, at the conclusion of letters. [17]

---

[16] Interestingly, the structure of the apostolic *parousia* as represented in Paul is found also in at least one of the letters emanating from a later pagan circle that worships Hermes Trismegistus; the archive in question, belonging to IV CE, includes PHermRees 2–6 and PRyland IV 616–51, and perhaps other unpublished papyri in the John Rylands Library as well (PHermRees, p. 2). The letter referred to is PHermRees 2: lines 3f. = (3a); lines 5f. = (3b); lines 7ff. = (3c); lines 15ff., unfortunately defective (see n., p. 4), = (3e); lines 26f. = (3f/4b). The entire archive deserves careful scrutiny in connection with the form of the Pauline (and Christian) letter.

[17] Walter Schmithals (1964: 299, 303) is of the opinion that personal remarks having to do with Paul's relation to the congregation are found only at the beginning and end of his letters. This opinion is based in part on his view of the composite character of several of the letters, for example, Philippians; 1, 2 Thessalonians. Even so, 1 Cor 4:14ff. constitutes a notable exception (explicable, in his judgment, on the basis of 1 Cor 16:19f.—the sending of Timothy is reported again at the conclusion of the letter). Whether this and his other provocative suggestions concerning the structure of the letter prove to be viable depends on establishing criteria for the form and structure of the Pauline letter. With regard to the position of personal remarks, (apostolic *parousia*), the question is: where do they occur in letters containing a paraenetical section? In 1 Corinthians, 1 Thessalonians and Galatians the apostolic *parousia* is found attached to the theological body of the letter, *before paraenesis.* Philemon has no *paraenesis* and 2 Cor 10–13 has only a paraenetical summary, which *follows* the apostolic *parousia* (13:11). The material must therefore be considered in conjunction with other collection passages (2 Cor 8, 9). The exceptions to the rule— body, apostolic *parousia, paraenesis*— are thus Romans and Philippians (on the view that Phil 1–2 is an independent letter). The structure of Philippians, as we

That the inclination is natural has been amply demonstrated by Koskenniemi in his ground-breaking study. He has shown that *philophronesis, parousia,* and *homilia* are basic motifs in both the conception and the form of the Greek letter from the beginning. The letter is designed to extend the possibility of friendship between parties after they have become physically separated. He traces the idea that friendship is dependent upon the presence of the parties to each other back to Aristotle's doctrine of friendship, which was taken up, extended, and applied to the letter by the Peripatetics. The fundamental structure of the letter—salutation, dialogue, farewell—corresponds to the meeting between friends.

Gustav Karlsson has further shown that the motif "absent in body, but present through letter" can be easily traced from the beginning of the Christian era well into the Middle Ages. He is of the opinion that the formulae found at 1 Cor 5:3 and Col 2:5 ("absent in body, but present in spirit") and elsewhere reflect well-known technical formulae of Greek epistolography.[18]

The motif of the presence of the parties to each other in one way or another is natural because it is constitutive of the conception of the letter. Koskenniemi has adduced compelling evidence from the language of the letter and from theoreticians to demonstrate that this motif is nearly universally presupposed in the situation to which the letter belongs. It would not be surprising, then, if the motif were to come to expression as a structural element in the composition of the letter itself, at least occasionally.

5.2   Neither the naturalness of the motif nor the Aristotelian doctrine of friendship accounts, however, for the significance that Paul accords to his own presence. Consider the startling statement in 1 Cor 5:3–5:

---

have tried to show, has its special explanation (parallel to the "letter of reconciliation"?). It remains to account for Romans. I agree heartily with Schmithals' program of sorting out the conflated letters in the Pauline corpus, but I am of the opinion that his specific proposals lack sufficient formal and structural control. Cf. further, 1960, 1957, 1959, 1956.

[18] The contrast occurs in Paul in one form or another at 1 Thess 2:17; Phil 1:27, 2:12; 1 Cor 5:3; 2 Cor 10:1f., 10:10f., 13:2, 10; cf. Col 2:5. Cf. Koskenniemi: 175ff.

For my part, though I am absent in body, I am present in spirit, and my judgment upon the man who did this thing is already given, as if I were indeed present: you all being assembled in the name of our Lord Jesus, and I with you in spirit, with the power of our Lord Jesus over us, this man is to be consigned to Satan for the destruction of the body, so that his spirit may be saved on the Day of the Lord. (NEB)

With this may be compared 2 Cor 10:3-4, in the context of his discussion of the alleged contrast between his boldness when absent and meekness when present (10:1-2): "Weak men we may be, but it is not as such that we fight our battles. The weapons we wield are not merely human, but divinely potent to demolish strongholds" (NEB).

Paul must have thought of his presence as bearing charismatic, one might even say eschatological, power. One is reminded of the power of the apostolic presence in Acts 5:1-11 and of the threatening character of the promise to appear in person in the letters to the seven churches (Rev 2:5b, 16, 25; 3:3b, 11). The appearance of both the motif of the apostolic presence and that of the presence of Christ, in the letter form and in similar language (Paul and Revelation), perhaps reinforces the eschatological overtones of the letter.[19]

Such an understanding of his personal *parousia* accords well with what Paul writes in 1 Cor 4:18ff. Those in Corinth who are behaving arrogantly, as though he were not coming, will have the opportunity when he does come to match their boasting with his power (4:19). Paul concludes, "Shall I come with a rod?" (4:21). Since he appeared in Corinth "in demonstration of Spirit and power" (1 Cor 2:4; cf. 2 Cor 11:12; Rom 15:19), the Corinthians may know whereof he speaks. It is possible, on the same basis, to understand his remark in 2 Cor 13:10 that he is writing to them to spare himself any sharp exercise of authority when he comes (cf. 2

---

[19] John Knox rightly warns against views that assign to Paul an exaggerated estimate of his own rôle in the eschatological plan of God (1964: 3ff.). Paul does not hold the view that the eschaton depends on him. He may have thought of himself as the supreme apostle to the Gentiles; and he appears to be willing to quit the scene himself (Phil 1:19ff.). It follows that he does not regard his presence as the presence of Christ.

Cor 1:23). Some Corinthian braggarts apparently advanced the
thesis that Paul wrote frightening letters, but that his bodily presence was beneath contempt. Paul replies, "People who talk that way
should reckon with this: when I come, my actions will show the same
man as my letters showed in my absence" (2 Cor 10:11, NEB).
Paul's power is bound to the weakness of Christ, it is true, but that
power, even in weakness, is capable of making itself felt: he promises
to show no leniency when he comes on his third visit (2 Cor 13:1–4).
The word of God spoken by Paul is indeed life-giving and death-
bringing (2 Cor 2:14–17), and this word is bound, so far as Paul is
concerned, to his personal presence.

Because Paul understands the significance of his apostolic presence in this fashion,[20] he gathers the items which may be scattered
about in the common letter or appended as additional information
into one more or less discrete section, in which he (a) implies that the
letter is an anticipatory surrogate for his presence—with which,
however, the letter is entirely congruent (2 Cor 10:11); (b) com-
mends the emissary who is to represent him in the meantime; and (c)
speaks of an impending visit or a visit for which he prays. Through
these media his apostolic authority and power are made effective.

6.1  The significance of the apostolic *parousia* as a structural
element in the Pauline letter may be considered for the bearing it has
on the date of Galatians. Paul announces an impending visit in Rom
15:28b; 1 Cor 4:19 (1 Cor 16:5); 2 Cor 12:14, 13:1; he expresses the
hope to make a visit (soon), circumstances permitting, in Phlm 22; 1
Thess 3:10; Phil 2:24 (1:25). Except for the letter fragments, if that
is what they are, in 2 Cor 1–7 and Phil 3:2ff., the only letter in which
Paul does not anticipate a visit to the congregation in question is
Galatians. In 4:20 he does write, "I wish I could be present with you
now" (ἤθελον δὲ παρεῖναι πρὸς ὑμᾶς ἄρτι), a wish which, however
one interprets the imperfect (see Moule: 9; Blass-Debrunner:
§359[2]), is clearly unattainable as expressed: he cannot be with
them at present because he is elsewhere. This wish nevertheless
evidences once again the significance that Paul attached to his presence.

---

[20] And, of course, the significance of their presence to him, for example, 2 Cor
7:6f., 13b–16; 1 Thess 3:6–8 (cf. 2:19f.); Phil 4:14–18.

In view of the magnitude of the crisis in Galatia, it is incredible that Paul would not have backed up his letter with the hint of a future visit—had he been in a position to contemplate one, however remote—or dispatching an emissary, had there been one available. It is just this omission which prompted John Knox to conclude that Galatians was penned relatively late in Paul's career, at a time when he could not return to Galatia because of other commitments (1962: 343). This can only mean that it was written at the time he had already set his face to the west. Surely nothing less than that would have prompted him to turn away with the mere wish that he could have been there!

6.2   The arrangement of the apostolic *parousia* in Romans may also be revealing for the character of that letter as a whole. It has been observed that Rom 1:8ff. corresponds virtually point for point to Rom 15:14–33. Paul has worked the ingredients of his characteristic treatment of the apostolic *parousia* into the thanksgiving of Romans, with a consequent modification of the typical form of that unit. As O. Michel has suggested, Rom 1:8ff. and Rom 15:14–33 serve as brackets to enclose the whole (325).

The parallelism between these two sections is striking up to the point of particularization: Rom 1:8ff., aside from the references to Rome in 1:7, 15, is general, whereas 15:14ff. is highly particularized. As John Knox has pointed out, a Roman reader would not have learned from 1:8ff., for example, that Paul was actually coming to Rome (only that he wanted and intended to come), that he was even now setting out, or that he intended to go on to Spain. Nor would he have learned of the Pauline itinerary which was to bring him to Rome via Jerusalem, and the further threat of delay posed by that route (1956: 191–3).[21] After reviewing the manuscript tradition which omits "in Rome" ἐν ʿΡώμῃ in 1:7, 15, T. W. Manson concludes that "the context, particularly verses 8–17, imperatively demands a particular reference to a well-known community not founded by Paul or hitherto visited by him" (229). Manson believes, of course, that the references to Rome in chapter 1 are original, but it is significant that the context, in his judgment, requires some reference to "a well-known community not founded by Paul or hitherto

---

[21] Knox observes (1956: 192) that Rom 1:10 is normally over-interpreted in view of Rom 15:14ff.

visited by him." Can we go so far as to say that this is *all* the context requires?

The double treatment of the apostolic *parousia* in Romans is exceptional for Paul,[22] and the appearance of one treatment in the thanksgiving is striking, to say the least. It is curious, moreover, that what is missing from this form is precisely the particular elements: (1), (3e), (3f). In this regard, Rom 1:8ff. is parallel to Galatians. And if, as I have attempted to show (1966), the apostolic *parousia* is normally attached to the theological body of the letter, preceding the *paraenesis*, this fact, too, makes the structure of Romans odd. Why did Paul anticipate the apostolic *parousia* in a general way in the thanksgiving and reserve a particular treatment of the same theme for the end of the letter?

The general character of the remarks in 1:8ff. (coupled with the possible absence of the references to Rome in 1:7, 15) and the near-epistolary style of the body (Romans approaches the treatise), together with the lack of certain personal references in the body of the letter, suggest that Rom 1:1-15:13 may well have been conceived by Paul as a general letter, to be particularized and dispatched as the occasion demanded to other well-known churches which he had not founded or visited.[23] The double treatment of the apostolic *parousia* and the position of the particularized form (15:14-33) at the end of the letter lend considerable weight to this suggestion, in my opinion: Paul needed only to fill in the address and, if the occasion required it, add a personalized form of the apostolic *parousia* at the end, in order to be able to dispatch this generalized summary of his gospel to yet another church. The customary form of the Pauline letter could scarcely be modified so easily, and the presence of the generalized apostolic *parousia* in the thanksgiving made it possible for him to send off another copy without doing more than adding his name.

---

[22] Unless 1 Cor 4 and 16 are to be regarded as doublets; see above.

[23] In his 1956 article Knox advances this view as something to be considered. In his 1964 essay (10, note 11), he appears to be more certain of its merits.

# Eight

# THE APOSTOLIC PRESENCE:
# JOHN THE ELDER

*0.* Twenty-one of the twenty-seven writings comprising the New Testament are customarily classified as letters, yet relatively little has been achieved in establishing the form and structure of the early Christian letter.[1] This deficiency is due, perhaps, to the failure to extend the study of the common letter as represented in the papyri in relation to the Christian letter. To put it briefly, the ground-breaking studies of F. X. J. Exler and Paul Schubert—to cite the two outstanding examples—have not been seriously followed up.

This chapter is a modest and tentative contribution to the renewal and furtherance of that neglected task. The focus will be on (1) the marks of the common letter to be found in 2 and 3 John; (2) the structure or the constituent elements of the two epistles; and finally (3) the relation of that structure to the structure of the Pauline letter.

*1.* In W. G. Kümmel's opinion, "No other NT epistle, not even Philemon, has so much the form of the Hellenistic private letter as 2 and 3 John" (1966: 313). Kümmel wishes to assert, of course, that these letters are actual and not fictive letters; yet his point can be taken to mean that 2 and 3 John sustain numerous points of contact

---

[1] Reviews of relevant work to date are to be found in Rigaux (164–203) and Funk (1966: 250–70).

with the common Hellenistic letter. It is in the second sense that I wish to support his assertion.

That the address and closing in general correspond to the common epistolary form requires no elaboration (2 John 1f., 12f.; 3 John 1, 13f.). The benedictory greetings of 2 John 2, customary in the Pauline and other Christian letters,[2] is replaced in 3 John 3 with a conventional health wish. The ὑγιαίνειν wish makes its appearance in the papyri in II CE in the basic form πρὸ πάντων εὔχομαί σε ὑγιαίνειν but with great variety in detail (Exler: 107–11).[3] Though the ὑγιαίνειν wish occurs frequently, a form with both εὐοδοῦσθαι and ὑγιαίνειν as it is found in 3 John is attested, to my knowledge, only in POxy XIV, 1680, late III or early IV CE.[4] The ὑγιαίνειν wish does not appear elsewhere in the New Testament or in the Apostolic Fathers. It is thus an item which 3 John alone has in common with the secular letter tradition.

According to Heikki Koskenniemi, the author of a recent brilliant study of the Greek letter, the expression of joy (ἐχάρην) at the receipt of a letter was common in replies during the Hellenistic-Roman period (75ff.). The letter was frequently begun with such expressions. Identical or similar expressions of joy were employed for a variety of other reasons as well, more often than not as a response to the receipt of good news. Good reports are acknowledged in 2 John 4 and 3 John 3 with the formula ἐχάρην λίαν, which is paralleled by PGiess 21 (II CE): λίαν ἐχάρην ἀκούσασα ὅτι ἔρρωσαι καὶ ἡ ἀδελφή σου Σοῆρις ("I rejoiced exceedingly when I heard that your sister, Soeris, was also well") (cited by Exler [112] as an initial phrase). The same opening formula is used in the Michigan papyri

---

[2] Of the New Testament letters, only James employs the common χαίρειν.

[3] Exler dates the appearance of this formula to early I CE on the basis of POxy II, 292, ca. 25 CE, where it appears at the *close* of a letter. Heikki Koskenniemi (134) therefore corrects the date to early II CE.

[4] Lines 2ff. Εὐοδοῦν in these wishes is rare in any case. The preposition is uniformly πρό (πάντων) in the papyri (so Exler), whereas in 3 John it is περί. The fact that the idiom does not appear to admit of variation and that περί in the sense "above all" is otherwise unattested (Blass-Debrunner: §229, 2) suggests that περί is a false reading. It must have been introduced by copyists who were familar with the Christian but not the pagan greeting.

The customary abbreviations are employed for published collections of papyri.

of the II CE, for example, VIII, 474, line 2. For λίαν may be substituted μεγάλως, for example, VIII, 495, line 11; or πῶς, for example, VIII, 473, line 4. Comparable formulae appear elsewhere in the letter, for example, in a postscript: VIII, 482, 113 CE, line 23. It is worthy of note that Polycarp opens his letter to the Philippians with Συνεχάρην ὑμῖν μεγάλως κτλ. ("I rejoice greatly with you"), by which he expresses his pleasure at their hospitality and faith.[5] With these phrases is to be compared, further, Phil 4:10: ἐχάρην δὲ ἐν κυρίῳ μεγάλως ὅτι... ("I rejoice in the Lord greatly that...").

Paul Schubert has noted that the ἐχάρην period is a by-form of the εὐχαριστῶ period so often used to open letters. In PGiess 21, cited above, the parallelism is made clear by line 15, where εὐχαριστῶ replaces ἐχάρην in a comparable phrase (177). Schubert further points out that the parallelism between the opening thanksgiving in Philippians (1:3ff.) and 4:10ff.; in the latter, which is a note of thanks, εὐχαριστῶ is replaced by ἐχάρην (77).[6] It would thus appear that the ἐχάρην λίαν periods in 2 and 3 John are the functional equivalents of the εὐχαριστῶ thanksgiving periods, well known from Paul and elsewhere.

Three tentative conclusions may be drawn from these observations: (1) ἐχάρην λίαν with adverbial variants is a common epistolary formula, often used to open letters; (2) it corresponds functionally to the εὐχαριστῶ thanksgiving period; (3) Phil 4:10 is not impossible as a letter opening, provided it can be established that the idiom was so used prior to 100 CE.[7]

Terence Mullins has called attention to the petition as a literary form in the letter (46–54). The characteristic form of the petition is:

---

[5] Pol. *Phil.* 1:1–2; cf. *Barn.* 1:12: ὑπερευφραίνομαι.

[6] One might also point to Phlm 7: χαρὰν γὰρ πολλὴν ἔσχον... ἐπὶ τῇ ἀγάπῃ σου, which is formally parallel to the thanksgiving period in v. 4: εὐχαριστῶ... ἀκούων σου τὴν ἀγάπην.... It is thus possible that χαρὰν πολλὴν ἔχειν is an opening formula and not the conclusion of the thanksgiving (cf. Sanders: 361). This would explain διό in v. 8 and would correspond to the pattern, ἐχάρην period (v. 7) followed by a petition (v. 8), which is attested for the common letter; for evidence see below. The thanksgiving motif is reiterated in the opening formula as the background for the petition that follows.

[7] The fragmentary evidence now available does not contain an example of the formula used as a letter opening to be dated with certainty earlier than 100 CE.

background; petition, introduced by one of four characteristic verbs; address in the vocative; courtesy phrase; desired action (47). One or the other of the elements may, of course, be omitted, and there is considerable variation in detail. One of the four common verbs of petition is ἐρωτᾶν. 2 John 5 is thus a petition in form: ἐρωτῶ σε / κυρία / ... ἵνα ἀγαπῶμεν ἀλλήλους. It exhibits the petition verb, the address, and the desired action. The ἐχάρην λίαν period in verse 4, furthermore, is probably to be understood as the background for this petition. It is unnecessary to introduce further evidence in support of Mullins' claim that the petition exhibits a formal pattern built around three basic elements (background, petition verb, desired action [46]). It should be noted, however, that the petition often occurs as the *second* element in the body of the letter, following upon a first period, or periods, that is to be construed as the background of the petition.[8] That is to say, it is not only the formal pattern of the petition that is significant, but its position in the body of the letter. It should be noted, furthermore, that the period which precedes the petition is sometimes the ἐχάρην λίαν formula noted earlier. Examples are PMich VIII, 474 (early II CE), lines 2ff.; 475 (early II CE), lines 8ff.; 484 (II CE), lines 3ff.

In sum, a petition preceded by a background statement that is occasionally introduced by the ἐχάρην λίαν formula, just as it occurs in 2 John 4f., appears to be an established epistolary convention, employed frequently as the opening gambit in the common letter.

The ἐχάρην λίαν period in 3 John 3f. is not followed, however, by an ἐρωτᾶν petition. What comes next is introduced by a vocative (ἀγαπητέ) and πιστὸν ποιεῖς (v. 5). The first part of the sentence, "You act faithfully whenever you render service to brethren and strangers at that"—with reference in this context to the service of hospitality—has a material parallel in Ignatius, *Smyrn.* 10:1: καλῶς ἐποιήσατε ὑποδεξάμενοι ("You did well to receive . . ."). Πιστὸν ποιεῖς therefore parallels the common idiom καλῶς ποιήσεις, used to introduce commendations of proper behavior.[9] It is undoubtedly a Christian counterpart of that idiom.

---

[8] The petition also occurs as the *first* element in the body, without explicit reference to the background preceding, for example, PMich VIII, 502 (II CE), lines 5f.

[9] Cf. Phil 4:14; Jas 2:1, 19; Acts 10:33; POxy I, 119 (II or III CE), lines 11f.

The idiom καλῶς ποιήσεις is also commonly used in the papyri in polite forms of petition (Koskenniemi: 134) and is to be translated there as "please" or "I beg you." It may be followed by a participle (Blass-Debrunner: §414, 5), an infinitive (Liddel-Scott: C. 5), or another finite verb, as a means of expressing the content of the request.

It is noteworthy that the second relative clause of 3 John 5f.—the sentence that follows the ἐχάρην λίαν period—is framed as a request, "whom I beg you to help on their way," which is introduced by καλῶς ποιήσεις. The main clause in the sentence, consequently, serves as the background ("You faithfully do that") for the petition contained in the relative clause ("Now I beg you to do this"). The request introduced by καλῶς ποιήσεις in 3 John 6b is therefore structurally parallel to the ἐρωτᾶν petition in 2 John 5, and the commendation introduced by πιστὸν ποιεῖς in John 5–6a serves as the immediate background for that petition.

Not only is the idiom καλῶς ποιήσεις (with variant forms of the verb)[10] commonly used in the papyri to introduce a polite request, but it also commonly occurs as the first element in the body of the letter with just this function, or it follows immediately upon relevant background information. Among numerous examples[11] is the following from PMich I, 35 (254 BCE):

Isingos to Zenon greeting. Concerning the money for which I was surety for Nouraios, the amount being 80 drachmas, he refuses to repay me. Be kind enough (καλῶς ἂν οὖν ποιήσεις) then to write Panakestor or Artemidoros to have it exacted from him and repaid to me.

Of course, καλῶς ποιήσεις as an idiom is not confined to letters. On the other hand, it occurs so frequently in common letters, especially as a polite way of introducing requests, and so often in the sequence indicated—background / καλῶς ποιήσεις / request— as to merit the characterization "epistolese."

---

[10] Εὖ may also be substituted for καλῶς.

[11] E.g., PMich I, 21 (257 BCE), line 4; 28 (256 BCE), line 23; 78 (III BCE), line 3; 80 (III BCE), line 2; 98 (III BCE), line 5; POxy I, 113 (II CE), lines 6f.; 116 (II CE), line 5; II, 294 (22 CE), lines 12f.; 299 (late I CE), lines 3f.; 300 (late I CE), line 5.

It was noted that the ἐχάρην λίαν period in 2 John 4 serves as the background for the ἐρωτᾶν petition. In 3 John, in addition to the special background provided by the recognition of Gaius' faithful act in receiving brethren "who testified to your love before the church" (vv. 5–6a), the ἐχάρην λίαν period also provides general background for the request, as is indicated by the parallel expression "I greatly rejoiced when some of the brethren arrived and testified to the truth of your life" (v. 3a). The favorable testimony of brethren in two respects is thus the platform from which the author advances his polite request. It may then be said that the letter bodies of both 2 and 3 John are opened with forms and structures entirely characteristic of the common letter tradition.

One further point of contact with the common Hellenistic letter may be noted in passing. In addition to the letter of recommendation proper, one finds commendations of third parties inserted in letters given primarily to other matters, for example, POxy IV, 743 (2 BCE), lines 33f.; cf. Polycarp, *Phil.* 14:1. In 3 John 12 there is just such a recommendation for Demetrius.

There are thus certain formal and structural respects in which 2 and 3 John follow the common letter tradition, more closely, perhaps, than other letters in the New Testament, including those of Paul.

2. The structure of 2 John as a whole is relatively simple and clear-cut: opening matters (vv. 1–3); body (4–11); closing conventions (12f.). Other than the sequence of formulae at the beginning, already noted, the body of 2 John is formally and probably materially continuous, unbroken from beginning to end. In closing (v. 12) the author expresses his preference for face-to-face conversation over the letter, a preference he hopes to indulge by coming to see them. This note approximates a recurrent theme in the Pauline letters, which has been designated the apostolic *parousia* (above, Chap. 7). By analogy, this element in 2 John might be called the presbyterial *parousia*. The nearly word-for-word repetition of the item in 3 John 13–14 suggests that the author is drawing upon a formulaic convention of his own, if not of wider usage.

The structure of 3 John, on the other hand, is more complex. Breaks are marked by the vocative, ἀγαπητέ, at verses 2, 5, 11. An expanded ἐχάρην λίαν period (in comparison with 2 John 4) occupies verses 3-4, following the conventional health wish (2). Other breaks in thought occur at verse 9 and verse 12. There are thus five parts to the body of the letter, excluding the health wish.

The first two parts are concerned, as already observed, with the author's basic request and its relevant background: just as you rightly walk in the truth, or receive brethren, please help them along the way also (3-8). The recalcitrance of Diotrephes respecting the reception of the brethren and the presbyter's proposal to deal with it form the subject matter of the next division (9-10). John has written to the church, but Diotrephes does not acknowledge his authority. If (or when?) he appears there, he will raise the question of what Diotrephes is doing. That is to say, he proposes to counter the suppression of his letter with the force of his personal presence. Once again there is thematic proximity to the apostolic *parousia* in the Pauline letter, especially 1 Cor 4:14-21, but with reference to a situation not directly involving the addressee of the letter.

The fourth section is comprised of a brief paraenetical summary (v. 11), and the fifth and final division is a recommendation for Demetrius (v. 12).

Reduced to structural outline, 3 John is contoured as follows:

(1) thanksgiving, which forms the general background for the request (vv. 3-4);
(2) body proper, with its request (5-8);
(3) presbyterial *parousia,* relevant to Diotrephes, who refuses a similar request (9-10);
(4) paraenesis (11);
(5) recommendation (12).

3.   The form and structure of 2 John conform in their idiom and simplicity largely to the common letter tradition. In these respects 2 John is quite comparable to Philemon, although Philemon may indeed be shaped to a greater extent by the distinctive Pauline touch of features diverging from the common letter format. Nevertheless, both letters are highly stylized in the idiom of their respective authors.

The conventional health wish in 3 John 2 marks this letter as the most secularized in the New Testament. On the other hand, the structure of 3 John exhibits more affinities with the Pauline—and thus the Christian—letter format than does 2 John. If, as I have endeavored to show (1966: 263–74 and Chap. 6 above), the character-istic structure of the Pauline letter is: thanksgiving; body, to which is attached apostolic *parousia;* and paraenesis—in that order—the structure of 3 John appears to correspond to the Pauline order. Because the Pauline structure, so far as is known, is a unique devel-opment in the history of the letter, it is possible that the author has been influenced by Paul or by the Christian letter tradition stem-ming from him. Of special significance is the sequence of body, paraenesis, which, of course, is not otherwise characteristic of the common letter but probably derives from the form of the homily.

The position of the section labeled presbyterial *parousia* (3 John 9–10) is suggestive but no more; it refers to a situation involving the letter, whereas the characteristic Pauline form bears directly on the parties to which the letter is addressed. Moreover, the more charac-teristic Johannine expression of the hope of his presence to the recipients is found in end position in 3 John (vv. 13f.), just as it is in 2 John. End position of this item is, I suspect, distinctive of the post-Pauline and common letter (cf. Heb 13:23). It is too much, conse-quently, to suppose that the author of 3 John is imitating the Pauline model in attaching the threat or promise of his personal presence to the body of a pastoral letter. It is more probable that the structural correspondence at this juncture is merely fortuitous.

As fortuitous as the structural correspondence may be, the motif of the significance of the presbyter's personal presence to his readers, given formulaic expression among closing matters in both 2 and 3 John and elaborated in 3 John 9f., echoes the Pauline preference for the oral word over the written word. And the paraenetical summary in 3 John 11, as a structural item in the letter, reflects the Christian letter tradition beginning with Paul and extending through Colos-sians, Ephesians, and Hebrews.

# Nine

# MYTH AND
# THE LITERAL NON-LITERAL

*0.* The study of theology ought to begin these days with a study of poetry. That is not merely to hand a rose to the poets, but to advocate a sane program of theological rehabilitation, certainly of theological repatriation. Theology seems to have gone a-whoring after the scientific flesh pots of Egypt. It has wandered so far afield that it has forgotten the wellsprings of its infancy. The antidote must be potent enough to restore sight to the blind and hearing to the deaf. Perhaps modern poetry is sufficiently strong medicine to enable the queen to shake off her torpor.

The route to a fresh beginning has not been and will not be direct but devious. I propose to map out one path that leads by way of Rudolf Bultmann's program of demythologizing, and thus starts off in the opposite direction, so to speak. Just how the course, which leads initially away from myth, comes round eventually to the literal non-literal, is not to be demonstrated by some logical artifice, but is to be shown if possible in its inevitability, given the original trajectory. In this way it will become clear why a theology that is hostile to myth can be friendly to, even intimate with, poetry.

*1. The theological repudiation of mythological language.* In recent theology Rudolf Bultmann has been the primary inspiration of the theological repudiation of mythological language. Under his tutelage a number of theologians have rejected the literal sense of myth. But unlike his liberal predecessors, who rejected the mythical language of the Bible as archaic and largely meaningless language, Bultmann has insisted that the Christian gospel came originally to expression in mythological language and nowhere else.[1] With respect to the old liberal antithesis between the (simple) message of Jesus and the theology of Paul (or, more broadly, the kerygma of the ancient church), Bultmann opts unequivocally for Paul (and the ancient church). In the proclamation of the death and resurrection of Jesus—to put it briefly—the import of the Christian gospel came authentically to expression.

It is strategically important to emphasize that Bultmann does *not* repudiate myth as such; in contrast to his liberal tutors (and liberalism generally), he takes his stand firmly on the primitive Christian kerygma, which is mythological through and through. He thus retains the scripture principle of orthodoxy as his theological foundation, albeit in a restricted sense; myth alone was appropriate to the expression of the transcendence inherent in the gospel.

The mythological scriptural foundation, however, is deceiving for modern theology and for the contemporary man of faith because mythological language now obscures its true import; modern man is offended by the language rather than by the real *skandalon* of the gospel. It is in order to permit the modern mentality to be confronted by the real scandal of the gospel that Bultmann proposes to demythologize the kerygma.

The false affront that mythological language makes inevitable for modern man is that this man can grasp myth only in a *literal* sense; he takes myth to be making factual assertions about the world in which he lives and thus about his worldview. He cannot square his worldview with that reflected in the New Testament myth, so he rejects the latter—rightly—out of intellectual honesty. He cannot sanction biblical cosmology, he does not believe in demons, he cannot credit the resurrection of a corpse, and he refuses to accept the principle of miracle as divine intervention in the ordered regularity of the cosmos. Insofar as aberrations occur in nature, they are aberrations—nothing more. Furthermore, he cannot swallow the notion

---

[1] I attempted to develop this point in *Language, Hermeneutic, and Word of God* (1966: 31ff., especially 35).

that the end of history as he knows it is a date fixed on the calendar, though known only to God. In sum, modern man proposes to give a *natural* account of every phenomenon, past or anticipated, that the biblical myth appears to project as direct, observable actions of God, and to reject those correlative features of the archaic mythical world-view that contradict his enlightened view of the way things really are.

Bultmann embraced the New Testament myth as his theological premise, but, like his contemporaries, he found he could not live with it literally. He therefore took myth to refer to nothing in the sensory world that could not be accounted for on a natural, or literal, basis. Bultmann does not, in my judgment, deny to myth all literal meaning; he denies only that myth is objectively descriptive. The difference may be put this way: myth is not literally literal, but it is in fact literally non-literal. It will be necessary to sort out the senses of the term literal subsequently. Meanwhile, Bultmann may be permitted to state what he takes the biblical myth to mean.

Myth refers to the acts of God only insofar as they are hidden, that is, not observable by ordinary sense perception. We do not learn anything descriptive about the world in which we live from myth; what we learn—and this is the crux of the Christian gospel—is to understand ourselves, in the context of the world, anew. A confrontation with the Christian proclamation may bring man, even modern man, to understand that he is dependent for his life on God, that authentic existence is faithful existence, which is made actual only by God's gracious act in Jesus Christ. This act is to be understood not as an open, verifiable event of the past, but as an event that takes place for the hearer in his confrontation with the proclaimed word. When this event takes place, when man is brought to faith, he will understand that God and God alone has freed him from the weight of his sinful past and opened the freedom of the future to him. But this act remains hidden: it cannot be looked back to as a past event any more than one can look back in this sense to the event of Jesus Christ; it has to be renewed again and again as an act of decision in confrontation with the gospel.

Demythologizing the Christian myth thus means shifting the locus of man's encounter with God from the world of empirical fact to language (one could also say to history, for language marks historical existence): insofar as the redemptive event occurs at all, it occurs in man's encounter with the word of God. That the event of Jesus Christ is borne by the proclaimed word, by language, is precisely what continues to make it eventful. Of course, this transposition has the effect of shifting the locus of the problem of God, and its execution brings the rôle of the prophet into closest proximity to the poetic act:

> The poet brings about the restitution of the word. He restores resonance to speech, he offers each word in a new situation, and in such a way that its original power reappears. (Gusdorf: 74)

Bultmann seeks only to restore original power to the word by subverting myth understood literally.

It may certainly be asked whether myth so understood affects how we perceive the world. Bultmann holds that myth does not modify or even touch the modern worldview in any of its particulars, but that it does make man free from dependence upon the modern or any worldview. Worldviews for the man of faith are relativized. The man of faith may opt for one or the other worldview for practical reasons, but he will accord to none the status of an ultimate account of the way things really are.

On Bultmann's view, then, understanding myth as literally literal is what robs it of its pristine power; literalism is a means of holding the power of mythic language at bay. On the other hand, he takes the Christian myth to be a literal non-literal paradigm of the way things really are. That is to say, myth is non-literal in a descriptive sense, but literal insofar as it impinges upon the really real. The inference to be readily drawn is that the two senses of literal involve a contest over the real.

Bultmann was driven in the direction of demythologizing because of the disease, assumed to be endemic to the modern mind, that prompts man to read everything, including the non-literal, literally, or descriptively. Bultmann takes literalism to be characteristic of the mind-set of the modern world.[2] Because of his consciousness of the presence of the church and society at large to theological work, he wanted theology to communicate, as well as perpetuate, a venerable but increasingly cloistered exercise. Then, too, as an interpreter of

---

[2] Modern world refers to the mentality that is informed basically by the Enlightenment; it is often attributed primarily to Descartes.

scripture, he found that the creative spirits in the New Testament were already onto the demythologizing game, for much the same reason he had discovered it. But he and the ancients were concerned that the gospel happen *to* as well as *for* man, and myth appeared to be a ready exit for the *to*. There are those, I know, including poets and literary critics, who contest the assumption that the present evil age is literal-minded, or at least that mythological language is mostly deceptive. Yet Bultmann appears to have been justified in his assumption, to judge from, among other things, the response he received from other theologians and the church. He was widely attacked from the one side because he was held to have destroyed the truth of the gospel: precisely its literal meaning. It may have surprised even him to learn how widespread and deep-seated literalism really was. Many of those who became his adherents were freed, moreover, from just that mind-set as a consequence of his work. One has to measure the cogency of the affliction by the numbers of both his friends and his enemies. Those who have to deal with the mentality prevalent in the church are therefore unmoved by the argument that modern man understands the non-literal character of biblical myth very well: insofar as he is in the church he understands it not at all—for him, myth that does not have a literal sense has no sense. And I know not a few scientific and literary savants, both in and out of the church, who are just as unrelenting in literalism where scripture is concerned.

Bultmann was attacked with equal vigor from the other side as well. The unregenerate liberals (those untouched by Karl Barth and neo-orthodoxy) thought Bultmann's demythologized version of the gospel as bad as the mythical form. They castigated him for not dispensing with myth altogether.

The line between the two fronts has been fine, and consequently difficult to negotiate. But Bultmann has steadily occupied the position defined initially by the opponents he chose to face on the right and left. Now that the smoke of the first war has cleared, it is possible to reconsider the issues and arrive at new definitions of the problem. A new phase will of course alter the nature of the contest. The theologians who have been through the war have largely abandoned the struggle with literalists and liberals alike and are looking in other directions, mostly outside the church, for fresh alliances and new opponents.

2. *Literal literalism. Literal* literally means *according to the letter (litteralis)*. The adverb *literally* in the preceding sentence reflects the etymological sense of literal, as given in the definition. Literal and its cognates are often used in this sense, particularly in working from one language to another. It is said, for example, that *hamartanein* literally means *to miss the mark,* although in post-Classical Greek it is never used in that sense. In the New Testament it is customarily translated *to sin.* Nevertheless, the etymological or literal sense of a word is accorded a certain priority, even where it is completely or nearly faded.

The etymological sense is often taken to be identical with the descriptive sense. This connection acounts for a second definition of literal: literal means true to fact, to things as they are commonly perceived, and hence, it is thought, to things as they really are. The descriptive sense of *ruach* or *pneuma* may be said to be *breath* or *wind*; it is only by extension, or by transposing the descriptive literalness of the word, that the terms come to mean spirit. This definition is undoubtedly related to the thesis that words originally have only a descriptive (literal) sense, after which they sometimes acquire figurative (non-literal) meanings. But the sophisticated philological theory of modern times appears to have ancient support. Philo, for example, allows that words and sentences have a literal or descriptive first sense, though he is primarily interested in the other thing *(allegoria)* they say. Like the medieval schoolmen, he thought it folly to stop with surface meaning.

The etymological sense of literal *(according to the letter)* also developed in another though proximate direction. It came to mean words or sentences taken in their usual or customary sense. "A sentence is 'literal' when it affirms what it means on the face of it, and nothing else" (Barfield, 1960: 48). What a sentence means "on the face of it" is, of course, a matter of convention, of tacit social compact. It might be assumed that literal as descriptive and literal as conventional regularly coincide. But that is not in fact the case. By common agreement *pneuma* came to mean *spirit*—I can use the English counterpart as a definition of the non-literal meaning because the English word has been virtually robbed of its literal sense—and so the common man understood it. The author of the Fourth Gospel was almost as hard put to make his word-play on *pneuma* (3:8) as the modern teacher is to explain the phrase pneumatic tire. There is no iron and no curtain in the current convention iron curtain. Fossilized metaphors are descriptively empty, but no less literal for that.

It is by virtue of the convention involved that Northrop Frye insists that a poem can never be anything literally except a poem, that is, an "inner structure of interlocking motifs" (1967: 77).[3] The poem is an autonomous verbal structure that turns, so to speak, around its own sun—or wanders, as the case may be, in its own sunless universe. This is because the language of poetry is centripetal and hence not assertive: it does not affirm anything directly about the external or sensory world. On this definition of poetry, to say that those who do not understand poetry are literal-minded is to surrender the meaning of literal to the descriptive sense. To understand poetry according to the letter, that is, according to the root meaning of the word *poiesis* (*artistic creation*), and according to the convention established by the poets themselves, is to understand poetry non-literally by the descriptive definition. The "imaginative illiterate," as Frye characterizes him (1967: 76), is thus a non-literalist in a double sense of the word.

The "imaginative illiterate" has come, however, to dominate Western culture; he is a decisive factor in both the naïve and sophisticated levels of culture. The ordinary churchman exemplifies the one level, the philosopical language analyst the other. It is difficult, as a consequence, to make the word literal stand for anything other than the descriptive, true-to-fact sense. The inference to be drawn is obvious: the sense of literal as convention has been assimilated to the sense of literal as descriptive because the latter has also become the prevailing convention.

Descriptive literalism is based on *common* sight, but, in this instance, a common mode of perception dictated by Everyman. The poets and philosophers have lost the right to be expansive with the word literal, to keep it fluid, as it were. As Norman O. Brown has remarked, "in the democrative academy truth is subject to public verification; truth is what any fool can see" (9). The ascendancy of literalism is no doubt coupled with the democratization of knowl-

---

[3] I am indebted to numerous provocative insights Frye offers in his work, as these remarks will indicate, yet I refrain from subscribing to his architectonic thesis.

edge, in conjunction with the rise of the descriptive sciences. One mode of perception has led convention captive, turned it over to the public trust, and there the convention, which began as the conquered, has become tyrant. Since Everyman sees descriptively, the poets are put down as harmless liars at worst, or amusing verbal jesters at best; in either case the poet has been discharged of his historic vocation and the democracy left in bondage to its own unchallenged perspective. The enormous virtues of the descriptive sciences are thus in imminent danger of running out into the sands of democratic mediocrity. The poet, meanwhile, either capitulates, goes underground, or assumes the rôle of buffoon.

The poet and the painter are the Gemini who once presided over the constellation *taxis kosmike*. Their common fall from the heavens makes them subject to the same demands: as any painter knows, "when the public demands likeness to an object, it generally wants the exact opposite, likeness to the pictorial conventions it is familiar with" (Frye, 1967: 132). And the public does make that demand. The poet knows, too, that when the public demands realism, what it generally wants is the exact opposite, likeness to the verbal images it is familiar with.

If the artist insists that he is painting only what he sees, he does so, of course, with tongue in cheek as an imitator of one or another of the established styles; but he does so as an iconoclast if he is prompted by a spontaneous vision of what is there. The classical perspective, as Maurice Merleau-Ponty suggests, is only one option and is neither confirmed nor contradicted by reality itself (48f.). If the artist cares to take out an insanity license, he may be given the liberty to contradict current pictorial conventions. But to the "imaginative illiterate" there is only one perspective, and that perspective is both true to fact and accords with the pictorial conventions with which he is familiar.

The "both ... and ..." is the clue to the artistic and poetic dilemma. Modern literal-mindedness has collapsed description and convention into one on a scale perhaps never before attained in the West. And the confluence of the two has produced a modern version of idolatry: the conviction that descriptive language corresponds, insofar as it is accurate, precisely to reality, to the really real. There is, consequently, a strong bias to discursive language just as there is a strong bias to representational painting: "In discursive writing what is said tends to approximate, ideally to become identified with, what is meant" (Frye, 1967: 81). The ideal form of visual representation is the photograph ("the camera doesn't lie"), and the ideal form of verbal representation is the objective description. So far as verbal representation is concerned, there is nothing left to do but clean up the language (verificational analysis).

The narrowing of the semantic range of the word literal, which is symptomatic of a broader cultural phenomenon, has precipitated, to be sure, a vigorous and growing revolt in literature (both in its production and in criticism), in the visual arts, and to a lesser degree in philosophy and related disciplines. It has also prompted a revolution of sorts in theology. Before attempting to make more explicit what that revolution has endeavored to achieve, its basis in scripture should be considered for the initial battle was waged ostensibly on scriptural ground.

3. *Towards a grammar of pauline rhetoric.* Paul is the first, so far as we know, to attempt anything like ordered reflection on the meaning of Christian faith. Because he stands at the head of a long tradition—and frequently at the head of turns in the tradition—it will be instructive to notice how he initiates theological reflection. Two samples of his language will suffice for our purposes: (1) mythical language that touches the redemptive event of Christ; and (2) metaphorical but non-mythical language used to characterize the native environment of man.

3.1 The redemptive event consists in God giving up his Son to death on the cross and in God rescuing his Son from death in the resurrection (Rom 8:32ff., to cite only one formulation of the two-pronged event characteristic of the earliest kerygma; cf. 1 Cor 15:3ff.). Paul utilizes language drawn from various traditions to convey the significance of this event. One source is Jewish sacrificial practice and the cultic-juristic thinking that goes with it. Paul echoes the earliest Christian tradition in characterizing the death of Christ as "an expiation by his blood" (Rom 3:25), or as a vicarious sacrifice (2 Cor 5:21; Gal 3:13). In the first case sin is canceled by virtue of an appropriate atoning sacrifice, in the second Christ takes on himself the guilt of man and suffers in his stead. These and closely related Jewish categories are developed by later theologians within a cultic-juristic frame of reference, which is to say, more or less literally. But

Paul transcends the boundaries of Jewish categories by holding that Christ's death not only cancels the penalty for sin, but actually effects man's release from the powers of sin and death ("the present evil age" Gal 1:4).[4] In order to develop this thought he draws upon the mystery religions, particularly the Gnostic myth, in which the redeemed are regarded as united with the redeemer in one *soma* (body) and thus participate in his history. The redeemer suffers death (or the illusion of death) and is raised from the dead; that is, he is tentatively subjected to the demonic powers only to finally triumph over them, as the old hymn in Phil 2:5–11 indicates. Accordingly, the believer's life is stamped by both the death (defeat) and the resurrection (victory) of the redeemer (2 Cor 5:14f., 17; Rom 6:5ff.).

By supplementing Jewish categories with mystery, especially Gnostic, language, Paul is able to express the redemptive event as a cosmic occurrence, and to allow for the significance of Christ's resurrection, which has no place in sacrificial categories.

The language utilized by Paul in depicting the significance of the redemptive event is thus a series of interlocking images, drawn from various contexts, modified in this respect or that, and superimposed upon one another in what, at the literal level, appears to be a careless polyphonic composition. The apparently inchoate state of Paul's language is the result of pressing logical language upon what is, literally, illogical language. The mythical categories he employs do not admit of logical review, as his willingness to juxtapose literally logical contradictions should suggest. That Paul was not merely a sloppy logician is demonstrated by the way he modifies the images, marshals them against each other, and deploys the whole in achieving a non-discursive unity.

One might think that no one would care to take the mythical images entirely literally, any more than one would suppose that Nicodemus was as dense as he is represented in the Fourth Gospel. Yet the demythologizing debate has been joined, in part, over whether this mythical language is something to be believed, regarded as true, on the basis of which faith as surrender to God then becomes possible (Bultmann, 1951: 300ff.). Bultmann has endeavored to show that the mythical language touching the redemptive event

---

[4] In this and other particulars I am drawing on Bultmann's brilliant analysis (1951: 297f.).

becomes true only as man submits to God in radical obedience and enters upon faith. The senses of true in the two cases are, of course, very different. The debate was then joined from the other side over whether true in the second instance was to be taken literally.

Had it been possible for Bultmann's opponents to recognize mythical language for what it is—non-literal—the issue would not have been joined as it was. One might then have asked what kind of theological exercise Paul was performing, and under what circumstances the significance of the redemptive event can properly be articulated in assertive language—except as a monastic exercise.

The "imaginative illiterate," who currently tends to dominate confessional theology of all varieties, assumes, of course, that if mythical language is not descriptive it has nothing to do with reality. In this he is half right, but his half is not the crucial half. He is correct in concluding that myth as metaphor has no basis in reality as commonly perceived. It flies in the face of the literal as convention, upsets the common mode of apprehension, breaks the idols of literalism. He is wrong regarding the potential that myth as metaphor lays upon the future. The mythical language of Paul, insofar as it is successful, opens a breach in the solidity of the everyday or received world and allows the eschatological reality of the future to break through. The kingdom comes, as it were, on the wings of myth.

The myth of redemption, as formulated by Paul, does not, however, give explicit expression to its own intentionality. It is possible that this is a crippling aspect of myth, so far as modern man is concerned. In any case, Paul's fundamental intention is clear, even with respect to myth, as his use of other types of language demonstrates. His use of the term flesh (*sarx*) confirms his intention and, at the same time, exhibits the inner opposition between the real significance of the redemptive event and reality as commonly perceived.

3.2 The natural environment of man is "in the flesh." So Paul assumes. Flesh (*sarx*) can denote, for Paul and generally, the corporeality of man, the meat on one's bones. When generalized it can refer to all humankind, everyone. Then by extension it comes to mean the earthly stage upon which life is played, the visible world of created things.

The literal sense of flesh is linked, by means of the observation that flesh is naturally subject to the ravages of disease, decay, and death, to the notion that things fleshly are weak and transitory by nature. This particular nuance remains within the boundaries of the literal, true-to-fact sense of flesh. But Paul parlays this notion into a sweeping generalization that is no longer to be taken literally: the flesh is that sphere which, when taken as the ultimate horizon of existence, becomes the context of spurious life. To live "according to the flesh" is to give oneself to the outward, visible, transitory, and weak, and in so doing to forfeit one's true destiny as man. This usage, which is characteristically Pauline, is metaphorical: there is no one-to-one correlation between flesh in the literal sense and flesh in the metaphorical sense. Paul does not characteristically regard the flesh itself as evil, on the one hand, and the most heinous form of life "according to the flesh" for the Jew, and thus for Paul, on the other, is a life devoted to the fulfillment of the law as the means of salvation (Phil 3:3ff.). To give allegiance to the norms of the flesh, whether in carnal (to use a Latin synonym which no longer has the metaphorical range of *sarx* as Paul uses it) or spiritual form, is the epitome of sin.

The literal and non-literal senses of flesh are related but not identified. The fleshly is the transitory, the unreal, but the flesh in itself is not evil. Flesh is equated with sin only insofar as the fleshly circumscribes the ultimate context of life.

The literal sense of flesh goes together with the letter (*litteralis*) that kills. The law, taken literally, brings death. The spirit leads to life because it redeems the law from literal-mindedness.

According to Paul, consequently, (1) flesh is sin only to the extent that it is taken literally—as descriptive of the really real; the true significance of the redemptive event is to free man from the literal. The redemptive event contradicts the real as the world understands it (to substitute the term world, which is Pauline, for the designation "commonly perceived"). (2) To understand flesh non-literally, as the ephemeral, is to accord flesh its rightful place as the natural environment of man but not his ultimate context, and thus to free him to enjoy it. The metaphorical sense of flesh is true because it points to the really real. On this view the literal sense of flesh by theological convention is precisely the metaphorical sense, but the metaphorical sense is literal also because it is the true sense. To bring the matter full circle, it would also have to be said that the metaphorical sense is the literal sense metaphorically, by virtue of the fact that the metaphorical sense represents the perpetual contest between the monolithic solidity of the received world and openness to the real which the future offers but does not guarantee.

Paul's understanding of flesh and the letter that kills suggest the following coupled formulations:

1a. The literal is ultimately deceptive, because unreal.
1b. The non-literal is ultimately true, because real.
2a. The literal is thus non-literal, precisely in a descriptive sense, in depicting how things really are.
2b. The non-literal is thus literal, precisely in a descriptive sense, in depicting how things really are.
3a. The literal in the sense of convention leads inevitably to deception, because convention constitutes a falling away from the real.
3b. The non-literal in the sense of convention is perpetually iconoclastic, in that it endeavors to shatter the idols of literalism.

The paradox in these formulations arises from the juxtaposition of the temporal and a-temporal horizons of reality. To put it in Bultmann's terms, the paradox is created by the superimposition of a view of man as a-historic upon one that seizes man in his full historicity.

In depicting the ontic situation of man, Paul thus uses language that is metaphorical but non-mythical. It is true, admittedly, that Paul occasionally speaks of flesh and sin as though they were demonic powers to which man has fallen prey. But man's fall is his own responsibility; man is *re-spons-able*. What gives this language its mythical cast is that, although man is responsible for his own bondage, he is powerless to free himself. He is powerless because he cannot bring a non-literal world quite around:

I cannot bring a world quite round,
Although I patch it as I can . . .

The chains which bind him are indeed magical (Brown: 11), but they are not magical in a mythical sense: the bondage of man consists in being born into a specific time and place under the weight of a particular tradition, without liberating poiesis (Bultmann: *word of God*). Such liberating poiesis ought also, in principle, to be non-mythical: man cannot assert his freedom until he is first spoken to, but this assertion, this word, is like any that passes between man and man except that it is liberating. Yet poetry is considered the inspiration of divine madness just because any word that liberates from the world must have its source in God: God spoke, and it was so.

The difference between the mythical language of redemption and the metaphorical but non-mythical language of man's situation indicates the dilemma into which Bultmann fell: can we speak non-mythically of redemption as well as of our human situation? Or, to locate the crux of the matter more precisely, can a non-mythical redemptive word be spoken?

4. *Myth, metaphor, and the modern mentality.* It has been asserted that Bultmann's primary aim was to break the strangle hold of liberalism on the theological mentality. One might have thought, as it occasionally has been suggested, that he should not—for that very reason—have opposed myth, but rather have advocated it. If Bultmann could have achieved his goal by reinstating the true nature of mythological language, why didn't he choose that route?

There are, perhaps, two basic reasons. First, he sensed—rightly, in my judgment—the profound hold that literalism has on the modern mind. Though the need for demythologizing was thereby made acute, he justified his procedure in principle by appealing to Paul and John within the New Testament, where demythologizing was already inaugurated in the face of literalizing interpretations. In the second place, because mythological language was out of the question as a vehicle for the gospel, he took his options to be limited to language understood as assertion and to the language of direct address. He made use of a third mode of language—discursive language—in articulating the problem, but his disposition to the language of direct address was dictated by Martin Buber and the assumption that the opposite of assertive language is personal address.

With respect to the first reason, Bultmann must be given his due—which is considerable. Nevertheless, even he has not fully grasped the radical crisis in which the modern mind finds itself, no doubt because he has not sufficiently developed the rationale for his own conviction. Had he done so and perceived the full dimensions of the crisis brought on by literalism, he might have proposed a different—and more radical—solution. As concerns the second reason, like every other critic, Bultmann brought to his creative work a certain amount of conceptual baggage that he was either not willing or not able to jettison. Among other things, he was and is oriented to language as assertion. He wanted to avoid assertive language in theology and preaching at all costs, but the only way he knew to do this was to turn in the direction of a more abstract language still: the existential categories of Martin Heidegger. He keeps talking about preaching as properly conducted only in the language of direct address, but he talks about it only in abstract language. So much is understandable, but he preaches just as he theologizes. His proclivity for ontological analysis and his reluctance to follow the course of the later Heidegger reveal his linguistic patrimony: he cannot shake his assertive legacy. He has been unable, consequently, to develop the category of direct address; and he can do no more with simile, metaphor, and parable than understand them as the decoration of language. In spite of his intense classical learning, he appears not to have a poetic bone in his body.

On both scores, then, it appears necessary to move beyond Bultmann—with gratitude, of course, for his having brought theology so far.

The tenacity with which literalism holds the modern mentality in its firm grip does not derive so much from the modern worldview (an explicit or conscious view of the world), as from the horizons of the lived world (*Lebenswelt, être au monde*). The two are not unrelated, of course, but worldview is always secondary, whether drawn directly from *Lebenswelt* as a more or less pure conceptual extrapolation, or whether conceived as a hypothetical construct in relative isolation from world as experienced. It is not unusual, for example, to find highly trained scientific minds with one worldview and a grossly contradictory *Lebenswelt*. One may experience the world in one way and conceive it abstractly in quite another. And it is not always the abstraction that is the more advanced or progressive.

One is born into a more or less coherent lived world, and in that world one is virtually condemned to live. World in the sense of *Lebenswelt* is not something one can modify or transform by taking thought. The lived world is transmitted, mostly sub rosa, from generation to generation and handed around within the discrete community as tradition that is embedded largely in language, but also in other forms of culture. Experience of world takes shape with the first words heard, the first sentences pronounced, the first childhood picture, inscribed or merely contemplated. From that point on, to change worlds one has literally to go out of the world.

The horizons of world in the modern West are blatantly secular, devoid of divinity. Modern man characteristically experiences the world as godless, often in spite of himself (in spite of his deliberate aspiration, founded upon a fading memory), and rarely as an immediate consequence of his first confrontation with the scientific worldview. The secular landscape of modernity is now a firmly entrenched tradition that reaches back at least as far as the Renaissance.

There are various means of taking the measure and tracking the rise of this world, not the least of which are the cultural barometers, the arts and letters. Taking literary fiction as a broad category, it is interesting to notice the scale proposed by Northrop Frye for classifying the fictive hero (1967: 33f.). The hero—the somebody who does something in the plot—may be classified, he suggests, not morally, but on the basis of his powers of action. If his power is superior in *kind* to other men and their natural environment, the hero is a divine being and the story about him a *myth*. If he is superior only in *degree*, the hero is typical of *romance*, whether of the secular (knight errant) or religious (saint) type. If the hero excels his fellows in degree but does not transcend their natural environment, he is a leader and belongs to the *high mimetic mode*. The *low mimetic* mode would then entail a hero who is simply one with his fellows, not really a hero in the classical sense at all. And finally, when the hero is looked down upon as inferior in power to other men and is at the mercy of his environment, he belongs to fiction in the *ironic* mode.

On the basis of these schema Frye makes the following illuminating observation: "We can see that European fiction, during the last fifteen centuries, has moved its center of gravity down the list" (1967: 34). The world as the writer of fiction experiences it has been gradually divested of its supermundane elements and the hero leveled accordingly. The development reaches its equilibrium, so to speak, with the low mimetic mode, where hero, humanity and environment are more or less balanced: no one has the upper hand. Fiction in this mode is designated realistic, Frye suggests, because the canons of fictive probability correspond to the canons of probability in the world of experience (1967: 34).[5] One might counter, perhaps, that realistic fictive probability allows the literal everyday world to come into ascendancy for the first time in the history of the West, opening the way for the common experience of world as realistic. That the world was commonly experienced as solidly realistic in the ages of myth and romance is difficult to credit. In any case, the pendulum has swung, during the last century, to the other side: the hero not only loses his superiority, but the balance is shifted in favor of the environment. In the ironic mode the powers of fate re-emerge, but in a context in which the hero is helpless before them, that is, where the gods have failed. Even though the spectator looks down on the hero, he is in no better position: his greater freedom, reflected in his judgment (Frye, 1967: 34), remains pure potential; he may intuit the trajectory of his true humanity, but he is without means of propulsion.

The interpretation here placed upon Frye's analysis[6] suggests the emergence of a realistic world as the common *Lebenswelt* beginning, roughly, in the seventeenth century.[7] This *Lebenswelt* is mirrored initially in fiction in the low mimetic mode and probably only gradually infiltrates the common mentality. The realistic world of low mimetic fiction is the literal world in the sense of the everyday world, the world of common convention, of the "they say" of Heidegger. This particular literal world by convention is a de-divinized world, a world shorn of its gods and supermundane heroes.[8] The

---

[5] This characteristic of realistic fiction Frye designates "displacement": plot is drawn from the mythical repertoire but "displaced" by being made more realistic. Mythologizing is therefore indirect (1963: 36). His analysis implies that writers of fiction felt themselves gradually constrained to "displace" myth, but that an entirely realistic fiction would be a contradiction in terms. The question Frye does not seem to have considered is whether non-mythical fiction is necessarily realistic.

[6] Frye is not unaware, of course, that his progression of modes lends itself to such interpretations. He takes for granted the present period as a "late" phase of Western culture (1967: 343).

[7] Frye dates the beginning of the low mimetic mode with Daniel Defoe in English letters, but fifty years earlier in French literature.

[8] See J. Hillis Miller (1963), in which the reaction of romantics to the loss of God is studied. Miller begins: "Post-medieval literature records, among other things, the gradual withdrawal of God from the world" (1).

counterpart of the disappearance of the gods is the emergence of man in his full humanity, but the new man soon finds himself helpless before his natural (secular) environment. The transition from the low mimetic to the ironic mode thus marks the consummation of man's bondage to the literal world.

If irony marks the final descent of man into the secular, it also offers him a modest instrument for loosening his bonds. His lever is ineffective, however, because he lacks a fulcrum and a place to stand. Nevertheless, tragic irony is the legitimate historic successor of low mimesis: realism is crowned with hyper-realism. To extrapolate from this development, it may be suggested that tragic irony should be succeeded in turn by comic irony. Comic irony is tragic irony recovering its sense of proportion: the first tangible assault on the hitherto impregnable strongholds of literalistic realism. But this is to anticipate.

If literary fiction is any clue to the way the world is experienced, Bultmann was justified in rejecting myth as anachronistic language, unable to score its point in the face of low mimetic and ironic realism. But Bultmann was not persuaded that myth was no longer true; he therefore sought, through demythologizing, to preserve the truth of the Christian myth, which he took to be the affirmation (confession) that God and no other effects man's (my) salvation. Although he takes this affirmation as not empirically verifiable, and thus as descriptively non-literal, he refuses to acknowledge that the *mode* of the affirmation remains mythical: the subject of the sentence is God, and Christ is retained as a hero of the mythical order. Such a confession, understood precisely in an existential sense, flies directly in the face of the common lived world. It is to be doubted whether such a confession is authentically possible short of a miraculous transformation of the *Lebenswelt*.[9] Perhaps that is what Bultmann means by saying that a new self-understanding (understanding of self, world, and God) arises with faith. If so, the locus of the problem is shifted to word of God, the means by which this transformation is to be effected. But word *of God* is equally mythological. Bultmann

---

[9] Bultmann's statement in "The Idea of God and Modern Man" (1965: 93f.) appears to identify the problem of God as a conceptual problem. But his more characteristic language indicates that he conceives it as a problem of our root experience of reality.

seems to have conducted us to the frontier of our linguistic crisis without indicating that we must go on alone.

Word of God in the sense of word from God (not word about God) is any word that has the power to transform the lived context of historic being-there-in-the-world—transform it, that is, by clearing away whatever obscures the really real. It is literally a world-creating word. Such a word cannot be raked up from just anywhere; it must erupt like a volcano from the heart of the heat of our history, lay an old world to waste, and then cool and crystallize in the chilly drafts of criticism as the threshold of a new world. In short, it must be authentic poiesis. And, if Matthew Arnold was right, the poet is to replace the priest as the bearer of this word.

Is it possible to contemplate a demythologized form of word from God?

It appears that history has brought theological language full circle: having begun with the poetry of parable, metaphor, simile, and aphorism, it seems that theology is being thrust back upon the language of its infancy. The reason may be that just as faith could not be presupposed then, it cannot be presupposed now. In such a context the redeeming word must lay its own foundation: by its power as word it must be able to bring that world into being in which faith is possible, indeed necessary. Only then is it possible for theology to extrapolate conceptually from faith's experience of the world as redeemed. If, in the intervening centuries, theology has grown less and less solicitous of its ownmost origin, it is now being forced to renew itself at its source—or perish.

The timeliness of comic irony links curiously with the foundational language of the Christian tradition, the parable of Jesus. The parable is secular in horizon and thus metaphorical but non-mythical; it is predominantly comic in mode—something new is born amidst the rubble of the old. Unlike absolute metaphor, which admits of no reference outside itself, tends to be esoteric, and by its very nature reflects the mood of waiting without hope, the parable is not exclusively centripetal, but connects with the everyday world while distorting that world in favor of a new, metaphorical view of reality. Absolute metaphor seems to go with tragic irony, for example, in Kafka; parable has fundamental affinities with comic irony. Absolute metaphor represents a suitable purgatory for the literalistic mind; parable offers kenotic redemption for those willing to venture beyond the precincts of the comfortable but illusory solidity of the received world.[10]

It is odd that this has not been noticed: in the parable as metaphorical but non-mythical, Jesus pronounces a demythologized word from God.

Parable holds the prospect of a timely mode of fictional language that breaks decisively with the solid realism of low mimesis and transcends the cul-de-sac of tragic irony.

It is unfortunate that nobody remembers how to hear or speak parables.

5. *Comic criticism of illusion and the resurrection.* Comedy is the movement from *pistis* (opinion) to *gnosis* (knowledge), from a society bound by law, custom, tradition, the old guard to a society given over to the avant-garde, youth, and freedom. It is a movement from illusion to reality. Frye goes on to define the two terms: "Illusion is whatever is fixed or definable, and reality is best understood as its negation: whatever reality is it's not *that*" (1967: 169f.). One is reminded of Kafka's parable "My Destination," which contains the lines:

"Where are you riding to, master?" "I don't know," I said, "only away from here, away from here. Always away from here, only by doing so can I reach my destination." "And so you know your destination?" he asked. "Yes," I answered, "didn't I say so? Away-From-Here, that is my destination." (189)

Away-From-Here is the poetic destination, now made acute by the intensification of illusion—the fixed, the definable, in sum, the literal.

Illusion as the fixed, definable, the status quo, and the cross go together. Stanley Hopper has summed up the matter admirably (1967: xix):

The drama of the Cross is implicit in our language whenever we cease to dwell poetically in the world: that is, whenever "meaning" is not disclosed, whenever the cliches of everydayness or abstrac-

---

[10] See Beda Alleman's provocative essay "Metaphor and Anti-metaphor" (103–123) in which he analyzes the history of metaphor as a clue to the dissolution of the received world for the modern poet.

tion fixate words. Fixation crucifies. The Cross occurs whenever Primordial Being is unheard, elided, or refused.

The messiah is crucified whenever the word he brings is reduced to its literal meaning. The inference to be drawn is that the messiah is risen from the dead whenever his word is given free play, allowed to strike like lightning, heard as the disclosure of the really real.

The poet, it is often said, has replaced the priest. The priest has become the mediator of dead words and an inert messiah; the poet seeks to mediate living language and thus a risen christ. Whether the poet ought to come off so handsomely is a moot point, but the church and its priestly hierarchy have been unequivocally indicted (Hopper, 1967: xix):

> Christianity, in its historic forms, has progressively destroyed its own meanings through the fixation of its language, brought about by reason of its capitulation to a grammar not its own.

The pristine grammar of the church is the parable, the similitude, the aphorism—a secular, literal non-literal language, comic in mode. The essentially comic quality of the language of Jesus has been obscured by an avalanche of moralizing commentary, which, significantly enough, has never been able to make much of the resurrection, except to invoke it as the literal sanction of the pious life. As Paul clearly discerned, theology that does not take account of the reality of the resurrection has nothing to commend it but religiosity.

It is customary to identify the cross as the illusion-dispelling factor in the Christian gospel. The cross seems solidly real. But of course it holds a dead man. The cross has the same realism as tragedy: submission to inexorable fate. It is hardly ever noticed that the inert figure on the cross has a smile on his lips: the world into which he entered and which was brought near through his poetry has made a mockery of fate because anchored in something transcending the demonic powers. The recognition scenes in the parables are humorous because they involve a reversal of the substantial, confortable, patent nexus of things and relations that constitutes the received world. We are obliged to laugh when the somber judge trips on his robe and knocks the bailiff across the clerk's lap, or when the local pastor is surprised making love to the first alto in the choir loft. Such reversals of the dignity of law and the moral earnestness of religion are not funny, of course, to the Pharisees, whose vocation it is to maintain the illusion.

Unlike tragedy, comedy is marked by a buoyancy that lifts it above the compulsions of the mundane world (Frye, 1967: 94). This is the reason comedy often seems unrealistic or romantic; it refuses to take the established order as immutable. Some comedy is merely wish-fulfillment, to be sure, but authentic comedy raises life above the confines of the merely conventional to reintegrate it, on the other side, into a new and strange world. This strange new world is the poetic vision, the apocalypse of the world that is to be.

To designate the poetic vision as apocalyptic is to suggest its temporal horizon. Apocalypse is ordinarily defined as the revelation of events that are to transpire at the end of history. Such a definition is literal. Nevertheless, apocalyptic has to do with futurity, with worlds aborning, but in the metaphorical sense. The poetic apocalypse catches a glimpse of a new world beyond the mundane horizon, bodies it forth in metaphor, and waits silently, because proleptically participant, for its deliverence.

The difference between the apocalypse of John and the apocalyptic language of Jesus is the comic character of the latter. John contemplates a pure future, unrelated, except negatively, to the present. Jesus indulges in the comic distortion of mundane reality as the means of evoking a vision of the approaching new world. The kingdom Jesus anticipates is the present world stood on its head. John is deadly serious and consequently tiring. Jesus is funny and therefore interesting.

The comic apocalypse, in contrast to the literal apocalypse, is its own antidote. Christian theology has never known quite what to do with the revelation of John, except to say as little about it as possible. The comic apocalypse, on the other hand, offers itself only for what it is, the ecstatic vision of a world waiting to be born. It requires a perpetual standing-out (*ek-stasis*) into the future. Just as it debunks the going order, it extends its vision with comic relief: he who looks and waits for that world deserves to be punished for blasphemy, is insane, or is to be put down as a fool and left to his own devices.

If we can no longer hear or speak parables, at least we can practice laughing—quietly—at the grand hoax to which we are parties. Perhaps then we will become parables.

*6. The poet and primitivsm: a codicil.* When offering a rose to the poets, one should, perhaps, extend it stem forward. At all events, a codicil to the original testament is in order, for the purpose of making the original terms clear so far as poetry is concerned.

There has arisen, it seems to me, a rather widespread hankering among poets after "the magico-religious experience of primitive man,"[11] after a pre-logical, pre-modern mythopoetic consciousness, through which, it is supposed, a greater contact with reality is established than through the modern scientific mentality. The antithesis, in fact, is often set up in just this way. The terms betray what the hankering is all about: scientism, it is alleged, has shorn modern man of his capacity to attend to the particular, has rendered him a statistic in the barren, arid desert of abstractionism, in sum, has robbed him of his humanity and left the world faceless. Anti-scientism undergirds and impels this poetic quest for the pre-modern, pre-Copernican, indeed pre-Christian mentality, together with its correlative world and language.

The present danger is taken to be evident. But is it really all that obvious and simplistic? In a half paragraph from "The Dyer's Hand: Poetry and the Poetic Process" (272), W. H. Auden wonders:

> At this moment it may look as if the artist's chance of dictatorship had passed forever, and that the only danger in the future will come, as it comes now, from the scientist; but one should never be too sure; one could hardly call nazism the work of scientists, whatever use it managed to make of them; and if a thermo-nuclear war were to destroy all the plumbing on earth tomorrow, who knows what strange sibyls and shamans might walk abroad again the day after?

We can, indeed, never be too sure. Even now latter-day sibyls and shamans aspire to reconstitute the sensibilities of the scientific mind in the name of a paganism that hearkens back beyond the fountain of the Judeo-Christian tradition. Whatever reservations theologians have with respect to scientism—there are many and they are vehement—it is the business of theology to inquire in the name of what the poetic protest against scientism is prosecuted.

---

[11] I draw this phrase from Wallace W. Douglas' essay, "The Meanings of 'Myth' in Modern Criticism" (124).

The poetic hankering after a pre-modern, pre-logical mythopoetic mentality ignores three points of reference that ought not to be lightly dismissed. They inform literate modern man, certainly the literate theologian.

We have learned, at no small price, to view man in his full historicity. The most important thing we have learned from modern historical consciousness is not the relativity of every point of view, of every spatial-temporal locus—as important as that is—but that no man or people can authentically enter in upon his or their own history except from where he or they are. The future is joined in tandem with the present, not some previous historic moment now lost forever. There is no going back, only forward. To attempt to go back means to ignore the concretions of time and place, and thus to lose contact with reality at the outset. Even if we agree that the modern mentality is not attuned to the really real, turning back the clock will not help recover vital sensibility; it will only postpone the reckoning.

Linked with the a-historical aspiration to rejoin the race in its infancy is forgetfulness respecting the rôle the Judeo-Christian tradition has played in the West. It is sometimes forgotten that Christ brought the principalities and powers to nought, putting them to death on the cross. That need not be taken as a partisan confessional statement, but it should be understood as an observation on our history. Somewhere between the golden age of Greece and the Renaissance, Western man was set free to explore, conquer, and even rape the world with impunity so far as the gods are concerned. Christian theologians have been inclined more recently, with some justification, to regard this freedom vis-à-vis nature to be the mandate of Christian faith: the God who incarcerated all his divine and quasi-divine competitors delivered the world into the hands of man, entrusted it to man's stewardship. For better or worse, the God of Jesus Christ took man in as a full partner in the unfolding of history. The poets who yearn to return to animism, totemism, shamanism, and the like thus intend nothing less than a reversal of the entire Western tradition. Secreted away in this poetic, eclectic religiosity with its primitive bent is a paganism which, although the underlying drive can be credited, has to be stoutly resisted by all those who do not wish to return to the Stone Age.

This brings us, finally, to the third point of reference: the scientific revolution, which freed the world of its load of supermundane baggage, bringing with it enormous benefits, like heart surgery and the electric refrigerator. Moreover, it infinitely expanded man's possibilities of subduing and having dominion over the creatures of the earth, even the earth itself—another old biblical mandate. What does the primitive poet wish us to do? Turn in our cards as moderns and begin the struggle all over again? This we could not do, even if we willed it. And it is not clear why it should be so willed. That is to say, the proposed return to primitivism and paganism seems even less desirable than scientific literalism. No, what we need are poets who are not afraid of modernity, who have the courage to take up the poetic enterprise within a secular landscape and show us the way toward a greater reality without the putative help of the dead gods.

There is, perhaps, an even more important reason why the impersonal, objectifying, manipulative scientific perspective is not to be rejected out of hand. Auden may be invoked once again (272):

> Mankind needs both the artist and the scientist, not only because both their worlds of study are real, but also for protection against the *hubris* by which each is tempted, for both, if unchecked, will lay claim to total mastery and create a chimerical universe. Without the check of the scientist, the artist, attempting to treat the world of mass as a world of faces, creates a magical universe in which prayers are said to the Dynamo. Without the check of the artist, the scientist, by attempting to treat the world of faces as a world of number, creates a positivist universe in which the Virgin is a statistic.

Henry Adams' World of the Dynamo, the world of number, should not be allowed to violate the Virgin, the world of metaphor, but it may, at the same time, serve to restrain her premature bodily assumption.

We should not aspire to be bold where poetry is concerned. It is too subtle a game to be played by amateurs. Yet, it is unclear why theologians should be reticent: poets are not reticent where theology is concerned. Let us then be foolishly bold.

The poetic revolt against literalistic scientism has been triggered for good reason but wrongly aimed. The reason for poor sight, I suspect, is the overly intellectual house in which poetry is forced to dwell these days. The contemporary poet does not inhabit the real, the everyday world, but spawns myths and metaphors in a book-lined closet, in a university or quasi-university context, in relation to a tradition that has run out into the sands of history. The problem is not so much to find the words (testimony to the contrary notwithstanding) as to shut off the flow arising from the way a now defunct tradition tickles the fancy below the ground, as it were. Good poetry writes itself, to be sure—for false as well as true prophets. The difference is notably difficult to establish, but for the poet—and here I speak with all due reverence—the right to speak comes when the poet can speak with his own voice, for himself, in his own time and place, with reference to the new world waiting to be born. The first step in the discovery of one's own voice is to shut off the flow.

> I remember vividly the first contact with reality that I got through my feet, so to speak. The million words or so which I had written, mind you, well ordered, well connected, were as nothing to me—crude ciphers from the old stone age—because the contact was through the head and the head is a useless appendage unless you're anchored in midchannel deep in the mud. Everything I had written before was museum stuff, and most writing is still museum stuff and that's why it doesn't catch fire, doesn't inflame the world. I was only a mouthpiece for the ancestral race which was talking through me; even my dreams were not authentic, not bona fide Henry Miller dreams. To sit still and think one thought which would come up out of me, out of the life buoy, was a Herculean task. I didn't lack thoughts nor words nor the power of expression—I lacked something much more important: the lever which would shut off the juice. The bloody machine wouldn't stop, that was the difficulty. I was not only in the middle of the current but the current was running through me and I had no control over it whatever. (Henry Miller: 284)

Theology and theologians are waiting for the poets to close the sluice-gates of antiquity *and* literalistic scientism and find their own tongues—probably in the form of silence broken by occasional stammering—in the horizon of our modernity. We may then be able to fund theological discourse once again with something approximating living language.

The substantive point made earlier with reference to poetry as the foundational language of theology is not thereby withdrawn. I only wish to stipulate that not all poetry will fill the bill. As for our own time, I propose to put in a call for demythologized poetry as well as a demythologized kerygma, and beyond that, I should like to demythologize language as well. By mythology in these contexts I of course mean the world viewed in complicity with its antique supermundane superstructure. I do not wish to assert that we can no longer speak of God; I stipulate only that God can be spoken of vitally now only within the horizon of the modern world. Whether talk of God or no, word from God will arrive in the guise of the merely human word.

Original participation, to use Owen Barfield's phrase (1957), is no longer a real possibility for us; the idolatry of literalism is to be shunned; final participation will bring us, I am convinced, to demythologized poiesis—powerful new language, in a secular horizon, ostensibly like any other language that passes between man and man, only liberating.

# Ten

# ON DANDELIONS:
# THE PROBLEM OF LANGUAGE

*0.1* Prima facie evidence indicates that language has become a problem.

Prima facie evidence is evidence taken on its unexamined face. It is evidence at first blush.

Here lies a murdered man, just at the edge of the driveway, close by the rosebush. Over him, with pistol still smoking in his hand, stands a neighbor. The prima facie evidence raises a presumption of fact: the neighbor has killed this man and is therefore guilty of murder. However, bystanders observe a stranger scurrying around the corner: did that stranger perhaps interrupt the pair in friendly conversation, attempt a robbery, fire the fatal shots, thrust the gun into the hand of the dazed neighbor, and flee? The fan of detective stories, but hardly anyone else, may be tempted by this more complex solution to a simple puzzle. For the most part, observers of the "facts" regard the neighbor as guilty.

Just then the "murdered" man gets up, feels his head and dusts off his clothes, while the neighbor apologizes for having failed to stop the assailant.

This contrived little melodrama suggests that prima facie evidence may be systematically misleading, not only with respect to the interpretation of the facts at one or more levels, but also with respect to the facts themselves. Evidence taken on its face is therefore to be read circumspectly.

Whether, in fact, language has become a problem may be left as an open question, at least for the moment. Meanwhile, it may be inquired: if language were a problem, in what sense would it be possible to make that very assertion? Within what horizon does it make sense to claim that language is a problem?

0.2 Things can be problems in a variety of ways. The dandelions in the lawn are a problem. A dull saw in a cabinetmaker's shop constitutes a problem. The heavy drinker is called a problem drinker, and the erratic student is called a problem student. There is the Middle East problem, the problem of cancer and diabetes, and the unemployment problem. The interpretation of a text and the mystery of the great work of art are also said to be problems. In the face of such variety, it is difficult to specify what constitutes a *problem* as such.

It will therefore be doubly difficult if the inquiry were aimed not just at language as a problem, but at language as a root problem. By qualifying problem as *root*, a dimension has been added that takes the inquiry beyond the ordinary sense of problem and beyond evidence taken at first blush. In asking whether language has become a root problem, one is asking whether language has become the problem of problems, the root of problems endemic to modern man and his age.

0.3 The horizons of an inquiry into language as a root problem are vast. The foreground of the inquiry is correspondingly cluttered with detail. One scarcely knows where to begin. And there appears to be no certain passage from one cluster of data to another. These considerations evoke the reservation: *The logic of investigations and reflections that seek the roots cannot be predetermined.*

It follows that the agenda of such an inquiry cannot be fixed in advance. One might look to the loci of ostensible evidence: the literary arts, including drama, the novel, poetry, and literary criticism; philosophy of language and linguistics; folklore and anthropology; the visual arts; phenomenology, theology, and biblical criticism. These spheres and others offer ample evidence for consideration.

It may be more important, however, to establish the *mood* of such an inquiry. Mood refers to how the investigator is predisposed to stand into the question; how one is inclined to lay hold of the issue.

On the other hand, it may be better to forsake that suggestion as an explicit part of the agenda and turn at once to the subject matter.

If a proper mood is to assert itself, the subject matter must be permitted to make its claim on the investigator; the inquirer will do well to release himself or herself toward the subject matter, toward the question. In so doing, the subject matter may take surprising initiatives of its own, initiatives that will lead the investigation into paths long since choked and obscured by the undergrowth of prior reflection.

*1.1* Initially it was said: "Prima facie evidence indicates that language has become a problem." What can it possibly mean that language has apparently become a problem?

The term that clamors for attention in the formulation is the word *language*. If we examine our preceptions closely, there is clearly no ordinary sense in which *our* language—the one we speak, read, and write daily—presses in on us as a problem. We have, at best, a faint sense that our tongue becomes a problem on special occasions and under certain circumstances. There is the political faux pas, familiar to us from television and the daily press. There is the annoying journalistic jargon of the news magazines and commentators. Occasionally, misunderstanding arises out of thoughtless words that pass between friends or among members of a family. And highly specialized, technical discourse produces non-understanding on the part of the uninitiated. And, of course, there is the near illiteracy that prevails in a vast segment of a society allegedly literate. But these evidences of problem language hardly indicate that language has become a problem as such, to say nothing of it as a root problem. The problems of which these evidences are symptoms are undoubtedly amenable to educational therapy or to the cultivation of a more restrained tongue. In any case, language as a problem in these senses does not merit substantial reflection.

The term language must therefore have been used in some odd or opaque sense in the formulation. Language as it is ordinarily experienced or used does not appear to constitute a real problem at all. And analytic philosophy tends to confirm the unstudied conviction of John Doe: language is a problem only to the extent that it masks pseudo-problems—clear up the careless, uninformed, or fanciful use of language and one clears up the problem.

*1.2* We have allowed ourselves to be carried away by the face of the question. The word *language* clamored for attention and the investigation capitulated. Perhaps what clamors for attention is to be denied, in the interests of truth, while clues that recede into the background are brought forward. We said that prima facie evidence is to be read circumspectly. What is most often overlooked is the obvious, which lies near at hand, that is, within the *readily understood*. Beware of the readily understood. If the term *language* does not convey meaning in any ordinary sense within the fabric of the formulation, it is possibly because the formulation is misconstrued: either some other term is being obscured by the ordinary sense, or the formulation has been put in the wrong horizon.

Language is obviously the subject matter of the formulation and the object of the investigation. If the assertion is to make sense, language is in need of sharp definition and extended attention. Indeed, it is only by discovering the meaning of the word *language* that the question can be understood at all. More precisely: when the question is understood in its full impact, then language will be understood in its essence.

*1.3* In contrast to the word *language*, which initially claimed our attention, the word *problem* escaped unnoticed. We assumed the meaning of *problem* and so found *language* to be troublesome. It may be more promising, in seeking to understand *language*, to approach the matter on the flank by looking away from the subject matter, so to speak. This we may do by exploring *problem*. If we expore the assertion "*X* is a problem" and then substitute *language* for *X*, we may chance upon a clearing: if this is what is meant by *problem*, then this is what must be meant by *language*.

*What is the essence of problem?* As I sit in my study and gaze out the window, I observe: dandelions are growing in the lawn profusely. My neighbor has already complained to me about their potential for his lawn. But dandelions are difficult to eradicate. That, we say, is the problem. Dull saws are inevitable in the cabinetmaker's shop. The problem is to keep them sharp. The meaning of *problem* seems unequivocal: how to get rid of the dandelions, how to keep the saws sharp. These are practical questions that pose themselves for resolution: by doing something, one solves the problem. Hence, in mathematics a problem is something to be done, worked. From these sedimented uses of the term is derived the dictionary definition: "a question posed for solution" (*Webster's New Collegiate*).

Sedimented word use preserves but also conceals the semantic horizon of terms. This is a lexicographical fact easily demonstrated: words enter a language at the hands of poets and philosophers fully charged with semantic richness; they invariably become habituated with use and so tend to fade, to become stopped down, with a consequent loss of depth. Ordinary usage demands that words be available without inhibiting forethought, and without excessive demands on the hearer's attention. Such words tend to be stopped down, moreover, in accordance with the predominant directionality of the culture in which they become habituated. The prerequisite of common parlance is that the words must be assimilated to what is already generally understood. Nevertheless, the sedimented or habituated meaning will echo, however, faintly, the original semantic overtones of terms: language is never used in a purely arbitrary fashion because it is carried forward with dirt still clinging to its historical roots as a result of the record left on the social memory to which every use must subscribe.

1.4   In what respects has the everyday understanding of *problem* obscured the essence of *problem*? Can the essence be brought to light by attending to the direction from which *problem* has come to its present resting place in habituated language? Clues may be sought all along the trajectory of its history, but especially at its rise and nadir.

The original formulation was: "the dandelions in the lawn are a problem." The assertion was subsequently rephrased: "How to get rid of them, how to eradicate them, is the problem." Which is it: the dandelions or the how? In everyday parlance the transition from one to the other is not even noticed. Native speakers regard the problem of dandelions and the problem of how to get rid of them as one and the same. When called to our attention, we account for the apparent discrepancy by rejoining: dandelions in the lawn pose a problem, the resolution of which is eradication.

How do dandelions pose a problem? The question in pure form will scarcely be understood. Dandelions do not, of themselves, pose a problem. In the open field they are a positive delight, especially in early spring. It is only *in the lawn* that they pose a problem. They do not belong in the lawn.

An innocent phrase in the fabric of the formulation thus calls attention, when omitted, to a forgotten dimension of the word *prob-*

*lem*. Dandelions can pose a problem when they are *out of place*. The essence of problem is displacement, in relation to which the question of eradication is derivative. If one were given to lawns aglow with dandelions, dandelions in the lawn would be no problem, and the question of eradication would never arise. And my neighbor would not be disturbed.

The hypothesis may be put to the test within the same frame of reference. Here is a fresh and somewhat surprising assertion: grass in the lawn is a problem. Such an assertion is nonsense: everyone knows that lawns consist of grass by definition. Indeed, they do. Whatever is in its place does not and cannot pose a problem precisely because it is not out of place.

A further step is now possible. If one looks out at the lawn and sees nothing but grass, what does one notice? Under normal circumstances, one notices nothing; there is, perhaps, a subconscious assurance that everything is in order, that nothing need be done. If, however, there are patches of dandelions here and there, we take note that something should be done to rectify the situation. The dandelions come explicitly to attention because they do not belong, and we jump to the conclusion: order must be restored. Something out of place *calls itself to our attention by virtue of its context*, which is taken to be unsuitable. Apart from the context, we could not say it was out of place, and we would not in that case notice.

1.5  The word *problem* is derived ultimately from Greek *problema*, which in turn comes from a verb, *proballein*, meaning *to cast, throw forward*. A *problem* is something thrown forward, cast in front of us. It is something that calls itself to our attention because it has been cast out of its familiar context and into an unfamiliar setting. Contextual displacement causes it to be thrown forward.

The predominant directionality of our culture has precipitated the particular sedmimentation of *problem*. The problem of dandelions in the lawn and the question of eradication have been collapsed into one because our predominant disposition is to *order* things. The essense of *problem* for us is the establishment and maintenance of the order we already take for granted. The dictionary definition of *problem* says as much: "a question proposed for solution." Such a definition has closed off other options and obscured the essence of *problem*. Something out of place calls itself to our attention, so "poses a *problem*" means to us: order must be restored. However, that is not the only possible meaning of *problem*. A *problem* (something which calls itself to our attention) may present itself, to be thought or contemplated. Or, a *problem* may call for celebration, enjoyment. But a technological society no longer understands pure contemplation or simple enjoyment, because it has forgotten that order is not necessarily managed. Disorder signals a breakdown in order, to be sure; but it may also herald the emergence of a new order. Minimally, disorder means that the collective representations called world are undergoing palpable changes through time; that world has a history. Optimally, disorder (*problems* aplenty) betokens variety, richness, largesse in the perceived world. Because unappreciated for what it is and promises, disorder so understood is intolerable where reality is managed, where nothing is permitted to be out of place. In that event, *problem* is something to be *worked, done,* or it is *no-problem.*

*1.6* Dandelions in the lawn suggest that displacement is the locus of problem. A dull saw in a carpenter's shop does not belong somewhere else; rather, because it is dull, it does not belong to the order of that shop, to the scheme of functions that tools at hand are designed to serve. As a consequence, one could say, "The saw is out of order," much as the vending machine or telephone gets out of order. On the other hand, if a student approaches the professor with a request to take the final examination a week late, the professor may well reply, "That presents a problem." Or, if a businessman goes to his banker and claims that he can't meet his obligations when they are due, he may be told that he has a problem. Thus, things that are non-functional and things that are out of sequence, out of time, are likewise said to be problems.

We approach something like the full semantic horizon of *problem* when we summarize: something out of place, out of time, out of order calls itself to our attention and thus poses a *problem,* particularly if we allow the words *place, time, order* to resonate in their own right. For example, the horn player who is a beat behind the conductor is out of time—not out of sequence, but out of rhythm.

*1.7* The mystery of the great work of art does not appear to be covered in the examples of problem given above. Mystery, enigma, puzzle, conundrum, not incidentally, are given in Webster's dictionary as near synonyms of problem. To say that the work of art is a mystery and a problem is, to a certain extent, redundant. In what sense is the work of art as mystery also a problem?

The question is usually taken as a question of interpretation and thus as a question of understanding. It is unclear what the work means. Insofar as art is prophetic, it anticipates what is not yet; it is out of season or ahead of the time. When the right time comes, the meaning of the work unfolds of itself. Nevertheless, art as mystery cannot be reduced to prophecy. As mystery, art is timeless, or, rather, timeful: it overrides the contingencies of history by illuminating all the ecstasies of time, past, present, future. The problem of the work of art is thus the problem of no-place, no-time, no-order: as mystery it refuses restriction to a place, a time, an order.

1.8   The loci of *problem* is out of place, out of time, out of order; no-place, no-time, no-order. But against what are the "out-of" and the "no" to be read? Against the place, the time, and the order that reign as the encompassing nexus of relationships called world. A problem is something cast forward, called to attention, by virtue of its disjunction with the order, the sedimented representations everyone takes for granted.

If now a culture reads *problem* only in the faded and derivative sense of the question of how the *problem* thing is to be put back in its place, restored to its habituated context, it is because that culture has allowed the word problem to become impoverished, because the *world* of that culture admits only problems of a certain order. Thus it happens that thinking *that* is correlative with that world (for example, certain forms of philosophy, literary criticism, scientific thought) regards the problem of problem as no-problem; it has no-place in a world in which problem has become fixed in one form, and where that one form guards the world to which that thinking belongs. A world as powerfully ordered as that undergirded by popular faith in the physical sciences closes off thought because it inhibits the occasions for world as such to come into view; order precludes problem from emerging as a root question, indeed, as a question at all. Thinking in that case has become a slave to itself: it can think only what thought already gives it to think.

2.1   We may now return to that point at which we determined to approach the matter on the flank. To say that $X$ is a problem is to say that $X$ is out of place, time, or order; or, that $X$ has no place, time, or order. If we substitute *language* for $X$, we may say that language has called itself to our attention, and thus poses itself as a problem in that it has come to be out of place, time, or order in relation to the world—the totality of interconnected relations—which is taken for granted. Or, language presents itself as a problem because it has no-place, no-time, or no-order in that received world.

It would appear that this formulation is as empty or as puzzling as the initial one that language is (has become) a problem. This would certainly be the case were our excursion taken as an arbitrary definition of the term *problem*. However, that would be to forget what was said about *problem* as such. Do our reflections on problem not afford some clues to the necessary course of thinking that must be followed in our original puzzling use of the term *language*? Is not the word *language* concealed under a veil of sedimented meaning? And is not the veil in the one instance of a piece with the veil in the other instance?

It may help to attempt to locate the thrust of the original statement. At what is the assertion "language has become a problem" aimed?

*2.2*   It does not seem cogent to think of language as out of place in the same way that dandelions in the lawn are out of place. Nor is it illuminating to suggest that language is out of time on the analogy of the horn player. And, if we think of language as a problem in the sense of having no-place, no-time, or no-order, in the sense of problem as mystery, our ordinary experience of language—the predominate disposition to language—refutes the thought. In short, the only sense in which it makes sense to speak of language as a problem, is in the sense that language is out of order, like the dull saw in the carpenter's shop.

But is it not curious that only in the one sense of problem does it appear appropriate to speak of language as a problem? In view of the history of man's experience of language, one would have thought that it would be perfectly appropriate to speak of language as mystery. And yet modern regard for language—or lack of it—even in high circles has squeezed the last ounce of mystery out of language. Language stands exposed in the full light of the familiar, the commonplace. But this is only to be noted for future reference.

Here is the cabinetmaker's shop. Various power tools lie around on their stands; the benches are covered with hand tools of every description, and in the drawers and cabinets are even more. At one end is a rack stacked with plywood and other stock. Glue, nails, screws, and clamps are at hand.

The craftsman takes up a hand saw to make a cut in a piece of stock he has clamped to the bench. It is difficult to make a proper start at the mark. He examines the saw, notices that it is dull. He hangs the saw on a nail by the door as a reminder to take it to the saw filer. He turns, finds another, sharp saw, and proceeds with the cut.

We are proximate to Heidegger's now famous hammer. Into the well ordered shop, where everything is more or less functional, there intrudes, for a fleeting moment, the tool that is out of order. The craftsman notices it, perhaps for the first time, as a mere thing, as something that does not belong to the order of things. But the project in which he is engaged is overwhelming: the context of ordered relations closes behind the incident and no further notice is taken.

In that fleeting moment, two prospects open up for the craftsman, not as craftsman but as man. He has the prospect of considering the thing, the tool, in and of itself because for the moment that thing is out of order. As a problem the tool calls attention to itself. It is a prospect otherwise open to him only on pain of carefully acquired habits of attention. He also has the prospect of glimpsing that totality of interconnected relations that governs the order of his shop. He may be prompted to consider: is it necessary to be dependent upon sharp saws? Or, is the production of cabinets worth the trouble it takes to keep the shop in order? If he has only one saw, and no prospect of either replacing or sharpening it, the question of the whole may become critical.

2.3 If we think of the problem of language in the context of that world where things are taken to be in order when they are functional, the problem of language takes on a very specific cast. And the problem of language appears to have contours analogous to the problem of *problem*, investigated earlier: language can be considered a problem only in the sense of out of order, because that is the only sense in whch the regnant world permits *problem*.

Language becomes a problem because it is taken to be non-functional in relation to the projects of the everyday world. It is taken to be non-functional because it keeps getting out of place, like dandelions in the lawn: it does not keep to its own functional terrain but is imported into odd places, like poetry and theology, and asked to perform in ways for which it is not designed. Further, language is taken to be non-functional because it keeps getting out of time: in spite of rigorous opposition, speech continually bursts the narrow corridor of the present and returns to borrow a phrase, a metaphor from some distant past, or it forges ahead into the uncharted seas of as yet undefined usage. A foray of either kind is especially odious to the sentinels of a well-ordered functional world. And, of course, language is out of order also in the direct sense: it does not work well because it is not fully explicit and not without ambiguity. But mathematics and computer tongues are conceived to combat that disease: speech is on the verge of being reduced to zeros and ones, to yes and no.

In sum, language is felt to be a problem in the reduced sense of out of order, into which the other dimensions or *problem* have been collapsed.

2.4 If thinking submits to the limitations just indicated, the question of language as a *root* problem is foreclosed from the outset.

The threshold of some question, however, lies precisely in what is given. And that threshold may open onto a larger vista, provided the imagination steals across when the guardians of sight and thought are looking the other way. One gains access to the hinterland of the question by uncovering the hidden dimensions of the problem as it presents itself.

Clues tacked to the lintel of the opening are two: (1) language regarded as a tool that has gotten out of order calls attention to itself; we are invited to consider the mere *thing*. Language is always encountered in connection with our projects, so that its thingness is seriously compromised at the outset. But the malfunction of language permits a glimpse—and only a glimpse—of language as a mere thing. That glimpse provides the occasion for thinking the essence of language. (2) The dysfunction of language also permits world to heave into sight momentarily. The horizon of language as a problem is world as a problem, and this in critical form: there is no prospect of replacing present language with another, more serviceable tongue. The prospect of honing the edge of present language in order to give it more bite is remote because the honing instrument we must use is more language. Nevertheless, the conjunction of the opportunity to consider language as a mere thing and the emergence of the question of world constitute a prospectus for considering the problem of language as *root*.

# Eleven

# THE NEW TESTAMENT AS TRADITION AND CANON

*1. Rise and development of the concept canon.* The Greek word ὁ κανών is derived from a Semitic root (Hebrew קנה; Assyrian, Ugaritic; ultimately a loan word from Sumerian) which meant "reed." The word developed a range of meanings which were related to the reed and its uses, as well as to the shape or form of the reed, some of which were literal, some metaphorical. In Greek, for example, the word can refer to the staves of a shield, a weaver's rod, a surveyor's rod, a plumb rule, a ruler. It can also denote a curtain rod or a bedpost (Judith 13:6). Because reeds, or objects in the shape of reeds, were used as measuring instruments, the word took on a spectrum of meanings related to the concept "rule" or "standard." Again in Greek it was used to denote a chronological table—that which "fixes" historical events (Kittel: III, 602.15), a boundary, a tax assessment, a tariff, and the like (cf. *IDB* I, 498f.).

The semantic value of the term was further extended in the direction of the metaphorical sense. In Greek usage "canon" became the norm which referred, on the one hand, to the perfect or complete form which, because it was perfect, was worth striving after. On the other, it referred to the absolute standard used in passing judgments on things; it was therefore the criterion (κριτήριον). The Greek strove for the perfect, the harmonious, the ideal, which represented the standard of judgment in relation to empirical phenomena. The canon as norm could thus be extended to the plastic arts, to music, to the use of the language (the Alexandrian grammarians referred to the Golden Age of Greek literature as canonical, thus giving rise to the concept of classics). Just as canon was brought into relation to aesthetics, it was referred to ethics. The law as an obligatory power became the canon, and specific ethical ideals were called canons. In philosophy, canon came to mean the rules of logic with which true and false could be determined. Here, as elsewhere, logic tended to be split off from the question of truth, with the result that a certain ambiguity attached to the concept of canon: it was unclear whether the standard of judgment lay in rules of thinking or in the subject matter itself. Heidegger has shown how this division gave rise to the correspondence theory of truth. In any case, it is clear that the term canon, by the Hellenistic period (New Testament times), had developed a full semantic complement of literal and metaphorical meanings (Kittel: III, 601f.).

It was canon in the sense of norm which the church took up into its language and used in relation to the Christian faith as a whole and in relation to particular spheres of Christian life. Omitting the New Testament usage, which is very limited (only in Paul and rarely by him), for three centuries the singular of the term predominated, denoting that which was regulative or binding for doctrine, cult, and life. Its use in three phrases played a significant rôle in the ancient church: (a) canon of truth, (b) canon of faith, and (c) canon of the church, or ecclesiastical canon. The last was inclusive of the first two (Kittel: III, 604.43ff.). A. Jülicher defined canon as understood in the ancient church in this way: "The canon is the norm by which everything in the church is determined; canonization means to recognize as a constituent element of this norm" (1931: 555). About 400 CE canonical meant approximately what we mean today when we use the terms divine, holy, errorless, unconditionally authoritative (Kittel: III, 605.15ff.).

The plural of the term came into use in IV CE to denote conciliar decrees (see Canon 2 of the Council of Constantinople in 381, with reference to the decrees of Nicea in 325). This usage was a logical development of the frequent meaning of the phrase "canon of the church" to denote what was binding upon the church. Out of this usage developed the comprehensive concept of canon law: beginning in V CE, the decrees of the councils were collected into one unified code. In IX CE, Papal decrees, which had long claimed the status of conciliar actions, were given the rank of canons. Out of the formal meaning of canon, "catalogue" (Canon 16 of the Council of Nicea), grew the practice of speaking of officers of the church as elders and deacons in the canon, or officially recognized list.

The ethical meaning of the term was also taken over into the church. Canonical meant the spiritual life, life in accordance with the rule of the church. This use was developed in relation to monks who lived in accordance with the canons of their order. It later referred to other orders and communities which were governed by strict canons. Canon was also used for the central, unalterable part of the mass. And finally, canonization came to mean the elevation to sainthood. It is unclear precisely how the connection with sainthood is to be understood; it is possible only through the solemn process of elevation, in which case participation in cultic honors may provide the link (Kittel: III, 605f.).

*1.2* It is significant that the term canon did not come to denote the collection of scriptures, both Old and New Testaments, until mid-IV CE. The Council of Laodicea in Phrygia (about 360), Canon 59, speaks of both uncanonical books and the canonical books of the old and new covenants (Kittel: III, 605.28ff.). Around 350 CE Athanasius spoke of the Shepherd of Hermas as uncanonical. Subsequently, the list of authoritative books "appointed to be read in the churches" was known as the canon. According to H. W. Beyer (Kittel: III, 605.34ff.), neither the fact that the Alexandrian grammarians spoke of a canon of authors representing literary Greek nor the formal meaning of canon as catalogue was decisive for this development. Rather, the normative concept attached to the term canon, and through it an understanding of the substantive content of the books as the canon of truth, was determinative. Latin theologians carried out the leveling of the terms canon and biblia, a leveling which reoccurred in Protestant Orthodoxy.

The judgment of Beyer is supported by the observation that the writings of the apostles and early disciples were regarded as normative long before they were collected into a canon. The authority that attached to such writings was transferred, perhaps, from the understanding of the Hebrew Bible that obtained in both Judaism and the early church. For whatever reasons, such a regard for early Christian writings did arise.

On the other hand, the church almost from the beginning was

engaged in a struggle to determine what was authentically Christian and what was not. It therefore found it necessary to establish norms for various spheres of Christian existence. Diverse Christian writings were invoked in the process of creating those norms. At the same time, the emergence of the norms made it possible to settle the question of a canon of scripture. That is to say, the church was obliged to project norms in order to determine which writings among those currently in use in the church could be recognized as normative. From this point of view, the saying "first the church and then the canon" is correct. Nevertheless, it was the insight of the Reformation that many of these same books, which were to be given recognition as canonical by the church, were actually employed to determine what was in fact normative. The reverse—first tradition (scripture, canon), then church—is also correct.

The problem of canon in relation to the New Testament is thus circular: the church invoked norms to determine what belonged to the canon (the norm), but the books of the New Testament, along with other traditions, substantively and for the most part provided the basis for the projection of the norms used to determine the norm (canon)!

2. *Character of the tradition: oral and written.* It has been said that Christianity was from the first a religion of the book. If so, its original book was the Hebrew Bible available to most early Christians in a Greek translation known as the Septuagint(LXX). The church's own book, the New Testament, did not come into existence for some time. Parts of it had not even been written by the end of I CE. It is not clear, however, that the primitive Christian movement was in fact a book movement. There is powerful evidence to the contrary. What requires investigation in this connection is how the church understood the tradition upon which it was primarily dependent, and specifically whether the church understood its tradition as written or oral. This question is correlative with the question of the content of the tradition the church took to be its own. For example, what portions of the Hebrew scriptures did the church claim? And what was the position of the Jesus tradition within the spectrum of tradition?

These questions require intense historical investigation. The brief sketch included here will be limited to the oral/written dialectic.

2.1    Jesus appeared as a rabbi. He proclaimed the will of God, taught in synagogues, gathered disciples, and debated with other rabbis in rabbinical manner and under the authority of tradition (Bornkamm: 57). However, he did not claim the authority of the tradition (the fathers) for himself. His word did not rest on the Old Testament text or on the oral tradition. In fact, he explicitly enters into controversy not only with the law, but also with the tradition (Bornkamm: 97ff.). The paradoxical way he relates himself to the law is indicated by the saying in Mark 7:9: "You have a fine way of rejecting the commandment of God, in order to keep your tradition!" And again in 7:13: ". . . thus making void the word of god through the tradition which you hand on." Here he appears to place tradition in opposition to the commandment and word of God. But elsewhere he criticizes the law itself with respect to the rules governing defilement (Mark 7:14–23) and with respect to divorce (Mark 10:1ff.; Bornkamm: 98).

The freedom of Jesus over against the law and the tradition goes together with the novelty of his speech forms (Wilder, 1962: 8; cf. 1971: 12f. and passim). He speaks with immediacy, directness, spontaneity (Wilder, 1962: 8). He does not appear consciously to be creating tradition in the manner of the scribes and Pharisees. His words are concentrated on the immediate situation, in direct encounter with the hearer. If it can be said that Jesus exhibits a strong preference for the oral word, it must be made clear that he sets this preference over against the formal oral tradition of the scribes as well as the formality of the written text. He seems to eschew conventionality in language in any form.

2.2    Jesus apparently left this legacy with his disciples. Like him, few of them wrote. (Matthew, John, Peter are credited with books, but the traditions have been called into question.) The church was content with the oral transmission of the gospel for at least a generation, and even then it did not immediately accredit the written form of the word. Helmut Koester has cogently argued that some of the Apostolic Fathers relied on the oral tradition rather than the written gospels, which were in existence by that time (at least the

Synoptics were). Eusebius has recorded an interesting comment of Papias, bishop of Hierapolis in Asia Minor, early in II CE:

> "And I shall not hesitate to append to the interpretations [the title of his five treatises was *Interpretation of the Oracles of the Lord*] all that I ever learnt well from the presbyters and remember well, for of their truth I am confident. For unlike most I did not rejoice in them who say much, but in them who teach the truth, nor in them who recount the commandments of others, but in them who repeated those given to the faith by the Lord and derived from truth itself; but if ever anyone came who had followed the presbyters, I inquired into the words of the presbyters, what Andrew or Peter or Philip or Thomas or James or John or Matthew, or any other of the Lord's disciples, had said, and what Aristion and the presbyter John, the Lord's disciples, were saying. For I did not suppose that information from books would help me so much as the word of a living and surviving voice."
>
> (*HE* 3.39.3–4; Loeb Edition)

Papias seems still to have preferred the oral word (at this late date), making some sort of vague connection between it and the truth itself.

Aversion to writing also appears in the epistolary literature. The words of the second epistle of John are well known: "Though I have much to write to you, I would rather not use paper and ink, but I hope to come to see you and talk with you face to face, so that our joy may be complete" (2 John 12; cf. 3 John 13). That Paul wrote letters only reluctantly is evident at many points, especially in 2 Cor 3 and the various passages which may be termed the apostolic *parousia*, where he invariably proposes to follow up the written word with an oral word. The apostolic *parousia*, in my judgment, occurs regularly after the body of Paul's letters because he felt keenly the inadequacy of the written communication. Origen, too, is known to have hesitated about writing at all (Vischer: 320–36; Overbeck: 417–72; Wilder, 1962: 11f., n. 3).

2.3  Over against the priority of the oral word, there is a tendency already evident in the New Testament to codify the teachings of Jesus as a new law corresponding to the authority of the Torah. This tendency is perhaps most evident in the Gospel of Matthew. But in Luke, too, early traditions have already come to be understood as written—as "records" of events gone by. By the time we reach the end of the New Testament period, other primal traditions and interpretations have come to be understood as fixed in the past and as part of the record. This proclivity goes together with an understanding of faith that makes it possible for faith to be seized, conceptualized, and then handed around and on. In one form, at least, the understanding of tradition as written comports with the understanding of faith as assent to right belief. Faith and orthodoxy are thus leveled.

It is a mistake to understand the fixing of tradition as entirely negative. Primal traditions were preserved, of course, out of respect. The inclination to formalize and crystallize arises with the natural need to hand the tradition on. Fixing in writing is thus born of regard. The preservation and circulation of the tradition presupposes its written character.

2.4 The difference between oral and written word is not, of course, a purely formal one (Ebeling, 1963: 312f., n. 1).

All language is formalized to some degree. To speak or write intelligibly, one must subscribe to the grammar of a language and at least in large part to its lexicon. The degree of formalization varies: there is a higher degree of conventionality in the written word than in the oral word, and an even higher degree in the published word. Lawyers exaggerate the formalization in order to reduce ambiguity to a minimum; poets, on the other hand, take liberties in order to illuminate. Written, oral, and published are viewed in this context as *acts* that have to do with how speakers or writers relate to the traditions on which they are ultimately dependent.

The oral word can be understood as oral, written, or published. Rabbi Aqiba (I CE) published his edition of the Mishnah orally, by teaching it to his students (Gerhardsson: 121). The speech of the rabbis in the schools of Tannaim was thus "bound" (Wilder, 1962: 9). It had written character. The oral speech of Jesus, by contrast, was untrammeled (Fuchs; Wilder, 1962: 9) in that he was not bound by the tradition and its conventions. This does not mean that Jesus was not dependent upon language with its grammar and lexicon, or that he did not use conventional modes of speech, such as parallelism, parable, aphorism, and dialogue. Nor does it mean that he was unfamiliar with the rabbinic tradition. Rather, it means that he subordinated all conventions in his language to the sole end of turning language into event. He was primarily interested in what his language set in motion, what it created.

2.5 The reduction of the biblical tradition to writing both aids and abets the transition from understanding the language of the tradition as word from God to understanding it as word about God.

If the difference between word from God and word about God is that the first is what God speaks to man and the second is what man has to say about God, it follows that the second only is subject to formalization. God presumably does not speak a particular language, nor is God subject to grammatical and literary conventions. But to put it that way is to speak in figures. The biblical text is made up of human words—Hebrew, Aramaic, and Greek. It is therefore preposterous that the biblical text should be confused with word from God. Nevertheless, it should be recalled that there lurks in the American tradition, as a legacy of Protestant scholasticism, the notion that the biblical text, literally, is word from God. As a consequence of this tradition, man's word about God—what the biblical writers say about God—has come to be understood as God's word to man. In the identification of the two the oral character of the word is lost; the text was turned into written traditions that could be handed around and on without understanding.

2.6 The distinction between God's word and word about God goes together but is not identical with the difference between God's word and human words.

God's word is always encountered concretely in the form of human words (Ebeling, 1967; 91). The character of the tradition is thus determined by whether God is speaking or man is speaking: if God is speaking, the word creates faith, reaches its goal, cannot fail; if man is speaking, the word is at best a demand, which cannot create that for which it calls (Ebeling, 1967: 93). God's word can be known, therefore, only by what it effects: God's word is a word-event that creates faith.

If word and faith go together in this way, then it has to be said that understanding of the tradition, of the biblical text, must also go with the understanding of faith. The correlation between word and faith gives the Christian (and Jewish) traditions their peculiar problem regarding its own tradition: do they regard that tradition as word-event or does it understand that tradition as written—as words that can be seized, taken possession of, and handed around and on?

2.7 Twenty-seven books—gospels, acts, letters, and an apocalypse—were eventually identified as special segments of the Christian tradition and set aside as a new canon, a new measure of faith. With the rise of the New Testament as canon, the question becomes: will the church hold fast to the insight that gave birth to the tradition that God's word is oral word, or will it sacrifice that insight to the certainties of a tradition reduced to writing and fixed in form? In sum, how will the church understand the New Testament as canon?

### 3. Circulation and use of the tradition: handing the tradition around

Moses received the Law from Sinai, and transmitted it to Joshua; Joshua to the Elders; the Elders to the Prophets; and the Prophets to the Men of the Great Synagogue, who said three things: Be deliberate in pronouncing judgment; train up many disciples; and make a fence for the Law. (Mishnah, Aboth I.1)

The Apostles received the Gospel for us from the Lord Jesus Christ, Jesus the Christ was sent from God. The Christ therefore is from God and the Apostles from the Christ. In both ways, then, they were in accordance with the appointed order of God's will. Having therefore received their commands, and being fully assured by the resurrection of our Lord Jesus Christ, and with faith confirmed by the word of God, they went forth in the assurance of the Holy Spirit preaching the good news that the Kingdom of God is coming. (1 Clement 42:1–3)

3.1 The church's body of authoritative tradition is something it appears to have had in common with Judaism: the similarity between the saying of Aboth and the statement of Clement is striking in this respect, although Clement characteristically places double emphasis on the tradition (gospel) and the office. Using this similarity as a basis, Birger Gerhardsson has attempted to develop the thesis that the early church transmitted its tradition in a way that corresponded to the process in Judaism of the same period. In so doing he has also created a picture of Jesus, interpreted the self-understanding of the primitive church, and attempted to define the church's understanding of tradition. (See 11ff. where Gerhardsson says, "Only the one who has a conception of Jesus *similar* to that produced by Dibelius and Bultmann can accept their view of the origins of the gospel tradition without reservations.") Gerhardsson is correct in asserting that the problem of tradition must be referred ultimately to who Jesus is.

That the church had a tradition is a fact to be accepted. That the primitive church created traditions for itself and passed them along is beyond dispute. How these traditions were transmitted in the earliest period remains open to dispute, as the difference between the form critics and Gerhardsson shows. But how the church understood its own tradition-creating and -transmitting processes is another matter, which is related to the question of how the tradition was transmitted. The church's understanding of tradition, moreover, is bound up with its understanding of faith.

3.2 We have observed how Jesus disposes himself to the traditions of the Fathers with a remarkable degree of freedom, refusing in fact to claim the authority of that tradition for his own word. Paul, on the other hand, appears to recognize a body of authoritative material which has come down to him as tradition (1 Cor 11:2; 2 Thess 2:15, 3:6). Receiving and passing this tradition along are indicated by the use of technical language ($\pi\alpha\rho\alpha\lambda\alpha\mu\beta\acute{\alpha}\nu\epsilon\iota\nu$, $\pi\alpha\rho\alpha\delta\iota\delta\acute{o}\nu\alpha\iota$: 1 Cor 11:2, 23, 15:1, 3; Gal 1:9; Phil 4:9; 1 Thess 2:13, 4:1; 2 Thess 3:6; Col 2:6; see Gerhardsson: 290). It is not always possible to tell whether Paul is referring to tradition which he himself has created or to tradition which he has received (for example, Phil 4:9; cf. Gerhardsson: 293). Nevertheless, as 1 Cor 15:3 indicates, Paul does pass on to his congregations tradition which he regards as of basic importance (cf. 1 Cor 11:23). The question is, how does Paul understand this tradition? The line of his argument in Gal 1:1–2:21 is crucial in this connection, for it is here that he insists that his gospel is not from or through man (Gal 1:11f., 16; 2:6). How are we to reconcile this claim to independence with his obvious dependence upon tradition in such passages as 1 Cor 15:1ff.? He avers that his apostleship is not dependent upon man (Gal 1:1). Though this assertion is not part of the gospel, it is not unrelated. Further, he insists that his gospel is not derived from tradition (he uses the technical term in 1:12), nor is it "according to man," that is, measured by human standards. Rather, he has received it by revelation (1:12).

It is obvious that Paul cannot be referring to the sentences of the kerygmatic tradition when he insists that he did not receive his gospel from man. When he turns to his own history before and after his conversion (1:13–2:2)—the subject which pops into his mind first— he is not denying that he learned the *kerygma* from those before him, but rather that he was not "taught" his *gospel* by them (1:12). What he was not taught was the *interpretation* of the kerygma; his predecessors did not hand down to him an interpretation as a rabbi hands down interpretations of the law to his disciples, so that both law and interpretation become part of the tradition. Paul is claiming that his interpretation was revealed to him directly in his encounter with the risen Christ (1:16f.).

That this is the case becomes clear when we consider his statement in 2:5 and 14: what he was debating with the Judaizers was not the traditional sentences of the kerygma, but the "truth of the gospel." Now the "truth of the gospel" means the contrast between justification by faith and the principle of law as expressed by circumcision (2:3) and segregated table fellowship (2:12–14). Paul sets out the fundamental contrast in 2:16ff.: ". . . who know that a man is not justified by works of the law but through faith in Jesus Christ, . . ." and then invokes the kerygma in support of his position (2:29–21)! In his restatement of the kerygma he uses himself as the model: the truth of the gospel for him as a Christian, the truth upon which his apostleship is based (law-free gospel to the uncircumcised), and the truth which comprises the content of his message are one and the same. It is this truth which rests on revelation and not on tradition.

Paul thus stands in paradoxical relation to tradition. He accepts the kerygmatic tradition as authoritative and passes it on, but he also allows himself to be interpreted by that tradition in a radically new way. Out of this new, revelatory interpretation he conceives his apostleship and his gospel. Unlike Jesus, he does claim the authority of the tradition for his own word, but he does not presume to hand on earlier interpretation of that tradition as a part of it.

This way of putting the matter leaves it full of ambiguity. Where does kerygmatic tradition end and interpretation begin? Is it not the case that the kerygma is already interpretation? Furthermore, does not Paul himself pass on interpretations as well as tradition, kerygma? For example, he sometimes invokes a "word of the Lord" (for example, 1 Thess 4:15, 4:2; 1 Cor 7:10), or says that he has no word of the Lord (1 Cor 7:25). And it is undoubtedly the case that his paranetical material is often traditional (for example, 1 Thess 4, 5; cf. Dibelius). Such passages as 1 Cor 13, too, may well have received their formulation prior to Paul. In any case, distinguishing tradition from interpretation requires more than formal analysis, than determining whether the words and sentences are Paul's own formulations or not. What is at issue ultimately is whether Paul views the tradition and its interpretation as something he comes across and is obliged to pass on, or whether he regards himself as basically dependent upon the tradition which goes back to Jesus but at the same time as compelled to allow it to come to expression anew as he interprets and translates it for himself and his congregations. In that case he may indeed use older linguistic formulations without being bound by their previous semantic horizons. Such a possibility warns us against rigid use of comparative lexicography: what Paul's words mean must in the end be determined by how *he* uses them.

3.3    If Paul regards the tradition as something which can be kept alive only by reinterpretation and translation, it is equally clear that tradition and interpretation are understood in the New Testament in a more formal sense. That is, the tradition comes to be understood as a deposit of teaching which has already been surrounded by a protective body of interpretation. Together they are to be handed on as tradition. The statement in 2 Tim 2:2 illustrates: "what you have heard from me before many witnesses entrust to faithful men who will be able to teach others also." Paul's "truth of the gospel" is here in the process of canonization, as is proved by the further statement:

> "But as for you, continue in what you have learned and have firmly believed, knowing from whom you learned it and how from childhood you have been acquainted with the sacred writings which are able to instruct you for salvation through faith in Christ Jesus."                                    (2 Tim 3:14f.)

"The faith once for all delivered to the saints" (Jude 3) is invoked as a hedge against heresy and distortion. Paul's writings, among other traditions, were open to abuse and misunderstanding (2 Pet 3:16). In the context of the struggle of the church to define its own faith and thus to identify what was heretical and what was not, the concept of tradition was formalized and its content crystallized in order to give clear lines of demarcation.

The Pastorals and 2 Peter stand near the end of the development within the New Testament. Nevertheless, signs of hardening are evident somewhat earlier. In Matthew there is the emergence of something similar to a school tradition (K. Stendahl, 1968), and Luke undertakes to guarantee the reliability of the tradition, as the Prologue to his Gospel indicates (Luke 1:1–4). What is significant about Luke's work is not that he attempts to "prove" the events which underlie the tradition, but that he attempts to guarantee the tradition and thus the interpretation of those events. The difference is critical.

3.4 In general, then, it may be said that the tendency of the church from the beginning was to allow its tradition to crystallize. It is inevitable that such crystallization will take place in handing tradition around and on. In the hardening process, however, it becomes increasingly difficult to maintain a fixed horizon of interpretation unless the tradition is buttressed by a corresponding body of fixed interpretation. The body has to be expanded with each new situation. The church wanted to build a hedge around the gospel in the same way that Judaism attempted to erect a fence about the law. If this process is understood as one in which the core of the tradition is preserved by being supplemented, then interpretation is never allowed to recognize that both the core and the amplification of the tradition are already interpretation. This makes it impossible for interpretation to be thrown back upon its own origin. The more the core is overlaid with protective tradition-interpretations, the more likely it is for the event which gave rise to the tradition to be lost to view. The fact that faith refers itself to Jesus as the one who creates the tradition is thus obscured by handing the tradition around and on: faith ceases to refer itself to Jesus, but refers itself to the tradition instead.

That Paul, and to a lesser degree the Fourth Gospel, have given rise to reformations, not to say heresies, within the church owes to the fact that Paul refers his gospel to revelation and not to tradition. He regards tradition as the path to, but not the destiny of, truth. His position with respect to tradition is fraught with risk, as the ancient church knew well and the Roman church learned to its regret.

Handing the tradition around—its circulation and use in the church—subsequently became a criterion for canonicity. Eusebius, following Origen, divided the books into three categories: (1) acknowledged, (2) disputed, and (3) spurious (Grant, 1963: 35). Referring, of course, to the church's disposition to the various rivals for recognition. Athanasius also apparently gave as his list those books which were in current use and firmly established in the tradition as tradition; in other words, he gave recognition to the tradition about tradition (Grant: 36). It is the habit of scholars to say that the New Testament canon was virtually determined by the end of II CE, meaning that a consensus had been reached in the church at large by then regarding which books would be received as authoritative (cf. Grant: 30). The precariousness of this criterion as a basis of canonicity, is recognized by Grant (37), not because he is dubious about its validity, but because he is not sure Eusebius and others really knew what was being read in the church in early II CE.

Our interest is not in whether the criterion of usage was valid, but in what it tells us about how the church understood its own tradition. If this criterion was the primary basis for determining whether a book was canonical, then it can be said that the church took as its norm for canonicity whether a tradition had passed into the public domain and could be considered as the opinion of the average Christian. In that case, the process of canonization would represent a crystallization of the tradition, in that the tradition would now be understood as something which one can come across and then pass on. In this respect canonization goes together with the transition from oral to written word. It thus becomes problematical whether the New Testament supports the concept of canon understood in this way. If we take Jesus and Paul as paradigms, it appears that it is precisely this view of canon which has to be broken in the interests of allowing the tradition to emerge in its own right.

It is necessary to guard against over-generalization at this point. In the first place, handing the tradition around and on and thus growing deaf to its claim does not totally efface the potentiality of the tradition, thus passed on, to become word-event again. There is always the possibility that the church can awaken to a new understanding of tradition. In the second place, circulation and usage was not the only criterion for canonicity. Other criteria were involved, and they also require analysis.

*4. The particularity and plurality of the tradition.* The particularity (for example, letters addressed to particular churches) and the plurality (for example, four Gospels) of the canonical tradition indicate that faith regards itself as historical: it refers itself to Jesus of Nazareth and it is realized by particular persons in particular times and places.

Plurality became a problem because it was not immediately evident why there were many and often divergent witnesses to the faith rather than a single, unified one. Of course, it could be said that all were "inspired by one and the same Spirit" (1 Cor 13:11; cf. *Muratorian Fragment,* line 19), but the one Spirit only makes the problem of dissident voices all the more acute. The problem of plurality applies to the whole of early Christian literature: Paul, for example, is "corrected" in the deutero-Pauline corpus, thus producing dissident voices. Nevertheless, the issue of plurality came to be focused in the fourfold gospel. That more than one gospel was felt to present a problem is indicated by the effort on the part of Ireneaus and others, toward the close of II CE, to limit the gospels to four. Interestingly enough, they insisted that there be no fewer than four. The establishment of the fourfold gospel meant that the unity of the four required demonstration (Grant, 1963: 30ff.). If the church came, in due course, to take the plurality of the tradition for granted, it must be recalled that this could happen only because the church believed an underlying unity pervaded the tradition. The rise of historical criticism in modern times called this unity once again into question.

Related to but not identical with the problem of plurality is the question of particularity. How is it possible to regard writings addressed to a particular situation at a particular time as universally applicable? How can such writings be regarded as binding upon the church universal, the *ecclesia catholica*? Even if it be allowed that the Spirit inspired such books, it remains unclear why and how that which is revelatory for a particular situation could still carry universal authority. This problem applies to the whole of early Christian literature: the Gospels, for example, were according to Matthew, Mark, and so on, and enjoyed special favor in limited spheres in the primitive church. Nevertheless, the issue of particularity can be focused in the corpus of Pauline epistles. If the church overcame the problem of plurality with a doctrine of unity, it met the problem of particularity with a doctrine of universality. In this case, too, historical criticism has undermined the solution by reasserting the particularity of the epistles, as of other early Christian literature.

By turning the questions around, it becomes evident that the church could not solve its problems by denying plurality and particularity. What if the tradition were not plural and particular? In that case it would not be historical either. Because the church had also to accept plurality and particularity in order to allow for the historical character of the tradition, it then became necessary to attempt to meet the hermeneutical problems arising out of diversity and specificity.

*4.1   The problem of particularity.* The Pauline letters are particular (each has a local address) in contrast to the so-called catholic epistles, which are addressed to the church at large (Barnett: *IDB* I, 542f.). Among the catholic epistles (James, 1–2 Peter, 1–3 John, Jude), 2 and 3 John were also, of course, addressed locally. Dionysius of Alexander (ca. 200) noted this difference and designated 1 John as catholic in contrast to 2 and 3 John (Eusebius, *HE* 7.25.7–10). The term catholic in the sense of general address had already been established in the second and third centuries (Apollonius, Eusebius, *HE* 5.18.5; Dionysius; Origen, Commentary on John 6:18 with reference to 1 Peter), and in IV CE Eusebius uses it to refer to the group of seven non-Pauline letters noted above (*HE* 2.23; 3.25.1–3). Although the catholic or general epistles came to be identified as a group, their catholic character, oddly enough, did not smooth the road to canonization. Eusebius reports that only 1 John and 1 Peter were among the recognized books in his time (*HE* 3.25.2f.); the remainder belonged among the disputed books.[1]

The particularity of the Pauline letters was a problem, nevertheless, as indicated by the effort of the anti-Marcionite author of the *Muratorian Fragment* to solve it. Following his predecessor John (of the Apocalypse), Paul wrote to particular churches, to be sure, but only to *seven*, and thus to the *ecclesia catholica* (lines 48–59). For one church is diffused throughout the world (lines 56f.). The effort of the author to invoke the pattern of the seven letters in Revelation,

---

[1] The *Muratorian Fragment* (ca. 200) recognizes only Jude and 1 and 2 John. Eusebius reflects the same opinion as Origen (ca. 250). The gradual and relatively late acceptance of the catholic epistles indicates, according to Barnett, that they belonged to a time subsequent to Paul's letters (*IDB* I, 542f.).

though unique to the *Muratorian Fragment,* shows that the apostolic status of Paul was not sufficient to rationalize including his letters in the canon. Their particularity had to be justified, and this was achieved on the basis of the parallel and the significance of the number seven (Stendahl, 1962: 239–45, especially 239–243; cf. Dahl: 261–71).

The problem of particularity is the overriding problem which concerns the author of the *Fragment,* as Krister Stendahl has shown (1962: 242). It touches the authors of the Gospels who wrote in their own names (lines 5, 15) but who were under the guidance of one Spirit (line 19). The book of Acts is characterized as the acts of *all* the apostles (line 34), presumably in the interests of catholicizing its report. The four pastoral epistles (including Philemon) are held in honor because they are profitable for the ordering of ecclesiastical discipline (lines 59–63). The epistles of Jude and two of John are also accepted in the church catholic (lines 68f.).

In a similar vein, N. A. Dahl points out that letters addressed to individuals would be even more problematical than letters addressed to churches (263). Victorinus of Pettau (died 304) utilizes the *argument* of the *Muratorian Fragment* to support the seven Pauline letters to seven churches (*Commentary on the Apocalypse* I.vii; *De fabrica mundi* xi; Dahl: 261, n. 7). He notes that afterward Paul wrote to individuals. By his time the Pastorals and Philemon were firmly established in the canon. Marcion, on the other hand, does not recognize the Pastorals, but he does accept Philemon. Tertullian takes note of the inconsistency (Dahl: 263f.). In any case, Philemon was the only letter to be rejected because of its limited scope (Dahl: 265). But Philemon was carried along on the tide, and the Pastorals seem to have been recognized quite early because of their subject matter, which has to do with church order. Content which lent itself to more general application undoubtedly made the personal address less of a problem.

The catholic perspective of Ephesians is one factor which gave rise to doubts about its authenticity in modern times. It is often said to be a catholic edition of Colossians (Dahl: 266, quoting W. Ochel). Romans, too, has a more general outlook, written, perhaps, to a church Paul did not personally know. That 1 Corinthians, especially chapters 5–15, gives the appearance of a *Kirchenordnung* may have paved the way for its wider use. It is not surprising, then, that these three epistles are most often cited by pre-Marcionite Christian authors (Dahl: 270f.). When one notes that the geographical designations in the salutations are omitted in certain textual witnesses, it is tempting to argue with Dahl that such omissions were in the interest of catholicizing the Pauline epistles (Dahl: 266–71). Dahl even speculates that these three circulated as an independent collection before publication of the Pauline corpus (271).

In an effort to bring these diverse and sometimes problematical phenomena into focus, Dahl's summary of the development can be cited (271):

> In a way, a generalization is unavoidable, if the Pauline letters shall at all be read as Scriptures relevant to the whole church and not simply as historical documents. It is also legitimate because there is an implicit catholicity of the Pauline letters.

Dahl's first point, that generalization is unavoidable, goes together with a certain understanding of the tradition. If the tradition is to be understood as universally applicable *as originally expressed*, there is no choice but to allow it to pass into the common understanding. Only in this way can it be handed around and on as relevant. That is, the particularity of the letters is converted to catholicity by giving over the language of the letters to what the church at large understands. The language is handed around and on until the spines of its specificity are worn smooth. When the particularity of the traditon has thus been delivered up to common opinion, the particularity is no longer a problem. In that case, of course, the tradition has also lost its critical power: the tradition no longer resists the common understanding but is taken over by it and submerged in it. The tradition that is created to preserve the tradition ends by effacing it.

It is correct to say that generalization is unavoidable, provided one is thinking of the inevitable and fateful loss of the power of tradition. On the other hand, the rediscovery of the particularity of the tradition has the consequence of making translation necessary for the interpreter. In periods of such rediscovery, like the Reformation, the problem of translation becomes acute, in the interests of allowing the tradition once again to have its say in the face of the public opinion that has given it a faceless universality.

Dahl's second point, regarding the "implicit catholicity" of the Pauline letters, is unclear. Does this mean that the letters lend themselves to generalization, as he has just suggested is unavoidable? Or does it mean that the letters are implicitly catholic in another sense—that they intend to be catholic? Stendahl has linked universality of intention with general usage in relation to the *Muratorian Fragment* (1962: 242). In the Fragment it is not just a question of wide usage, however important that may be, but of the intention of general address (243). Here again we meet with the peculiar phenomenon which shows up again and again in the church's understanding of the New Testament as canon: it is not sufficient justification to make a claim on behalf of the New Testament unless that claim can be shown to inhere in the text itself. Thus, even if wide usage pointed to a catholicity of understanding, such usage had to be justified on the basis of Paul's own intention. Stendahl reads this as a post-rationalization of a *fait accompli* (243). Indeed, it is just that, but it points at the same time to the uneasy juxtaposition of a tradition fixed in its particularity in writing with the need to call upon that tradition as normative. If the early church solved the problem of particularity with fanciful arguments involving sacred numbers and the like, the solution suggests that the church was attempting to grapple with a root problem from a remote locus.

The letters in their particularity had to be shown to be intended for the church universal. This reflects the effort to make the intention of the New Testament square with the church's understanding of it as canon. The effort has to be made, if the New Testament as norm is to be honored. In the understanding of the author of the *Fragment*, however, the hermeneutical problem posed by the particularity of the letters is glossed over, and the question of the New Testament as norm is reduced to receiving and handing the tradition on, understood now as universally applicable. If the intention of the New Testament and the understanding of the *Fragment* do not square, we have grounds for rethinking the claim in the face of the New Testament itself.

One further observation is in order. Stendahl has pointed out that inspiration, like apostolicity, was not enough for canonization (1962: 245). Inspiration is nowhere used as a divisive, discriminating standard. The church did not take the stand of Judaism, that the spirit of prophecy had departed from Israel. It could not in this way either chronologically or qualitatively distinguish "inspired" from other writings. Inasmuch as it did not have the Spirit ready to hand, it had to develop other criteria, and these became more "historical" in nature (243). Inspiration was available as a label only after the canon had already been identified, in which case it was not a differentiating criterion.

These observations again afford certain clues. The reticence on the part of the church to invoke inspiration in relation to the selection of canonical literature indicates that it understood well its inability to control the Spirit. Though the church sometimes linked the Spirit with an office, it apparently guarded itself against the fatal error of linking it with scripture. On the other hand, once the canon was formed, the doctrine of inspiration arose as a means of justifying the selection. Inspiration means that the text is true or contains the truth; truth in this context means what is generally applicable. The doctrine of inspiration goes together with the doctrine of catholicity: both are designed to preserve the tradition by delivering it over to common understanding and thus to make it possible to hand the tradition on without considering whether it had real catholic intent.

To recapitulate: particularity becomes a problem on the assumption that particular expressions of faith, when written and canonized, are regarded as normative and thus universally applicable. This problem is customarily met by allowing the tradition to pass into the common understanding. The common understanding gives particularity either a literal and rigid applicability—a precedent setting character—or a faceless generality, which permits it to be assimilated to regnant cultural modes. The two ways of obscuring the problem of particularity are held in solution in the common understanding.

*4.2 The problem of plurality.* Plurality looks to the unity of the subject matter, the single gospel, the solitary Christ-event. Particularity looks to the proclamation of the gospel in relation to a concrete situation. Plurality considers how the Christ-event leaves its imprint upon the primitive Christian consciousness. Particularity reflects upon how its imprint is expressed anew in varying contexts. Insofar as the Christ-event is viewed as giving rise to the phenomenon of faith in which the Christ-event has already received interpretation, and insofar as the proclamation of the gospel is interpretation of the Christ-event, the two are identical. Nevertheless, it is necessary to make the distinction for the reason that primordial interpretation in relation to the Christ-event undergoes metamorphosis when it is redirected as proclamation. This is only to say that confession is not the same thing as proclamation.

It is not accidental that the question of particularity should adhere in a special way to the Pauline epistles, or that the question of plurality should belong especially to the Gospels. The Gospels allegedly hold the Christ-event specifically in view; the epistles are concerned ostensibly with proclamation. If subsequent analysis tends to blur this formal distinction, it is because the ostensible subject matter of the gospel and the epistle is misleading. It may, in fact, prove to be the case that it is Paul who holds the Christ-event strictly in view, whereas the Gospels tend to major in proclamation, or perhaps in tradition.

Oscar Cullmann has observed that Matthew and Luke, on the basis of the two- or four-document hypothesis, are already rudimentary Gospel harmonies (1956: 45). Thus, though not designed to supplant other Gospels (cf. Luke 1:1–4), they intend to improve upon their predecessors.[2] This double tendency is latent from the first: the effort to improve the primary tradition led to a multiplicity of gospels, but, by the same token, the desire to present the "pure" gospel meant taking up the work of predecessors into every new version and thus represents a counter tendency to reduction. The Fourth Gospel holds a special place in the development in that it apparently represents an independent tradition. Though it was possible to grasp the underlying unity of the synoptic tradition rather easily, it was not so easy to account for the pecularities of the Fourth Gospel. For this reason the Gospel of John was often played off against the Synoptics, as, for example, by the Valentinians (Irenaeus, *Adv. haer.* 3.11.7). Yet it was also posible for one of the Synoptics to enjoy special privilege within a local tradition (Matthew among the Ebionites, Luke with Marcion, Mark in Docetism: Irenaeus, *Adv. haer.* 3.11.7). The point to be observed is that the tendency to multiplicity, which was strung out endlessly in the apocryphal gospels, was corrected by the counter-tendency to reduction, which was also triggered also by heretical movements.

The fourfold gospel represents a compromise in the internal

---

[2] Cullmann has rightly argued, I think, that the question supplement or supplant is an arbitrary dichotomy (see 43ff.).

struggle of the church to identify its primary tradition. Because no one gospel was sufficient, a number had to be received; as unlimited multiplicity would lead to chaos, the number had to be limited. Various criteria had to be invoked in settling on the four canonical Gospels, but from a political viewpoint it can be said that the church agreed in excluding the marginal witnesses and in compromising on those which enjoyed the widest support. Such support rested, of course, on wide usage, access to apostolic traditions, and conformity to accepted doctrine.

Irenaeus' argument for the number of the gospels is as fanciful as that of the *Muratorian Fragment* for the catholicity of Paul. That there are four zones in the world and four principal winds, and that the Cherubin have four faces is neither here nor there (Irenaeus, *Adv. haer.* 3.11.8). Yet, like the author of the *Fragment,* he witnesses to a problem which was deeply felt: why were there four canonical Gospels, no more and no less? The number, of course, is unimportant. The restricted plurality of the tradition is significant.

Cullmann's explanation of this phenomenon combines a theological point with historical circumstance (1956: 52). On the one hand, it was necessary to collect and preserve all the available materials stemming from the apostolic age. This the church did: there were few if any reliable traditions outside of the fourfold gospel which could rightly claim apostolic authority (cf. the Gospel of Peter, etc.), and the traditions of the apostolic period had already been collected into four different versions. The church merely accepted the fact. On the other hand, the richness of the truth about Christ could not be exhausted by any one evangelist, with the result that a diversity of tradition and interpretation was necessary. The unity of the multiple witness thus defined was guaranteed by the one Spirit (cf. *Muratorian Fragment,* line 19; Irenaeus, *Adv. haer.* 3.11.8; Origen, Commentary on John 5.7 [IV, 104f.]: "it is one Lord who is preached by all" [Cullman, 1956: 43 and n. 38]).

It may be observed that Cullmann's point about the need for a plurality of witnesses argues for an unlimited plurality: the richness of the truth about Christ cannot be exhausted (cf. John 21:25). Only an infinite number of finite witnesses can preserve an infinite truth. He hedges the thrust of this argument with a historical consideration: the witnesses must have some legitimate point of contact with the truth to which they bear witness. Inasmuch as that point of contact is limited to the Christ-event, only those witnesses who have apostolic connections, so to speak, may be admitted. In this form of the argument we get the mixture of two items: (1) the Christ-event gives rise to an unlimited number of futures, and thus requires an unlimited number of witnesses. In this sense, every act of faith is witness to the Christ-event. (2) The Christ-event was a historical event: it transpired in space and time. Access to it requires participation in the event itself. For this reason primary witnesses are confined to the apostolic circle.

Is it proper to conclude, then, that the number of canonical witnesses might have been six, twelve, or even seventy, had they all been of the apostolic circle? The answer must be both yes and no, for it is now apparent that some further criterion is needed. We have observed that the claim to apostolic authority was not sufficient to raise a book, not even a gospel, to canonical status. Apostolic authority had to be matched by consensus on content (cf. Bishop Serapion of Antioch and the Gospel of Peter: Eusebius, *HE* 6.12 [Cullmann, 1956: 46 and n. 13; 52]). That the fourfold gospel in fact represents the sole apostolic authorities preserving the gospel tradition may be the rationalization of the church,[3] or it may be historical accident. In any case, it is not the basis upon which the fourfold gospel was canonized. The church had to take into account the content of the competing books in relation to their claim to apostolic authority. The content was measured (a) by use in the church, and (b) by conformity to accepted doctrine. It is difficult to distinguish (a) and (b) because use presumably indicated doctrinal acceptability. As a consequence, it may be said that the church was projecting the canon upon its own understanding of faith. But if the "upon which" is its own prehension of faith, that which was being projected was drawn from the tradition. Viewed circumspectly, the community of faith was laying hold of the tradition on the basis of its own prehension of faith, but in so doing it was also setting the tradition over against itself, in two respects: (a) it was refusing to narrow the tradition to a single, logically coherent interpretation; (b) it was refusing to ex-

---

[3] Cullmann (1956: 52) rightly notes that the attempt to establish the apostolicity of the four Gospels was an attempt to confirm the rightness of the original judgment. He does not attempt to press the point, but accepts it at face value.

pand the tradition indefinitely without reference to the ground of the tradition.

*4.3* To recapitulate the essential points: plurality becomes a problem for the primitive church on the grounds that a variety of expressions of faith, when written and canonized, are regarded as normative, but must be taken to refer to just one gospel and one lord. This problem was met generally by excluding marginal witnesses to the faith and settling on those traditions which enjoy the widest circulation. At the same time, divergent witnesses are harmonized in the common understanding, in the interest of a unified ground and object of faith. And, as in the case of the problem of particularity, inspiration is invoked to insure the unity of the witnesses: the Spirit prompts the witnesses to say the same thing.

Nevertheless, the church fought off efforts to reduce the plurality of witnesses to a written unity (for example, Marcion), on the one hand, and to expand the list of classical expressions of faith indefinitely, on the other. In so doing, the church was attempting to hold to a single ground of faith, while permitting that ground to give rise to innumerable authentic and inauthentic future witnesses to itself.

The church likewise resisted efforts to efface the particularity of the written tradition, as noted earlier. In so doing, it was refusing to settle the hermeneutic problem on the basis of the common understanding.

In refusing both to expand the canonical tradition indefinitely or to narrow it to a single, internally consistent tradition, the church settled on a spectrum of witnesses that held the two poles together: (1) the unity of the ground of tradition and (2) the particularity and hence plurality of appropriate interpretation.

*5. The canon as spectrum of tradition and interpretation.*

*5.1* The unity of the ground of the tradition provided the canon with outside limits: the primal witnesses had to be tethered to their ground; they had to be "apostolic."

In refusing to expand the tradition indefinitely, the church was attempting to hold to the ground of that tradition, Jesus, in order to maintain the unity of intentionality: faith has a single object, it always refers itself to Jesus. If the church subsequently invoked the one Spirit as a guarantee for the unity of the tradition, it did so only in retrospect, making the Spirit an accessory after the fact. The tradition finds its unity in the one Lord who is preached by all (Origen, Commentary on John 5.7 [IV, 104f.]).

5.2 The particularity and plurality of appropriative interpretation provided the canon with inside limits: because the ground of faith would admit neither a monolithic tradition nor non-particular appropriations, the canon was made to consist of a plurality of diverging apostolic witnesses.

In refusing to narrow the tradition to a single, internally coherent interpretation, the church perceived that the Christ-event gives rise to innumerable futures just because it is a historical event and is to be appropriated historically: the meaning of the Christ-event is disclosed only in the faith to which it gives rise. Like the Christ-event, faith, too, is historical. It follows that the Christ-event can be appropriated faithfully only in relation to particular contexts. A single, monolithic tradition would yield a-historical faith and an a-historical Christ. A historical Christ and historical faith necessarily give rise to a multiplicity of traditions and interpretations.

In the face of this polarity, the church was driven to settle on a *spectrum* of witnesses in which these two poles were held together: the single ground intended by the tradition, and the particularity and hence plurality of appropriation. The first provided outside limits for the canon, the second set inside limits.

5.3 This spectrum may be viewed from a second perspective. The early Christian memory of its own faith is that Jesus set faith in motion: Jesus called for faith, indeed, gave his hearers the right to have faith, by invoking the reality of God's reign in aphorism and parable.

The response to Jesus is twofold: the earliest disciples confessed the faith to which they came at the behest of Jesus; they also fastened onto and repeated the words spoken by Jesus. One of the forms of confession, consequently, was the creation of the gospels: the confession of faith utilizing the words of Jesus now taken up into a retrospective narrative. But confession is also expressed as the interpretation of faith in relation to the language horizons of the person or community that comes to faith.

Confession is subsequently redirected as proclamation: proclamation is confession translated into alien language worlds for the benefit of those seeking to come to faith. Paul, for example, found it necessary not only to pass along the kerygma as tradition, but to interpret the kerygma, to translate it, and that means to bring it into the language horizons of his hearers. The response to his preaching is new confession and therefore new articulation of the interpretation of faith.

Finally, the church came to reflect on its confession and its proclamation in relation to the object of its faith, Jesus: faith reflecting on its linguistic history is theology. Paul is preeminent among New Testament authors as a theologian.

The spectrum represented by the New Testament therefore embraces the language tradition created by Jesus, confession as faith coming to expression, proclamation as translation, and theology in rudimentary form. The New Testament reflects not just a single cycle of this order, but a number of cycles, and these cycles tend to be conflated because the previous stages are preserved as the traditions from which subsequent cycles depart. We have to allow, of course, for relatively isolated traditions in which the mixture is less severe.

5.4 The canon as a spectrum of interpretations and traditions has a third dimension.

Every interpretation excludes other possible interpretations. Insofar as it is genuine interpretation and not mere traffic in words, particular interpretation narrows down access to what is being interpreted by bringing it into relation to a specific context. Interpretation turns text into event, crowding the "meaning" of the text into the circle of context. The claim of context keeps expressions of faith historical.

Particular interpretation, because it takes place in a specific linguistic horizon, pulls alien traditions into its orbit as a means of understanding its object in that horizon. By permitting its object to be interpreted concretely in relation to new and different terms and symbols, faith runs the risk of losing the thread which provides its own continuity. Though this risk is necessary, it is potentially corrupting.

Misunderstanding and non-understanding enter into and threaten the tradition at every level. Even originative—or especially originative—expressions giving rise to new traditions are articulated in language which has a pre-history, and which is therefore freighted with elements that may be hostile to a new voice. As primary expressions become frozen (as, for example, Jesus' words do in the Gospels), those expressions are reduced and threatened in the common understanding by both misunderstanding and non-understanding. Non-understanding permits the full measure of words, sentences, figures to be stopped down, narrowed, and referred to what everybody already knows. Misunderstanding invites the vestiges of borrowed but deformed language to reassert themselves. To put the matter in its extreme form, the common understanding is prone to reduce Jesus to his predecessors and to conflate his words with everyday parlance. Nevertheless, *understanding* is also preserved in a particular tradition when that tradition preserves expressions of its vision in written form. It can then not be entirely deceived by its memory; the interplay between and among layers of tradition will serve to recall what tends to be forgotten: the original impetus of that tradition.

Transmission thus both preserves and corrupts interpretation. The fact of corruption was observed long ago by Marcion, who wanted to purge the tradition by reducing it to an emasculated gospel and a collection of Pauline letters freed from interpolation. What makes Marcion's move heretical is that he thought he could reduce the truth of the gospel to a single undistorted vision, which could then be reintroduced into language and passed on as tradition without need of further interpretation, without corruption. He aspired to tailor the canon to his own understanding of the faith and thus cut himself off from correction. In this respect he was functioning as the archaeologist who excavates the entire tell as a means of insuring that his or her interpretation of that particular site will be uncontested.

These observations may be ordered in a slightly modified fashion. When authentic interpretation is handed around and on, the transmitter tends to forget that interpretation is both narrowing and corrupting: the narrowing and the alien elements are passed on as though they had come with the original package. This is because the common understanding traffics in tradition as an undifferentiated mass. As a consequence, the whence of tradition is obscured.

On the positive side, reinterpretation may be said to be the effort to recover the primal voice of the tradition by attending to particular interpretations. This process involves raising back to the surface the understanding of the ground of faith that is implicit in particular interpretations. Reinterpretation is the attempt to cleanse the arteries of transmission of the cholesterol of interpretation. Reinterpretation is no differently situated than original interpretation, though: it, too, is narrowing and corrupting.

The canon thus consists of originative interpretation, interpretation, and reinterpretation. These acts are ordered in relation to their proximity to the ground of faith.

It has already been observed that the New Testament as spectrum of interpretation and tradition has inside limits: the particularity of interpretation requires multiple witnesses to faith—as many witnesses, as it were, as there are contexts in which faith is to be given its concrete meaning. Particularity thus leads, willy-nilly, to plurality. On the other hand, the immediate intention of particular interpretation is to recover the primal voice of faith for a new time and place. Particular interpretation is consequently drawn to the oral face of the tradition and to the "truth of the gospel." It will invariably take on messianic pretensions simply because it deigns to proclaim the word of God anew.

The real counterweight to particularity is not universality, but more particularity, or plurality. Particular interpretations compete with each other, the tradition gains a written character to guard the integrity of its memory, and the common understanding transmits the tradition more or less dumbly, until moved to a new understanding by a new (particular) prophet. Both particularity and plurality function as a bulwark against Marcionite messiahs who wish to preempt the canon by reducing the spectrum of interpretation to a single voice, and by fixing the meaning of that voice.

6. *The ground of the tradition.* There are three criteria for canonicity in II CE: apostolicity, conformity with received teaching, and circulation and use in the church. A closer look at apostolicity permits us to examine the church's intention to cling to its ground.

6.1 The authority of the words of Jesus was anterior to the authority of the apostolic tradition (Beare: *IDB* I, 521f.). It has already been observed that Paul invokes a word of the Lord upon occasion. Luke, *via* Paul, invites the reader to recall the words of the Lord Jesus (Acts 20:35). In the Fourth Gospel, the officers of the chief priests and Pharisees are permitted to testify: "No man ever spoke like this man!" (John 7:46). That the words of Jesus were treasured in the earliest community is demonstrated by the eventual appearance of the Gospels. The sayings traditions which were taken up into the Gospels, especially the Synoptics, evidently circulated orally in the community for a generation or more. The authority accorded the Jesus tradition (including the narrative tradition) in the earliest community is evidently transferred to the Gospels in the later community.

The Gospels, nevertheless, were not ultimately canonized because they contained the words of Jesus (Stendahl, 1962: 241). Of more importance for the second century church was whether the Gospels could claim apostolic authority, as the *Muratorian Fragment* and Irenaeus indicate. In the first place, apostolic authority came to parallel the authority of Jesus, so to speak, as quickly as the church passed out of the apostolic age and began to look back upon its own heroes and founders. The epistle to the Ephesians could already conceive of the church as "built upon the foundation of the apostles and [Christian] prophets" (2:29), and Jude can speak of "the faith which was once for all delivered to the saints" (Jude 3). It is remarkable that Luke's presentation of the foundations of the church embraces, in a two-volume work, the ministry of Jesus and the ministry of the apostles. Hans Conzelmann has sought to show that Luke's work reflects a threefold periodization: the time of preparation; the time of Jesus; the time of the church. But this division is basically wrong for Luke. On Luke's view, the time of the Twelve (those who accompanied Jesus from the baptism of John) is inseparably linked with the time of Jesus; the real break is between the Twelve and those who follow. In any case, in Luke's work we have the double foundation: Jesus and the apostles. And Acts gives the warrant for taking the epistles into the canon. It was not without cause, then, that the canon was thought, for example, by Marion, to consist of gospel and epistle (cf. the Lectionary).

In the second place, the authority of Jesus tended to be taken up into the authority of the apostles for the same reason that Paul had to be taken up into his orthodox interpreters: to protect him from misunderstanding (cf. 2 Peter 3:16). With the rash of late gospels and interpretations of Jesus, the church found it necessary to protect itself against the abuse of the Jesus tradition. It did this, of course, by restricting the Gospels to four, and by arguing that these four represented trustworthy interpretations of Jesus. According to Irenaeus, this move was directed against the would be correctors of the apostles (*Adv. haer.* 3.1.1); as much may be inferred from the *Muratorian*

*Fragment.* Two aspects of this line of argument are worthy of note. First, the church did not seek to prove its case by reference to Jesus himself; it took for granted that the Jesus tradition was open to a variety of interpretations. Second, the church chose to vest its case in the apostolic origins of the Gospels, by which it implied (a) that only apostolic interpretations of Jesus had any claim to authenticity, and (b) that the historical link between the apostles and Jesus provided the basis for this claim. If this claim was buttressed with the doctrine of inspiration (cf. Irenaeus), this was done only in a secondary way.

6.2 In the development, the appeal to Jesus himself disappears quite early, and the temporal proximity of the apostles to Jesus soon goes underground. From the vantage point of the later church (second and third centuries), it looks as if it was entirely sufficient to ground the tradition in the apostles. Irenaeus' statement may be taken as exemplary:

> So Matthew among the Hebrews issued a Writing of the gospel in their own tongue, while Peter and Paul were preaching the gospel at Rome and founding the Church. After their decease Mark, the disciple and interpreter of Peter, also handed down to us in writing what Peter had preached. Then Luke, the follower of Paul, recorded in a book the gospel as it was preached by him. Finally John, the disciple of the Lord, who had so lain on his breast, himself published the Gospel, while he was residing at Ephesus in Asia. All of these handed down to us that there is one God, maker of Heaven and earth, proclaimed by the Law and the Prophets, and one Christ the Son of God. If anyone does not agree with them he despises the companions of the Lord, he despises Christ the Lord himself, he even despises the Father, and he is self-condemned, resisting and refusing his own salvation, as all the heretics do. *Adv. haer.* 3.1.1–2.
>
> (Library of Christian Classics, I, 370)

Irenaeus neatly establishes his point by showing that Mark and Luke represent apostolic authority through Peter and Paul, respectively, whereas Matthew and John are taken to be apostles in their own right.[4] It would appear that Irenaeus has elevated apostolic authority above that of the Jesus tradition (cf. Eusebius' statement in *HE* 3.25.6–7). Yet it should be observed that those who disagree,

---

[4] Only the historical connection of John with Jesus is given notice.

according to Irenaeus, despise not only the companions of the Lord, but the Lord himself. Irenaeus witnesses the decay of the link between the apostolic and Jesus traditions, yet he does not forfeit that link entirely.

In the *Muratorian Fragment* an apostolic claim for Luke is less explicit (lines 2–8). Yet John, who is called a disciple and not an apostle (cf. Stendahl, 1962: 301, n. 13), writes on behalf of the whole apostolic circle (lines 9–34). He testifies to what he has seen and heard, and the other apostles are his witnesses (lines 13–16, 29–31). Given this link to the apostolic circle and to Jesus, it was perhaps unnecessary for John's apostolic status to be made explicit.[5]

In Acts, Luke posits a link between the apostles and Jesus, indeed, he makes it the fundamental criterion for admission to the apostolic circle. With respect to a replacement for Judas, he writes:

> So one of the men who have accompanied us during all the time that the Lord Jesus went in and out among us, beginning from the baptism of John until the day when he was taken up from us— one of these men must become with us a witness to his resurrection. (Acts 1:21f.)

These words, attributed to Peter, square with what Luke has Peter say in chapter 10:

> And we are witnesses to all that he did both in the country of the Jews and in Jerusalem. They put him to death by hanging him on a tree; but God raised him on the third day and made him manifest, not to all the people but to us who were chosen by God as witnesses, who ate and drank with him after he rose from the dead. (Acts 10:39–41)

Lest there should be any mistake, Luke has Paul repeat the point:

> But God raised him from the dead; and for many days he appeared to those who came up with him from Galilee to Jerusalem, who are now his witnesses to the people. (Acts 13:30f.)

If Luke reads Paul out of the apostolic circle in the narrow sense, he does so in the interests of preserving this historical link between the apostles and Jesus. For Luke, then, an apostle is one who by definition can bear witness to the ministry of Jesus.

---

[5] Line 1 of the *Fragment* is also interesting: the author(?) of the preceding Gospel (Mark?) sets down events at which he was present.

*6.3* If the church from III CE on invoked primarily the criterion of apostolicity to justify its selection of canonical gospels (Kümmel, *RGG*[3] I 1136), it did so in memory of its historical rootage. It is not too much to say that the church sought to ground its tradition in the apostles and Jesus. When apostolicity is turned into an overt criterion, however, it becomes entirely relative—a fact not always noticed by the Fathers. Nevertheless, the interest in apostolic authorship, or at least in the antiquity of the testimony, bears oblique testimony to the linkage required by Luke. In this struggle between liberals and conservatives in the modern period over the relative dates of New Testament books, it was the conservatives who felt that they had to maintain early dates for every book. They were driven, of course, by the fear of having the canonical tradition severed from its historical root. If the liberals were less concerned about the early dates of books, it was because they knew a better way to track the tradition to its ground through the Synoptics and through Acts and Paul. The latter were no less concerned about "wie es eigentlich gewesen ist" (what actually happened).

The interest in apostolic authorship goes together with an interest in place of origin. Birger Gerhardsson (214–220; 274-280) has noted that both Luke and Paul defer to Jerusalem as the source of all tradition. In Luke's presentation, everything leads up to Jerusalem in the Gospel and everything out from Jerusalem in the Acts. As the holy city with its holy temple, Jerusalem is the center of the church, as of Judaism. The rôle it plays in history corresponds to the rôle it will play in the new age. In the same way, Paul refers his case to Jerusalem in Galatians (see especially Gal 2:2). How significant Jerusalem is for Paul is indicated by the fact that he describes his ministry as beginning in Jerusalem (Rom 15:19; cf. Acts 1:8), and at the close of his ministry in Greece he feels he must return to Jerusalem with an offering for the poor saints there. The reason he gives in Rom 15:27 is that Jerusalem has shared its spiritual blessings, and now the Gentiles must share their material blessings. This final and fateful trip to Jerusalem evidently weighs heavily in Paul's mind as he thinks of his future plans. [6]

The reference to the apostolic origins and antiquity of the traditions, as well as the secondary reference to their provenance, point

---

[6] Cf. Irenaeus, *Adv. haer.* 3.3.2, where *the* place has shifted to Rome.

to the ground of the tradition. It is necessary to say "point" rather than "name" because in looking at the content of the tradition, rather than statements about the tradition, it is evident that faith refers itself to Jesus. This is not a characteristic peculiar to the apostolic period, but it continues to dominate the Christian understanding of faith. If faith refers itself to Jesus, it follows that the tradition out of which faith lives must be grounded in Jesus, that is, in a particular place (and time).

Yet it is noticeable that the Fathers fail to give central importance to this point. Of course, it may be claimed that the effort to establish apostolic origin was a means of guaranteeing the link between the tradition and Jesus. This inference would be valid, however, only if it could be taken for granted with Luke that the apostles were, by definition, from the circle of Jesus' disciples, and that the Fathers understood that every canonical book was directly or indirectly dependent upon an apostle thus defined. On any reading Paul constitutes a major block to this line of reasoning. The problem is further complicated by the fact that we can no longer naïvely accept the old traditions respecting apostolic authorship.

It is nevertheless the case that the criterion of apostolicity intends the historical rootage of the tradition in Jesus. An understanding similar to Luke's must lie behind the development of the tradition. What was not always recognized by the Fathers, in applying the criterion rigidly to the literature, was that apostolicity—proximity to Jesus—does not guarantee the link desired. An additional element is required, one already implied in the term apostle. Not only were the apostles witnesses to Jesus, they were *faithful* witnesses to Jesus. In the end we are thrown back upon the fundamental circularity of the process: the church had to gather its norms out of the tradition so as to determine what was in fact normative. That the apostles whose writings were taken up into the canon were faithful witnesses is, in a sense, both the point of departure and the end product of this circuit.

6.4 If the criterion of apostolicity intends, in spite of its obliqueness, the historical rootage of the tradition in Jesus, why did the church not adhere to the point in its explicit form? Why did it allow the essential link to be suppressed? In a general way, it can be said that the distinction between written and oral word with respect to the core of the tradition, the canonical books, applies also to the traditions which grew up about the core of the tradition. That is, the secondary traditions regarding scripture were also crystallized in the process of handing them around and on, with the result that their intent was also lost to view.

The point can be illustrated with reference to the Gospels. The Gospels evidently reflect an understanding which deems it necessary to preserve and hand the Jesus tradition on. Those who were historically able to introduce the Jesus tradition into the life of the primitive church were the original disciples, those who had known Jesus. They were the necessary link in its transmission. As the necessary link, the disciples and apostles could also be taken, uncritically, to be the actual and immediate link (they were responsible, directly or indirectly, for writing down the Jesus tradition). An uncritical tradition which is readily handed around as the common opinion does not have to give a strict account of itself. It may even stand in contradiction to other elements in the general tradition. Thus, in the *Muratorian Fragment* the tradition with respect to Luke (lines 2–8), for whom apostolic authority is not explicitly claimed, stands in curious tension with the reason given for excluding the Shepherd of Hermas (lines 73–80): it cannot be included because it cannot be read among the prophets or the apostles. It is also curious that the Wisdom of Solomon, written by anonymous friends in honor of the royal sage, is acceptable within this framework (lines 69–71).

These inner contradictions in the secondary traditions provide the clue to the intent of the tradition concerning the apostolic origins of the canonical material: the intent was to hold to the historical rootage of the canonical tradition in Jesus. With the tendency to identify the oral word with the written word, however, it was an easy if not inevitable step to ground the tradition in the apostles rather than in Jesus. Once the transfer had been made, the secondary grounding was formalized as tradition and treated in a mechanical way. The result is that the intent of the tradition regarding the apostolic origins of the canonical books was obscured, and the now crystallized tradition was twice removed from its ground. Thus, though "apostolic" at one point intended the historical link with Jesus (Luke), in the process of handing the "apostolic" tradition around a line was drawn, so to speak, immediately behind the written tradition, cutting it off from its ground.

7. *The canon within the canon.* These observations and reflections on the New Testament as tradition and canon may be

rounded off by bringing the matter full circle: what is the New Testament as canon?

In principal the limits of the canonical New Testament are entirely arbitrary. Because faith must always be open to its own ground, it must also be open to other, non-canonical witnesses. Another way of making that assertion is to say: the ground of faith will produce innumerable futures, some authentic, some inauthentic, without respect to the limits of the twenty-seven books of the New Testament. To its authentic futures faith must always be open; it cannot therefore in principle confine itself to a specific body of tradition as its final and complete expression.

On the other hand, the identification of what is canonical (normative) depends on a fresh appropriation of faith mediated by what is already taken as canonical. The formal canon thus has a limiting function, although it is also subject to discriminating appropriation, to the identification of a canon within a canon.

If the canon is subject in principle to expansion, on the one hand, and to reduction, on the other, insofar as the limits of the spectrum of witnesses depend upon faith's prehension of itself the canon has been theologically relativized. But the canon has also been relativized by historical criticism: every witness is discrete chronologically and geographically, no matter how proximate two witnesses may be, and every witness articulates an understanding of faith that is particular to him as witness. The internal unity of the canon has thus been broken by the recognition that the authors and language of the New Testament books are historical.

These reflections on the problem have attempted to show that the relativization of the canon in a formal sense opens the way to understanding the canon in a material sense: the difference between formal and material goes together with the difference between written and oral, between received tradition and the "truth of the gospel." As a purely formal concept, canon conflates ground, tradition, and interpretation. In a material sense, canon distinguishes layers of tradition and adjudicates among them. In that way canon provides access to the ground of faith through a plurality of diverging traditions: the word which once occurred, which once produced faith, may be permitted to occur again. The nature of the recurring word is oral: it sets faith in motion once again.

As oral word, the faith that comes to expression anew will appear over against the canon as written. For the imagination that seizes a new canon within the canon and permits the word of faith to occur again will be "secular": it will emerge "outside" the tradition and yet draw upon it, it will claim the tradition for itself and yet appear to contradict it. Such is the risk attached to word of God.

# Bibliography

Alleman, Beda
  1967    "Metaphor and Antimetaphor." Pp. 103-23 in *Interpretation: The Poetry of Meaning*. Eds. Stanley Romaine Hopper and David L. Miller. New York: Harcourt, Brace & World.

Auden, W. H.
  1957    "The Dyer's Hand: Poetry and the Poetic Process." In *The Anchor Review* 2. Garden City, NY: Doubleday and Co.

Barfield, Owen
  1957    *Saving the Appearances. A Study in Idolatry.* London: Faber & Faber.
  1960    "The Meaning of the Word 'Literal'." Pp. 48–63 in *Metaphor and Symbol*. Eds. L. C. Knights and Basil Cottle. London: Butterworths Scientific Publications.

Black, Matthew
  1967    *An Aramaic Approach to the Gospels and Acts.* 3rd ed. Oxford: At the Clarendon Press.

Blass, F. and A. Debrunner
  1961    *A Greek Grammar of the New Testament and Other Early Christian Literature.* Trans. and rev. Robert W. Funk. Chicago: University of Chicago.

Bornkamm, Günther
  1960    *Jesus of Nazareth.* Trans. Irene & Fraser McLusky, with James M. Robinson. New York: Harper & Row.

Brown, Norman O.
  1967    "Apocalypse: The Place of Mystery in the Life of the Mind." Pp. 7–13 in *Interpretation. The Poetry of Meaning*. Eds. Stanley Romaine Hopper and David L. Miller. New York: Harcourt, Brace & World.

Bultmann, Rudolf
  1957    *Kerygma and Myth.* Trans. R. H. Fuller. Vol. 1. London: S.P.C.K.
  1960    *Existence and Faith.* Trans. Schubert Ogden. New York: Meridian Books.
  1951    *Theology of the New Testament.* Trans. Kendrick Grobel. Vol. 1. New York: Charles Scribner's Sons.
  1965    "The Idea of God and Modern Man." *JThC* 2: 83–95.
  1968    *The History of the Synoptic Tradition.* Rev. ed. New York: Harper and Row.

Burrows, Millar
 1955 "Thy Kingdom Come." *JBL* 74: 1–8.
Buttrick, G. A.
 1962 *The Interpreter's Dictionary of the Bible.* 4 vols. Nashville:
  Abingdon.
von Campenhausen, Hans, et. al.
 1957 *Die Religion in Geschichte und Gegenwart.* 5 vols. Tübingen: J.
  C. B. Mohr (Paul Siebeck).
Cassirer, Ernst
 1957 *The Philosophy of Symbolic Forms.* Vol. III. *The Phenomenology
  of Knowledge.* Trans. Ralph Manheim. New Haven: Yale
  University.
Conzelmann, Hans
 1968 "Present and Future in the Synoptic Tradition." *JThC* 5: 26–44.
Crossan, John Dominic
 1973 *In Parables.* New York: Harper & Row.
 1974a "The Good Samaritan: Towards a Generic Definition of the
  Parable." *Semeia* 2: 82–112.
 1974b "Parable and Example in the Teaching of Jesus." *Semeia* 1: 63–
  104.
 1974c "The Servant Parables of Jesus." *Semeia* 1: 17–62.
 1974d "Structuralist Analysis and the Parables of Jesus." *Semeia* 1: 192–
  221.
Culley, Robert C.
 1976 *Studies in the Structure of Hebrew Narrative.* Philadelphia:
  Fortress, and Missoula, MT: Scholars Press.
Cullmann, Oscar
 1950 *Christ and Time.* Philadelphia: Westminster.
 1956 "The Plurality of the Gospels as a Theological Problem in
  Antiquity." Pp. 39–54 in *The Early Church: Studies in Early
  Christian History and Theology.* Philadelphia: Westminster.
Dahl, N. A.
 1962 "The Particularity of the Pauline Epistles as a Problem in the
  Ancient Church." Pp. 261–271 in *Neotestamentica et Patristica.*
  Leiden: E. J. Brill.
Deissmann, A.
 1910 *Light from the Ancient East: The New Testament Illustrated by
  Recently Discovered Texts of the Graeco-Roman World.* Trans. L.
  R. M. Strachan. London: Hodder & Stoughton.
Denniston, J. D.
 1952 *Greek Prose Style.* Oxford: At the Clarendon Press.
Dibelius, Martin
 n.d. *From Tradition to Gospel.* New York: Charles Scribner's Sons.
Dodd, C. H.
 1936 *The Parables of the Kingdom.* 3rd. ed. London: Nisbet & Co.

Douglas, Wallace W.
1966    "The Meanings of 'Myth' in Modern Criticism." Pp. 119–128 in
        *Myth and Literature: Contemporary Theory and Practice.* Ed.
        John B. Vickery. Lincoln: University of Nebraska.
Dundes, Alan
1964    "Texture, Text, and Context." *Southern Folklore Quarterly* 28, 4
        (December 1964): 251–65.
Ebeling, Gerhard
1963    *Word and Faith.* Trans. James W. Leitch. London: SCM.
1967    *The Nature of Faith.* Trans. Ronald Gregor Smith. Philadelphia:
        Fortress.
Exler, Francis Xavier, Jr.
1923    *The Form and Function of the Ancient Greek Letter: A Study in
        Greek Epistolography.* Washington: Catholic University of
        America.
Fackenheim, Emil L.
1961    *Metaphysics and Historicity.* Milwaukee: Marquette University.
Frye, Northrop
1963    "Myth, Fiction, and Displacement." Pp. 21–39 in *Fables of
        Identity: Studies in Poetic Mythology.* New York: Harcourt, Brace
        & World.
1967    *Anatomy of Criticism.* New York: Atheneum.
Funk, Robert W.
1964    "'How Do You Read?' (Luke 10:25–37)." *Int* 18: 56–61.
1965    "The Old Testament in Parable: A Study of Luke 10:25–37."
        *Encounter* 26,2: 251–267.
1966    *Language, Hermeneutic, and Word of God.* New York: Harper &
        Row.
1974a   "Structure in the Narrative Parables of Jesus." *Semeia* 2: 51–73.
1974b   "The Good Samaritan as Metaphor." *Semeia* 2: 74–81.
Gaston, Lloyd
1973    *Horae Synopticae Electronicae: Word Statistics of the Synoptic
        Gospels.* Sources for Biblical Study 3. Missoula, MT: Society of
        Biblical Literature.
Gerhardsson, Birger
1961    *Memory and Manuscript: Oral Tradition and Written Trans-
        mission in Rabbinic Judaism and Early Christianity.* Lund: C. W.
        K. Gleerup, and Copenhagen: Ejnar Munksgaard.
Gleason, H. A., Jr.
1968    "Contrastive Analysis in Discourse Structure." Georgetown
        Monograph Series on Languages and Linguistics 21: 39–63.
Grant, R. M.
1963    *Historical Introduction to the New Testament.* New York: Harper
        & Row.
1961    *The Earliest Lives of Jesus.* New York: Harper & Brothers.

Grässer, E.
1957    *Das Problem der Parusieverzögerung in den synoptischen Evangelien und in der Apostelgeschichte.* Beihefte zur *ZNW* 22. Berlin: Alfred Töpelmann.

Gusdorf, Georges
1965    *Speaking.* Trans. Paul T. Brockelman. Evanston, IL: Northwestern University.

Heidegger, Martin
1962    *Being and Time.* Trans. J. Macquarrie and E. Robinson. London: SCM.

Hopper, Stanley R.
1965    "Wallace Stevens: The Sundry Comforts of the Sun." Pp. 13–31 in *Four Ways of Modern Poetry.* Ed. Nathan A. Scott, Jr. Richmond, VA: John Knox.
1967    "Introduction." Pp. ix–xxii in *Interpretation: The Poetry of Meaning.* Eds. Stanley Romaine Hopper and David L. Miller. New York: Harcourt, Brace & World.

Jeremias, Joachim
1963    *The Parables of Jesus.* Rev. ed. New York: Charles Scribner's Sons.

Jülicher, Adolf
1931    *Einleitung in das NT.* Tübingen: J. C. B. Mohr.

Kafka, Franz
1961    *Parables and Paradoxes.* New York: Schocken Books.

Karlsson, Gustav
1956    "Formelhaftes in Paulusbriefen?" *Eranos* 54: 138–141.

Käsemann, Ernst
1969    "Blind Alleys in the 'Jesus of History' Controversy." Pp. 23–65 in *New Testament Questions of Today.* Philadelphia: Fortress.

Kittel, Gerhard and Gerhard Friedrich
1933–   *Theologisches Wörterbuch zum Neuen Testament.* Stuttgart: W. Kohlhammer.

Koskenniemi, Heikki
1956    *Studien zur Idee und Phraseologie des griechischen Briefes bis 400 n. Chr.* Annales Academiae Scientiarum Fennicae (Sarja-Ser. B. Nide-Tom., 102,2). Helsinki: Akateeminen Kirjakauppa.

Knox, John
1956    "A Note on the Text of Romans." *NTS* 2: 191–193.
1964    "Romans 15:14–33 and Paul's Conception of His Apostolic Mission," *JBL* 83: 1–11.

Kümmel, W. G.
1957    *Promise and Fulfilment.* Trans. Dorothea M. Barton. London: SCM.

Kümmel, W. G., P. Feine and J. Behm
1966    *Introduction to the New Testament.* Trans. A. J. Matill, Jr. Nashville: Abingdon.

Leach, Edmund
1972    "Anthropological Aspects of Language: Animal Categories and
        Verbal Abuse." Pp. 39–67 in *Mythology. Selected Readings*. Ed.
        Pierre Maranda. Baltimore: Penguin Books.
Liddel, Henry George and Robert Scott
1940    *A Greek-English Lexicon*. 9th ed. by H. S. Jones and R.
        McKenzie. 2 vols. Oxford: The Clarendon Press.
McKenzie, John L.
1974    "Primitive History: Form Criticism." Pp. 87–99 in SBL Seminar
        Papers I. Missoula, MT: Scholars Press.
Manson, T. W.
1962    *Studies in the Gospels and Epistles*. Ed. M. Black. Manchester:
        Manchester University.
Merleau-Ponty, Maurice
1964    *Signs*. Trans. R. C. McCleary. Evanston, IL: Northwestern
        University.
Michel, O.
1957    *Der Brief an die Römer*. Göttingen: Vandenhoeck & Ruprecht.
Miller, Henry
1961    *Tropic of Capricorn*. New York: Grove.
Miller, J. Hillis
1963    *The Disappearance of God: Five Nineteenth Century Writers*.
        Cambridge, MA: Harvard University.
Moule, C. F. D.
1953    *An Idiom-Book of New Testament Greek*. Cambridge: At the
        University Press.
Moulton, J. H. and G. Milligan
1949    *The Vocabulary of the Greek Testament, Illustrated from the
        Papyri and Other Non-Literary Sources*. 2nd ed. London: Hodder
        & Stoughton.
Mullins, Terence Y.
1962    "Petition as a Literary Form." *NovT* 5: 46–54.
Olrik, Axel
1965    "Epic Laws of Folk Narrative." Pp. 129–41 in *The Study of
        Folklore*. Ed. Alan Dundes. Englewood Cliffs, NJ: Prentice Hall.
Olsson, B.
1974    *Structure and Meaning in the Fourth Gospel. A Text-Linguistic
        Analysis of John 2:1–11 and 4:1–41*. Lund, Sweden: CWK
        Gleerup.
Overbeck, Franz
1954    *Über die Anfang der patristischen Literatur*. Wissenschaftliche
        Buchgesellschaft = Historische Zeitschrift 48 [1882] 417–472.
Patte, Daniel
1974    "An Analysis of Narrative Structure and the Good Samaritan."
        *Semeia* 2: 1–26.

Perrin, Norman
1963    *The Kingdom of God in the Teaching of Jesus.* Philadelphia:
        Westminster.
1967    *Rediscovering the Teaching of Jesus.* New York: Harper & Row.
1971    "The Modern Interpretation of the Parables of Jesus and the
        Problem of Hermeneutics." *Int* 25: 131–48.
1976    *Jesus and the Language of the Kingdom.* Philadelphia: Fortress.
Propp, Vladimir
1968    *Morphology of the Folktale.* 2nd ed. Austin: University of Texas.
Rigaux, Béda
1964    *Paulus und seine Briefe: Der Stand der Forschung.* Biblische
        Handbibliothek II. Munich: Rösel-Verlag.
Sanders, Jack T.
1962    "The Transition from Opening Epistolary Thanksgiving to Body
        in the Letters of the Pauline Corpus." *JBL* 81: 348–362.
Schmithals, Walter
1971    *Gnosticism in Corinth: An Investigation of the Letter to the
        Corinthians.* Trans. John E. Steely. Nashville, TN: Abingdon.
1957    "Die Irrlehrer des Philipperbriefes." *ZThK* 54: 297–341.
1959    "Die Irrlehrer von Rm 16:17–20." *ST* 13: 1–19.
1960    "Zur Abfassung und ältestem Sammlung der paulinischen
        Hauptbriefe." *ZNW* 51: 224–45.
1964    "Die Thessalonicherbriefe als Briefkompositionen." Pp 295–315
        in *Zeit und Geschichte. Dankesgabe an Rudolf Bultmann zum 80.
        Geburtstag.* Ed. E. Dinkler. Tübingen: J. C. B. Mohr (Paul
        Siebeck).
Schubert, Paul
1939    *Form and Function of the Pauline Thanksgivings.* Beihefte zur
        *ZNW* 20.
Spitzer, Leo
1967    *Linguistics and Literary History: Essays in Stylistics.* Princeton,
        NJ: Princeton University.
Stanford, W. B.
1967    *The Sound of Greek. Studies in the Greek Theory and Practice of
        Euphony.* Berkeley: University of California.
Steiner, George
1967    *Language and Silence: Essays on Language, Literature, and the
        Inhuman.* New York: Atheneum.
1971    *Extraterritorial: Papers on Literature and the Language Revo-
        lution.* New York: Atheneum.
Stendahl, Krister
1962    "The Apocalypse of John and the Epistles of Paul in the
        Muratorian Fragment." Pp. 239–245 in *Current Issues in New
        New Testament Interpretation.* Eds. W. Klassen and G. F.
        Snyder. New York: Harper.

1968     *The School of St. Matthew and Its Use of the New Old Testament.*
Philadelphia: Fortress.

Stevens, Wallace
1954     *The Collected Poems of Wallace Stevens.* New York: Alfred A.
Knopf.

Strack, H. L. and P. Billerbeck
1956     *Kommentar zum Neuen Testament aus Talmud und Midrash.*
Munich: C. H. Beck.

Taber, Charles Russell
1966     *The Structure of Sango Narrative.* 2 vols. Hartford Studies in
Linguistics 17. Hartford, CT: The Hartford Seminary Foundation.

Theissen, Gerd
1974     *Urchristliche Wundergeschichten. Ein Beitrag zur formgeschicht-
lichen Erforschung der synoptischen Evangelien.* Gütersloh: Gerd
Mohn.

Toelken, J. Barre
1969     "The 'Pretty Language' of Yellowman: Genre, Mode, and
Texture in Navaho Coyote Narratives." *Genre* II, 3: 211–235.

Via, Dan O.
1967     *The Parables. Their Literary and Existential Dimension.*
Philadelphia: Fortress.

1971     "The Relationship of Form to Content in the Parables: The
Wedding Feast." *Int* 25,2: 171–84.

1974     "Parable and Example Story: A Literary-Structuralist Approach."
*Semeia* 1: 105–33.

Vischer, Lukas
1956     "Die Rechfertigung der Schriftstellerei in der alten Kirche."
*Theologische Zeitschrift* 12: 320–336.

Wilder, Amos
1959     "Eschatological Imagery and Earthly Circumstance." *NTS* 5: 229–
245.

1962     "Form-History and the Oldest Tradition." Pp. 3–13 in
*Neotestamentica et Patristica.* Ed. W. van Unnik. Leiden. E. J.
Brill.

1971     *Early Christian Rhetoric: The Language of the Gospel.*
Cambridge, MA: Harvard University.

Yselling, Samuel
1970     "Structuralism and Psychoanalysis in the Work of Jacques
Lacan." *International Philosophical Quarterly* 10: 102–117.

# Index of Parables

Bold numbers refer to chapters. Numbers following a colon indicate sections and sub-sections. For example, **11**:2.3 means chapter 11, section 2, sub-section 3.

Narrative Parables
  Good Samaritan (Luke 10:30–35) **3**;
    **4**; **5**:2, 4, 6, 7
  Great Supper (Luke 14:16–
    24//Matt 22:1–10) **4**; **5**:2, 4, 6;
    **6**:3
  Laborers in the Vineyard (Matt
    20:1–15) **2**:3.1, 4.1, 4.2, 4.32; **4**;
    **5**:2, 4, 6; **6**:3
  Prodigal Son (Luke 15:11–32) **2**:3.3;
    **4**; **5**:2, 4, 6; **6**:3
  Rich Man and Lazarus (Luke
    16:19–31) **4**:1, 2, 8.3, 8.4
  Talents (Matt 25:14–30//Luke
    19:12–27) **2**:3.1, 3.3; **4**, esp. 8.1;
    **5**:2, 3
  Ten Maidens (Matt 25:1–13) **2**:3.1;
    **4**, esp. 8.1, 8.4; **5**:1, 2, 3
  Wicked Tenants (Mark 12:1–
    9//Matt 21:33–41//Luke 20:9–
    16) **4**:1, 2, 3.31, 4, 8.2, 8.3; **6**:4
  Unmerciful Servant (Matt 18:23–
    34) **2**:3.3; **4**
  Unjust Servant (Matt 18:23–34)
    **2**:3.3; **4**

Other Parables
  Leaven (Matt 13:33//Luke 13:20–
    21) **6**:3
  Lost Coin (Luke 15:8–10) **4**:1; **5**:6;
    **6**:3
  Lost Sheep (Matt 18:12–14//Luke
    15:4–7) **4**:1; **5**:6; **6**:3
  Mustard Seed ((Matt 13:31–
    32//Mark 4:30–32//Luke

  13:18–19) **6**:3
  Pearl of Great Price (Matt 13:45f.)
    **6**:3
  Pharisee and Publican (Luke 18:9–
    14) **4**:1
  Seed Growing of Itself (Mark 4:26–
    29) **6**:3
  Servant's Wages (Luke 17:7–10) **4**:1
  Sower (Mark 4:3–8//Matt 13:3–
    8//Luke 8:5–8) **4**:1; **5**:6
  Treasure in the Field (Matt 13:44)
    **6**:3
  Two Debtors (Luke 7:41–43) **6**:3
  Two Sons (Matt 21:28–31a) **4**:1
  Unjust Judge (Luke 18:1–8) **4**:1
  Wheat and Tares (Matt 13:24–30)
    **6**:3

# Index of Citations

Bold numbers refer to chapters. Numbers following a colon indicate sections and sub-sections. For example, **11**:2.3 means chapter 11, section 2, sub-section 3.

Matthew
  3:7–10 (par)—**6**:4
  10:23b—**6**:4
  12:39—**6**:3
  18:27—**2**:3.3
  18:28—**6**:3
  18:32—**2**:3.2
  18:34—**2**:3.3
  20:1—**2**:3.1
  20:8—**2**:3.1
  25:6—**2**:3.1
  25:11—**2**:3.1
  25:15—**2**:3.1
  25:19—**2**:3.1
  25:26—**2**:3.3

Mark
  2:18ff.—**6**:4
  7:9—**11**:2.1
  7:13—**11**:2.1
  7:14–23—**11**:2.1
  8:12—**6**:3
  10:1ff.—**11**:2.1
  10:35–45—**1**:1
  13—**6**:2
  13:30—**6**:4

Luke
  1:1–4—**11**:3.3
  10:33—**2**:3.3
  11:20—**6**:3
  11:29—**6**:3
  11:32—**6**:3
  14:21—**2**:3.3
  15:28—**2**:3.3

John
  7:46—**11**:6.1
  21:25—**11**:4.2

Acts
  1:8—**11**:6.2
  1:21f.—**11**:6.2
  5:1–11—**7**:5.2
  10:33—**8**:1 n. 9
  10:39–41—**11**:6.2
  13:30f.—**11**:6.2
  20:35—**11**:6.1

Romans
  1:1–15:13—**7**:6.2
  1:8ff.—**7**:1, 2, 4, 6.2
  3:25—**9**:3.1
  6:5ff.—**9**:3.1
  8:32ff.—**9**:3.1
  15:14–33—**7**:1, 2, 4, 6.2
  15:19—**7**:5.2;—**11**:6.2
  15:27—**11**:6.2
  15:28b—**7**:6.1

1 Corinthians
  2:4—**7**:5.2
  4:1–21—**7**:6.2 n. 22
  4:14–21—**7**:1, 2, 3, 4; **8**:2
  4:18ff.—**7**:5.2
  4:19—**7**:6.1
  5–15—**11**:4.1
  5:3—**7**:5.1 and n. 18
  5:3–5—**7**:5.2
  7:10—**11**:3.2
  7:25—**11**:3.2

11:2—**11**:3.2
13:1-13—**11**:3.2
13:11—**11**:4.0
14:37f.—**7**:4 n. 11
15:1—**11**:3.2
15:3—**11**:3.2
15:3ff.—**6**:4; **9**:3.1
16:1-24—**7**:6.2 n. 22
16:1-11—**7**:1, 2, 3, 4
16:5—**7**:6.1
16:12—**7**:1, 2, 3, 4
16:21—**7**:4 n. 14

2 Corinthians
1-7—**7**:6.1
1:1-2:13, 7:5-16—**7**:1 n. 1
1:10—**7**:2 n. 4
1:23—**7**:4 n. 9, 5.2
1:23ff.—**7**:4
1:24a—**7**:4 n. 9
2:3f.—**7**:4 n. 9
2:9—**7**:4 n. 9
2:14-17—**7**:5.2
3:1ff.—**11**:2.2
5:14f.—**9**:3.1
5:17—**9**:3.1
5:21—**9**:3.1
7:6f.—**7**:5.2 n. 20
7:13b-16—**7**:5.2 n. 20
8:16-23—**7**:1, 2, 3, 4
9:1-5—**7**:1, 2, 3, 4
10:1f.—**7**:5.1 n. 18
10:3-4—**7**:5.2
10:10f.—**7**:5.1 n. 18
10:11—**7**:5.2
11:12—**7**:5.2
12:14-13:10—**7**:1, 2, 3, 4
12:14—**7**:6.1
13:1-4—**7**:5.2
13:1—**7**:6.1
13:2—**7**:5.1 n. 18
13:10—**7**:4 n. 9, 5.1 n. 18, 5.2

Galatians
1:1-2:21—**1**:1; **11**:3.2
1:4—**9**:3.1

1:9—**11**:3.2
2:2—**11**:6.2
3:13—**9**:3.1
4:12-20—**7**:1, 2, 4
4:20—**7**:6.1
6:11—**7**:4

Ephesians
2:29—**11**:6.1

Philippians
1:1-2:18—**7**:4.2
1:3ff.—**8**:1
1:3-11—**7**:4.2
1:12-26—**7**:3
1:25—**7**:6.1
1:27—**7**:5.1 n. 18
2:2—**7**:5.1 n. 18
2:5-11—**9**:3.1
2:17f.—**7**:3
2:19-24—**7**:1, 2, 3, 4
2:24—**7**:6.1
2:25-30—**7**:1, 2, 3, 4
3:2ff.—**7**:6.1
3:3ff.—**9**:3.2
4:9—**11**:3.2
4:10ff.—**8**:1
4:14—**8**:1 n. 9
4:14-18—**7**:5.2 n. 20

Colossians
2:5—**7**:5.1 and n. 18
2:6—**11**:3.2

1 Thessalonians
2:13—**11**:3.2
2:17-3:13—**7**:1, 2, 3, 4
2:17—**7**:5.1 n. 18
2:19f.—**7**:5.2 n. 20
3:6-8—**7**:5.2 n. 20
3:10—**7**:6.1
4-5—**11**:3.2
4:1—**11**:3.2
4:2—**11**:3.2
4:15—**11**:3.2
5:27—**7**:4 n. 14

2 Thessalonians
2:15—**11**:3.2
3:2—**7**:2 n. 4
3:6—**11**:3.2
3:17—**7**:4 n. 14

2 Timothy
2:2—**11**:3.3
3:11—**7**:2 n. 4
3:14f.—**11**:3.3
4:17f.—**7**:2 n. 4

Philemon
4—**8**:1 n. 6
7—**8**:1 n. 6
8—**8**:1 n. 6
21f.—**7**:1, 2, 4
22—**7**:6.1

Hebrews
13:23—**8**:3

James
2:1—**8**:1 n. 9
2:19—**8**:1 n. 9

2 Peter
3:16—**11**:6.1
2 John
1-13—**8**:0, 1, 2, 3
1-3—**8**:2
1f.—**8**:1
2 —**8**:1, 3
4-11—**8**:2
4f.—**8**:1
4—**8**:1
5-6a—**8**:1
5—**8**:1
12f.—**8**:1, 2
12—**8**:2; **11**:2.2

3 John
2—**8**:2
3-8—**8**:2
3-4—**8**:2
3f.—**8**:1

3—**8**:1
3a—**8**:1
5-6a—**8**:1
5f.—**8**:1
5—**8**:1, 2
6b—**8**:1
9-10—**8**:2, 3
9—**8**:2
11—**8**:2, 3
12—**8**:1, 2
13f.—**8**:1, 2, 3
13—**11**:2.2

Jude
3—**11**:3.3, 6.1

Revelation
2:5b—**7**:5.2
2:16—**7**:5.2
2:25—**7**:5.2
3:3b—**7**:5.2
3:11—**7**:5.2


Apostolic Fathers

Barnabas
1:12—**8**:1 n. 5
1 Clement
42:1-3—**11**:3

Ignatius
Smyrnaeans 10:1—**8**:1

Polycarp
Philippians 1:1-2—**8**:1 n. 5
14:1—**8**:1


Church Fathers

Eusebius
H.E. 2.23—**11**:4.1
2.25.1-3—**11**:4.1
3.25.6-7—**11**:6.2

3.39.3-4—**11**:2.2
5.18.5—**11**:4.1
6.2—**11**:4.2
7.25.7-10—**11**:4.1

Irenaeus
Adv. haer. 3.1.1-2—**11**:6.2
3.1.1—**11**:6.1
3.11.7—**11**:4.2
3.11.8—**11**:4.2

Muratorian Fragment
lines 2-8—**11**:6.2, 4
5—**11**:4.1
9-34—**11**:6.2, 4
15—**11**:4.1
19—**11**:4.0, 2
34—**11**:4.1
48-59—**11**:4.1
59-63—**11**:4.1
68f.—**11**:4.1
69-71—**11**:6.4
73-80—**11**:6.4

Origen
Commentary on John 5:7—**11**:4.2,
    5.1
6:18—**11**:4.1

Victorinus of Pettau
Commentary on the Apocalypse
    I.vii—**11**:4.1
De fabrica mundi xi—**11**:4.1

# Index of Authors

Bold numbers refer to chapters. Numbers following a colon indicate sections and sub-sections. For example, **11**:2.3 means chapter 11, section 2, sub-section 3.

Alleman, Beda **9**:4 n. 10
Arnold, Matthew **9**:4
Auden, W. H. **9**:6
Barfield, Owen **9**:2, 6
Barnett, Albert **11**:4.1
Barth, Karl **9**:1
Beare, Frank W. **11**:6.1
Beckett, Samuel **2**:5.21
Beyer, H. W. **11**:1.2
Black, Matthew **2**:4.3
Blass, F. and Debrunner, A. **7**:6.1; **8**:1 and n. 4
Bornkamm, Günther **6**:1, 2, 3; **11**:2.1
Brown, Norman O. **9**:2, 3.2
Buber, Martin **9**:4
Bultmann, Rudolf **4**:1.1, 3; **6**:3, 4; **9**:0, 1, 3.1, 3.2, 4; **11**:3.1
Burrows, Millar **6**:5
Cassirer, Ernst **6**:5
Conzelmann, Hans **6**:3, 4; **11**:6.1
Crossan, J. Dominic **3**:0; **4**:3.1
Cullmann, Oscar **6**:5; **11**:4.2
Dahl, Nils **11**:4.1
Deissmann, A. **7**:3 n. 5
Denniston, J. D. **2**:4.3
Dibelius, Martin **11**:3.1, 3.2
Dodd, C. H. **3**:1.1; **4**:1
Douglas, Wallace W. **9**:6
Dundes, Alan **2**:5.2
Ebeling, Gerhard **11**:2.4, 2.6
Exler, F. X. J. **8**:0, 1
Fackenheim, Emil **6**:5
Frye, Northrop **9**:2, 4, 5
Gaston, Lloyd **2**:2.1

Gerhardsson, Birger **11**:2.4, 3.1, 3.2, 6.3
Gleason, H. A., Jr. **3**:2
Grant, Robert M. **11**:3.4, 4.0
Grässer, E. **6**:4
Greimas, A. J. **5**:1
Heidegger, M. **6**:5; **9**:4; **11**:1
Hopper, Stanley **9**:5
Ionesco, Eugene **2**:5.21
Jeremias, Joachim **3**:1.1; **6**:3, 4
Jülicher, Adolf **3**:1.1; **11**:1
Kafka, Franz **2**:5.21; **9**:4, 5
Karlsson, Gustav **7**:5.1
Käsemann, Ernst **6**:1
Knox, John **7**:5.2 n. 19, 6.1, 6.2
Koester, Helmut **11**:2.2
Koskenniemi, Heikki **7**:4 n. 12, 5.1, **8**:1
Kümmel, W. G. **6**:3, 5; **8**:1; **11**:6.2
Lacan, Jacques **1**:5
Leach, Edmund **1**:3.2
Manson, T. W. **7**:6.2
Merleau-Ponty, Maurice **9**:2
Michel, O. **7**:6.2
Miller, Henry **9**:6
Miller, J. Hillis **9**:4 n. 8
Moule, C. F. D. **7**:6.1
Mullins, Terence **8**:1
Orlik, Axel **4**:3
Overbeck, Franz **11**:2.2
Patte, Daniel **5**:1
Perrin, Norman **6**:1, 2, 3, 4
Propp, Vladimir **5**:1
Rigaux, Beda **8**:0 n. 1
Sanders, Jack T. **8**:1 n. 6

Schmithals, Walter 7:5.1 n. 17
Schubert, Paul 8:0, 1
Spitzer, Leo 2:5.22
Stanford, W. B. 2:4.3
Steiner, George 1:1
Stendahl, Krister 11:4.1, 6.1
Taber, Charles 2:4.1
Toelken, J. Barre 2:5.2
Via, Dan O. 3:0; 4:2, 2.1, 3.1, 4, 6.2
Vischer, Lukas 11:2.2
Wilder, Amos N. 6:5; 11:2.1, 2.2, 2.4

# Index of Subjects

**Bold numbers** refer to chapters. Numbers following a colon indicate sections and sub-sections. For example, **11**:2.3 means chapter 11, section 2, sub-section 3.

actants
  as functions **4**:5; **5**:4, 6
Acts **1**:1; **11**:6.1
alliteration **2**:4.3
animals, classification of **1**:3.2
apocalyptic
  eschatology **6**:1, 3, 4
  Son of Man **6**:2, 4
  as comic **9**:5
apostles (and apostolicity) **11**:6.0, 6.1,
  6.2, 6.3, 6.4
Apostolic Fathers **11**:2.2
Aqiba, Rabbi **11**:2.4
assonance **2**:4.3
Athanasius **11**:1.2

canon (and canonicity) **11**:1, 3.4, 6.0
  relativization of **11**:7
  within the canon **11**:7
  relation of inspiration to **11**:4.1, 4.3
Colossians **8**:3
comedy **9**:5
commentary **1**:4
cross **9**:5

demythologizing **9**:1, 3.1, 4, 6
Dionysius of Alexander **11**:4.1
dissimilarity
  as criterion **6**:1

Ephesians **8**:3; **11**:4.1
epistles, catholic **11**:4.1
eschatology **6**
  consistent **6**:3.5
  as historical problem **6**:1, 3

realized **6**:3, 5
  as theological problem **6**:1, 3, 5
everydayness **5**:3, 4, 5
  as leveling **6**:1, 4, 5; **9**:2; **10**:1.2, 1.3,
    2.1; **11**:4.1

fiction **9**:4
flesh (sarx) **9**:3.2

gospels **1**:1
  four **1**:2.42; **11**:4.0, 4.2, 4.3
  of John **9**:2, 3.1; **11**:4.2
  of Luke **11**:2.3, 4.2
  Mark **11**:4.2
  Matthew **11**:2.3, 4.2
  plurality of **11**:4.0
Greek, Hellenistic **2**

Hebrews **8**:3
hero **9**:4
hiddenness **9**:1
history
  as event **1**:2
  as mystery **1**:2.41, 2.42

illusion **9**:5
Irenaeus **11**:4.0, 6.1
irony **9**:4

James **8**:1 n. 2
Jesus
  authentic tradition **6**:2, 3
  criteria for **6**:1
  and contemporary Judaism **6**:2
  founder of Christian tradition **1**:5

identification of **11**:3.1
as instigator of faith **11**:5.3
and law **11**:2.1
message of **4**:7; **9**:1
as name **1**:4
and novel speech forms **11**:2.1
and oral word **11**:2.1
as referent of tradition **11**:3.4, 4.0,
  5.1, 5.3, 6.3
and social space **1**:3.3
understanding of time **6**; 6:3
words as tradition **11**:5.3, 6.1
Jerusalem
as center of mission **11**:6.2

kerygma
of earliest church **6**:4; **9**:1; **11**:3.2
humiliation/exaltation **6**:4
hiddenness/openness **6**:4
kingdom of God **1**:1
temporality of **6**
tension between present and future
  **6**:2, 3
as future **6**:2
as comedy **6**:3
knowledge, pre-conceptual **3**:1.2
kyrios **1**:1

language
abstract **1**:5; **9**:4
as assertion **9**:4
discursive **9**:4
drift **1**:3.2, 3
event **9**:1
as grid **1**:3.2, 3
and idolatry **9**:2, 3.1, 3.2
mode of **3**; **9**:5
mythological **9**:1, 3, 4
and names **1**:3.1
as perception **1**:3; **9**:1
as problem **1**:4; **10**
as promise **1**:5
and reality **1**:0; **3**:1.2; **9**:1, 2, 3.2, 6
and religion **1**:0
and social space **1**:3.2
study of **1**:0

and taboos **1**:3.2
tradition, see tradition
and world **1**:0; **9**:2, 3.1, 3.2, 4
letter, common Hellenistic **7**:3 nn. 5, 7,
  4.1 nn. 12, 16, 5.1; **8**:0, 1, 2
thanksgiving **8**:1
petition **8**:1
letter of recommendation **8**:1
letter, Pauline **8**:0
apostolic *parousia*
as personal presence **7**:0, 4.1, 5.1, 5.2
as structural element **7**:5.1, 6.2; **8**:2,
  3; **11**:2,2
significane of **7**:5.1, 5.2, 6.1
apostolic emissary **7**:0, 4, 5.1
body of **7**:1 n. 1, 5.1 n. 17; **8**:3
Galatians, date of **7**:6.1
as homily **8**:3
paraenesis **7**:1, 4.2, 5.1 n. 17, 6.2; **8**:3
Romans, character of **7**:6.2
thanksgiving **7**:4.1, 4.2, 6.2; **8**:3
travelogue **7**:0
liberalism **9**:1, 4
literal and literalism **3**:1.1; **9**:1, 2, 3, 4,
  5, 6
literally literal **9**:1, 3.1
literally non-literal **9**:0, 1
non-literal **3**:1.1
biblical **1**:3.3
logic **1**:5; **4**:7; **9**:3.1

Marcion **11**:4.1, 4.3, 5.4, 6.1
metaphor **3**; **9**:3, 4
miracle story **5**:1
myth **9**:0, 1, 3, 4
Gnostic **9**:3.1

narrative
participation of auditor in **3**:1.2
perspective **1**:2.41; **3**:2, 3, 4
repetition in **2**:4.1, 4.2
wordplay **2**:4.2

oral word **8**:3; **11**:2
Origen **11**:2.2

painter, painting 9:2
parable 1:1
  as allegory 6:3
  application of 3:4
  and auditor 5:3, 7
  composition in Greek 2:5
  as declension of reality 4:7
  episode of 4:4
  as example story 3
  as foundational language 9:4
  of grace 3:2, 5; 5:4
  interpretation of 3:5
  as invitation 3:4
  as message 4:7
  as metaphor 3; 6:3
  narrative 2; 3; 4; 5
  participants in: see participant
  plot 2:2.3; 4; 5:2
  reading 3:2
  as satire 6:3
  scenes in 4:1
  as surprise 3:5; 4:5.2, 5.4, 6.1; 5:4, 7;
    6:1
  as unfinished 3:4; 4:7
  vocabulary of 2:2, 5
paronomasia 2:4.3
*parousia* 6:2, 4
  delay of 6:3
  presbyterial 8:2, 3
participant 4
  as actants (functions) 4:5; 5:4, 6, 7
  principal 2:3.2
  determiner 4:2, 3, 4, 5, 6.2, 7; 5:3, 4,
    5, 6, 7
  as authority figure 4:6.2; 5:6
  change in scale 4:1.3
  respondent 4:2, 3, 4, 5; 5:3, 4, 6, 7
  subordinate 4:1.2
  response of the just 4:5.1, 5.4, 6.1,
    6.2, 6.3, 7; 5:4, 6, 7
  recipient of grace 4:5.2, 5.4, 6.1, 6.2,
    6.3, 7; 5: 4, 6, 7
  sets 5:2, 6
  instrument of justice/grace 4:5.3,
    5.4, 6.2, 6.3; 5:5, 7
  reversal of expectations 4:6.1, 7; 5:4;
    9:5

expectation confirmed 5:3
Pastorals 11:4.1
Paul
  apostleship 11:3.2
  letters, particularity of 11:4.0, 4.1
  theology of 9:1, 3, 11:3.2
Philemon 8:1, 3; 11:4.1
Philo 9:2
plot 5:1
poetry, poet 1:5; 9:0, 1, 2, 5, 6
poiesis 9:2, 3.2
pronouncement stories 1:1

realism 9:4
redemptive (salvation) event 9:3.1, 3.2
referent
  as accessible and inaccessible 1:2
resurrection 9:5
Revelation of John 9:5

scientism 9:6
semantic code 1:0
Shepherd of Hermas 11:1.2, 6.4
Son of man 6:4
spirit (pneuma) 9:2
symbol system 1:0

temporality
  coincidence of horizons 6:3
  indefiniteness of future 6:3
  everyday understanding of 6:3, 4, 5
Tertullian 11:4.1
theology 9:0, 2, 6
tradition
  authoritative 11:3.2, 6.1
  building 1:1
  and common understanding 11:4.1,
    4.3
  as confession 11:5.3
  continuity/discontinuity 6:1
  as criticism of itself 11:4.2
  crystallization of 11:3.4, 6.4
  in gospels 11:6.4
  ground of 1:2.42, 5; 9:4; 11:4.3, 5.1,
    6, 7
  interpretation of 11:3.2, 3.3, 3.4, 4.3,
    5.4

layers 1:2; 11:5.4, 7
and memory 1:2.2, 2.3, 2.4; 6:1
New Testament as 1:1
oral 1:2.42; 11:2, 6.4
particularity 11:4.0, 4.1, 4.3, 5.2, 5.4
plurality 1:2.42; 11:4.0, 4.2, 4.3, 5.2,
  5.4
referent of 1:2
see also Jesus, as referent of tradition
and reflectivity 1:1
religious 1:0, 1
secular 11:7
written 1:2.42; 11:2, 6.4
and understanding 11:5.4
translation 1:4

Wisdom of Solomon 11:6.4
word of God 9:4; 11:2.5, 2.6, 7
cf. poiesis, poetry
world 3:1.2; 10:2.2, 2.4
as godless 9:4
as lived 9:4
as new 9:5
received 4:7; 9:5
secular 9:4
worldview, modern 9:4
written word 8:3; 11:2